Charles Jensen

# SPLICE OF LIFE

A Memoir in
13 Film Genres

sfwp.com

Library of Congress Cataloging-in-Publication Data

Names: Jensen, Charles, 1977- author.
Title: Splice of life : a memoir in 13 film genres / Charles Jensen.
Description: First edition. | Santa Fe, NM : Santa Fe Writers Project, 2024. |
    Summary: "Movies and memory intersect in this compelling and
    unconventional memoir from queer writer, film aficionado, and Jeopardy!
    contestant Charles Jensen. Splice of Life follows Jensen from his upbringing
    and struggles with sexual awareness in rural Wisconsin to his sexual liberation
    in college and, finally, to the complex relationships and bizarre coincidences
    of adulthood. Exploring what it means to be male and queer, each essay splices
    together Jensen's lived experiences with his analysis of a single film. Deftly
    woven, Splice of Life shows us how personal and cultural memory intertwine,
    as well as how the stories we watch can help us understand the stories we all
    tell about ourselves" — Provided by publisher.
Identifiers: LCCN 2023019580 (print) | LCCN 2023019581 (ebook) |
    ISBN 9781951631338 (trade paperback) | ISBN 9781951631345 (ebook)
Subjects: LCSH: Jensen, Charles, 1977- | Poets, American — 21st century —
    Biography. | Gay men — United States — Biography. | LCGFT: Autobiographies. |
    Film criticism. | Essays.
Classification: LCC PS3610.E56256 Z46 2024 (print) | LCC PS3610.E56256
    (ebook) | DDC 811/.6 [B] — dc23/eng/20230926
LC record available at https://lccn.loc.gov/2023019580
LC ebook record available at https://lccn.loc.gov/2023019581

Published by SFWP
369 Montezuma Ave. #350
Santa Fe, NM 87501
www.sfwp.com

In memory of Pat Oliver

I would have never become who I am
if she hadn't told me I could

*Cinema is a mirror by which we often see ourselves.*
—Alejandro González Iñárritu


*Anything that is not autobiography is plagiarism.*
—Pedro Almodóvar


*A film is never really good unless the camera
is an eye in the head of a poet.*
—Orson Welles

# MAIN TITLES

This book contains spoilers.

# ESTABLISHING SHOT

The rotor antenna on top of my rural childhood home extends the reach of our consciousness, pulling in more stories, more voices, more imaginaries.

There is no cable television this far in the country. Corn fields seem morally opposed to such luxury. The cattle have their needs, too. But when my father learns about a special box that brings paid television to your home, he buys it. He buys a Betamax, then the height of innovation. These two devices birth a litter of black tapes, names of films scrawled upon them. They eventually number so many volumes that we index them with adhesive letters and numbers, write up a reference list so that we can find the movie we want when we want it without having to slide each tape in and out of its plastic sleeve.

It's a holy room, this room with the tapes and the glass screen. It's the closest we have to a church we can believe in, all of us huddled together to experience other lives. We didn't agree on much, but we agreed the TV was our once and future king.

When cable finally does stretch its wires to our village, we upgrade, but it's short lived. My teen brothers blow out a TV's speakers listening to MTV at top volume despite the presence of four to five stereos in the house. My dad cuts the cable and replaces the television. We exist only on broadcasts and what we sorted into the library of tapes.

This is how the history of film braids itself into my thinking. As a kid, I was often alone, the youngest person in the house by nearly a decade. I watched every movie I could, sometimes repeatedly, sometimes so often I could recite the movie as it played, sometimes so often I could recite the movie without any cues. To me they weren't entertainment. They were real lives I was living. I could travel from my tiny town and surface in an instant in New York, Rome, Alaska, South America, India, anywhere. I could be anyone. I could desire anything.

Movies caulked in the spaces between each cell in my body. I became whole.

Life is decidedly non-narrative as it happens. It's only in the looking back we make movies of the memories. We are the never the director. We are sometimes the star.

We are always—for better or worse—the editor.

But movies—the ones we watch and the ones we splice together in our minds—never tell us who we are. They only show us who we have been, who we want to be. We trim away anything that doesn't suit us in the moment and there, scattered around our feet, are the remnants we thought we didn't need.

The cutting room floor.

I wondered what would happen if I reached into those forgotten strips and reassembled them into something that somehow made sense to me—the intersection of movies and memory. Splices of life, both real and imagined. An essay that reads and critiques. A memory that is mine and—somehow—also yours.

# ACT I

# POLITICAL SATIRE

## HERE COMES THE HOTSTEPPER

Mrs. Frederick's nasal voice, pinched tighter by the rickety PA system, echoed down the cinderblock halls of Palmyra-Eagle High School. It was a Monday in the spring of my junior year. Among her list of morning announcements, Mrs. Frederick noted Prom Court elections would be held that day.

The qualifications required of Court members were strict. You had to be a junior "in good standing," meaning you paid class dues each year of high school. You needed a GPA above 2.0. And you needed to be involved in some kind of school activity or club. In a class of just over one hundred students, these stipulations left about twenty-five possible nominees. I was among them, along with the entire slate of popular kids and a mishmash of folks from other cliques in the school.

PEHS educated just over four hundred students total, drawn together from a sprawling region that included two small towns (the eponymous Palmyra and Eagle), a number of unincorporated areas, and the rolling hills and dairy farms of southeastern Wisconsin. Palmyra suffered from depression, economic and emotional. Main Street bisected the little town from lakes located on either end. Century-old buildings lining it featured Western false front architecture, the squared edges of the facades cloaking the pitched roofs behind. Anchor businesses included bustling bar, Sadie's, and a basement bowling alley. The high school perched on the far edge of town, the last major development before the land opened to endless fields of grass, corn, and wild forest. As a resident of Eagle, ten miles down Highway 59, I bussed to school those first two years, then carpooled with friends. Halfway between the two towns, the Waukesha/Jefferson County line split the highway. On the Eagle side, the road was smoothly paved with bright paint. The Jefferson County road was stippled with pockmarks and scars, faded to a washed out gray. While both towns seemed firmly blue collar, the marked difference in this infrastructure spoke volumes about the gap between Palmyra and Eagle. Neither featured a single stoplight.

That afternoon, a couple of our junior class officers pulled a lunch table out of the cafeteria and set out ballots, photocopied and trimmed into little handbills. The names of the girls and boys in the running formed two columns, a blank box next to each one. I voted for myself, a testament to my optimism.

The following week, Mrs. Frederick announced the nominations in alphabetical order, boys and then girls. The results were mostly what you'd expect: popular kid after popular kid, and then I heard my name sandwiched between Jeff Iverson and Jeff Merrill. Things were about to get weird.

## THE SCHOLASTIC INDUSTRIAL COMPLEX

Tina Fey adapted the script for *Mean Girls* from an unlikely source: a book about high school bullying and social hierarchies written to help parents raise their children through those pressures. *Queen Bees and Wannabes* bears almost no resemblance to the iconic film it would become, but you can see its underpinnings throughout the culture of North Shore High. When Janis Ian (Lizzy Caplan) draws Cady (Lindsay Lohan) a map of the cafeteria to help her find where she belongs, Janis identifies each highly specific clique by table. The social sorting is comical in part because no matter when and where we were in high school, we recognize this topography and its power structures. What's important is that Cady has been accepted by the school's queerest student, Damien (Daniel Franzese), and Janis, who was accused of being a lesbian because she focused too much energy on her friendship with Regina George (Rachel McAdams), the school's reigning social queen and member of its most influential clique, The Plastics.

Janis and Damien are misfits. Their clique has no highly specific identifier beyond "the greatest people you ever meet," and that's because cliques are not defined from the inside out. They are named and characterized by nonmembers. Sexually Active Band Geeks and Unfriendly Black Hotties don't self-identify with those labels because from the inside, they are *all* The Greatest People You Will Ever Meet, each and every group in that cafeteria. Internally, identities get to be complex and nuanced. But from the outside, each group becomes labeled by its greatest common denominator.

## WHAT'S MY NAME?

Almost no one spoke to me on my first day of ninth grade at PEHS. I'd spent the year prior living on an island off the tip of Door County, Wisconsin's geographic thumb. The combination of twelve months of absence with the reconstructive work of adolescence rendered me unrecognizable to people I had known for almost my entire life. They looked me in the eye and didn't say a word. On the second day, I stood nearby while Jenna Castle talked to Mr. Bearden. I saw a flicker of recognition flash through her eyes. "Wait. Are you Charlie Jensen?"

Almost as soon as that happened, the torment began.

Kids called me "gay" long before I knew what the word meant. Their words became seeds in my mind. The thoughts that blossomed from them augured fear and anxiety in me not only about actually being gay, which even in those early years felt like it rang true, but even being perceived as gay. I started doing whatever it took to deflect the allegations. I dated any girl who would go out with me. My closest friends that first year were girls. Lindsey, Julie, Meggan, Jill. My locker was halfway down a back hallway near the music room, and in the mornings before school began, we congregated there. People messed with me less if I wasn't alone, so I found as many ways as possible never to be alone. Along with my flock of female friends, I dove into extracurriculars, joining the yearbook, the newspaper, the drama club, the technology club, the track team, National Honors Society, student government. I never had a free minute. I never had a solitary minute. I couldn't take the risk.

## DARK HORSE

No one knows Cady when she arrives at North Shore High for her first day of public school after a life lived in a place the film only identifies as "Africa." All of her childhood socialization took place there, so this is her very first encounter with American teenage culture. Cady makes the slow walk from the sidewalk to the school's entrance to a cover of Blondie's "Rip Her to Shreds," slicing through the throng of adolescents whose dress, talk, and style are completely alien. Everything overwhelms her: rules she doesn't understand, social conventions she's never had to learn. Cady even bumps into Ms. Norbury (Tina Fey), splashing coffee all over her math teacher in front of the entire class. She ends up eating her lunch alone in a bathroom stall, the only place she finds peace.

Cady's loneliness permeates the film's opening scenes. She doesn't understand that she'll need to fit in, but once she does, she longs for it. This emotional need ultimately hooks her to Damien and Janis. Damien, the only out homosexual student, is deeply alone, unable to express the natural romantic feelings of adolescence while yearning to be seen for who he is. We intuit from his almost co-dependent relationship with Janis that no one else in the school is ready to offer what Damien wants and needs. Janis, for her part, embraces her outsider status, even though she was in large part pushed into it by Regina's rejection. She dresses aggressively, a confrontational style that dares anyone to see her as anything but an outsider. Her rejection of high school's fashion norms is an expression of her artistic nature. We understand her look expresses her embrace of uniqueness, which, like Damien's longing, desires to be seen as is.

When Regina George takes an unexpected interest in Cady at lunch during that first week, Cady abandons Damien and Janis, recognizing even in that moment that with social status comes power and privilege. Even though she doesn't know anything about Regina, Gretchen (Lacey Chabert), or Karen (Amanda Seyfried) as people, Cady understands Regina's invitation will put her in proximity to that power. We see Cady pause for a moment to consider what to do, but the thrill of being acknowledged by the school's most influential person is influence in and of itself. Later, Cady agrees to spy on Regina and the Plastics for Janis, but like any agent who goes undercover, she'll risk losing herself by believing her own lies.

## LOSER

I spent the first two years of high school wondering if I should kill myself.

My suicidal thoughts fired from my brain like curved arrows, circling immediately back to my body. They percolated through the soup of anxiety, depression, and self-loathing I fell into when I went to bed. I talked in my sleep almost nightly, often waking myself up with the sound of my own voice. The symptoms included body disruptions, too. If I dreamed about being in class, I'd wake in my dark room sitting up in bed as though in a desk, my arm raised. I'd rise from the bed and stand near the closet door, thinking it was a threshold I needed to pass through. Or I'd speak to the faces in the movie posters that hung opposite my bed, the combination of moonlight and subconscious thought transforming them into teachers, students, even strangers.

The stress tore its way through me even as my body was breaking itself apart and shapeshifting. In the six months after my thirteenth birthday, I grew six inches. The growth spurts continued the following year. My legs ached in the mornings, especially at the joints. Stretch marks appeared on my knees because my skin wasn't keeping up with lengthening bones. And my weight fluctuated but kept me, generally, very thin. I suffered from headaches so routinely, I kept an industrial bottle of Tylenol in my locker.

A few weeks into freshman year, I walked into the den where my mom stared at the television. I wore a ratty black bathrobe, black sweatpants, and a black t-shirt. I plopped down on the couch next to her. "I'm depressed," I said.

She didn't pull her eyes away from the TV. "Oh? What about?" She was forty-seven years old and despite having smoked for her whole adult life and some of her teenage years, she looked younger and healthier than that. In twenty years, she'd be dead of lung cancer. She was a beauty in her youth, which is one of the reasons my dad relentlessly pursued her, proposing to her nine times before she finally said yes. Their marriage was on the rocks that year. We didn't talk about it, but I knew. My mom was also depressed. Her family moved her from Belgium to America when she was twelve, telling her they were just going on a vacation to see her aunt. Then they never left. My mom ended up in an American grade school, not speaking a word of English, weathering the taunts of her classmates before she even understood what they meant.

I didn't know what to tell her in that moment. I couldn't reveal what they said about me at school because I was afraid *they* were right. I worried if I said it out loud, she'd say, *You know, you probably are gay, and get out of this house.* But I also knew I had to say something or there was a very real chance I wouldn't live through the year. "I have problems," I managed. "I think I need to go to therapy."

She turned to me, her face blank. "You're fourteen. What kind of problems could you possibly have?" A laugh track filled up the room as if to punctuate her point.

I didn't say anything.

The conversation ended.

The darkness found its way out of me anyway. In my English class, doing a unit on creative writing, I wrote poems about killing myself and the kind of release I'd experience by doing it. I took pains to craft them with perfect rhyme and meter. I put so much effort into shaping those sentiments I didn't even notice how plainly they made it onto the page. Ms. Oliver asked me to stay after class after I turned in one of those pieces.

A stack of my poems sat on the corner of her desk. "These are really good," she said, patting them with her palm. "You have a talent for writing." I'd been writing stories since I was a kid, and poems since a poet visiting my school the previous year led a weeklong workshop on writing. I never stopped. Poetry, as it does for a lot of kids, became the repository of my complex adolescent feelings. "Why don't you keep writing and show the work to me. I'll give you feedback. We can work outside of class."

I thanked her and agreed I would. The recognition made something click. The suicidal thoughts didn't leave me for more than two decades after that morning. But that was all it took to save my life.

## ABSOLUTE POWER CORRUPTS ABSOLUTELY

*Mean Girls* makes explicit many of the tacit social rules teens follow, whether it's the "girl code" of not dating your friend's ex or how to create a Halloween costume (lingerie worn with animal ears). Cady, having grown up entirely outside this system of rules and restrictions, ultimately finds solace in them. When Ms. Norbury hands back Cady's math assignment, she's outed to Janis and Ian as a brain. Cady realizes "nerd" status could eject her from their group, isolating her further. She ignores Ms. Norbury's repeated encouragement to join the Mathletes, a group only whose name is cringier than their activity. Ms. Norbury is the only figure in the film encouraging Cady to be the person she is, not the person they want her to be.

Cady knows Janis and Damien, who elect to exist outside all these rules, have full freedom to be themselves and do what they want, while anyone who lives within the system, like the Plastics, must follow the rules or risk social isolation. Gretchen wears pink on Wednesday as is required of her as a Plastic, but we learn there's a personal rule applied to her. She's not allowed to wear silver hoops, not even the expensive ones she got for Hanukkah, because Regina—it's no coincidence her name is Latin for "queen"—arbitrarily decided those were "her thing." Gretchen could break the rule, but then where would she be? No longer atop the pyramid. And that's the fear all of the characters in the high school share: no one wants to fall even a single rung on the social ladder.

You could argue *Mean Girls* bears more resemblance to *V is for Vendetta* than, say, *Can't Hardly Wait*, the only similarity to the latter being the ages of the characters. The former focuses on destroying an oppressive regime through radicalization, resistance, and action, and this is the plan Janis, Damien, and Cady put into motion. Their goal? To dethrone Regina George and her "army of skanks" so that normal people like them can have a little peace again.

Cady is the tool of this plan. She infiltrates the Plastics to earn their trust and destroy them from the inside out. She enjoys being popular, having influence, being envied. She enjoys it so much that in order to sell it, she starts bombing math class to appear weaker to a boy she likes, hoping he'll like her back. But as Cady burrows deeper into her new identity, she risks losing the person she used to be.

## MR. VAIN

A month stretched out between the announcement of Prom Court and the actual dance itself. I was flabbergasted I'd been elected to the court, considering the years of bullying I'd experienced. In a way, the attention embarrassed me. I'd avoided being seen or acknowledged for so long, now that something positive happened to me, I didn't know how to accept it.

By my junior year, only one class of kids made me miserable. Over the course of that last year, many of them dropped out of school once they'd hit their eighteenth birthdays, kind of a rite of passage in a high school for communities of rural poverty. As fewer and fewer of my bullies remained in the school, I came out of my protective shell. To survive, I'd learned to be nice to as many people as possible—though, like all kids, I made fun of people too, without any awareness that my impact on them might be as devastating as the impact others had on me. This realization would be waiting for me later, in adulthood, when I understood the people who tormented me didn't realize their impact, and probably didn't intend it, either.

I sat down in Ms. Pyle's classroom for AP American History the afternoon of the court announcement. Her classroom had a high ceiling and giant windows overlooking the old football field.

Jill Bonnett sat in the desk across from me and we talked about going to Prom as a group with her and her boyfriend from another school. Cari Gallagher overheard us. "Charlie, you're on Prom Court! That's so exciting."

"Yeah. Are you coming to Prom to see me get crowned King?" I deadpanned.

My candidacy for King was a joke. I had a snowball's chance in a very hot place of winning this popularity contest and, while I knew it, I let everybody around me know I knew it too. I acknowledged the honor and acknowledged the unlikely odds, like I'd been handed a Powerball ticket on the night of the largest jackpot and was wished good luck.

But rather than accept the honor of my nomination, I repeated this line—"Are you coming to Prom to see me get crowned King?"—over and over and over, any time the conversation naturally landed on Prom, and any time I could wrangle it there. I could tell people were getting tired of it, but I couldn't stop.

I treated all of it like a joke. I thought everyone was in on it with me. But the joke would ultimately be on me.

## SOMETHING WICKED THIS WAY COMES

Cady learns about the Burn Book as soon as she weasels her way into the Plastics. If the Plastics are three witches, the Burn Book is their sacred Grimoire, full of the kind of leverage they use to maintain their power over others. The popular girls have filled it with rumors, cruel observations, and jokes about their classmates, often pasting in the students' photos alongside the content. Their words become spells that make the Plastics powerful, and the power they feel then radiates back out to others, confirming their superiority.

Regina tells Cady to put a funny comment she makes about Ms. Norbury into the book to memorialize it and, in part, earn her membership in the group. Doing so makes Cady a Burn Book co-conspirator. Cady takes Ms. Norbury's encouragement of her, reframes it as "pushing," and then uses that word to imply her teacher sells drugs. This becomes the spilled blood that initiates Cady into the Plastics, earning their trust.

When Cady tells Janis and Damien about the book, they're surprised but they're not surprised. Of course the Plastics would do something like this. But when Janis demands to know what's in the book about her, Cady lies and says there's nothing there. Janis believes it because she already feels invisible to the powers that be.

Despite the Burn Book's significance to the integrity of the Plastics, we don't see it much throughout the film. It fades into the background of the politicking and sabotage that comprises the main arc of the film. Destroying Regina becomes Cady's sole focus, but why? Janis and Damien encourage her to do it. For Janis, it offers revenge for the middle school ostracization that has kept her on the margins. For Damien, he'll have the chance to control who becomes the chair of the Student Activities Committee.

That *Mean Girls* convinces us the title refers only to the Plastics without including Janis and Damien underscores how much we as the audience buy into this power struggle. Cady participates in this war not because it's her war; she fights only to fit in *somewhere*. Whether she's sitting with the Plastics or hanging out with Janis and Damien, Cady becomes their pawn, shifting back and forth between light and dark.

Cady plays the role of a Plastic so well, she becomes one. There's a scene of the four Plastics walking in slow motion down a school hallway while Missy Elliot's "Pass that Dutch" plays over it, the thumping bass and clicking of drumsticks adding the kind of percussive fervor that sounds both celebratory and militaristic. The student body idolizes these four girls not for who they are, but for what they represent. Regina George, for instance, has an entire mythology about her unpacked in the first fifteen minutes of the film, including everything from being in a Japanese car commercial to John Stamos telling her on a plane that she was pretty. When we see Regina at home, occupying the main bedroom of the house, her mother (Amy Poehler) seems desperate for her daughter's approval by embracing her "cool mom" identity and trying to be her friend instead of her parent. Regina is the queen of all she surveys. Gretchen, scion of toaster strudel, represents wealth and prestige, two traits that give everyone a significant boost of privilege and influence. Karen, when she isn't speaking, becomes the kind of fresh-faced, no-makeup beauty sold to teen girls in Neutrogena commercials. Her lack of intellect prevents her from being too threatening to other girls, and so she gets to be popular.

Cady, in this hallway shot, fits in with them seamlessly. It isn't long before non-Plastic girls talk about her the way they do Regina, taking cues from her wardrobe choices and gossiping about her past. The Plastics aren't popular for who they are—*Mean Girls* makes that clear over and over—but for what they represent: opportunities, experiences, or resources other girls want, from dating a star athlete to sleeping in the main bedroom of their parents' home. The Plastics are human metaphors.

Their influence hinges on a level of social isolation from others. If people knew Karen much better, for instance, they'd realize she's so dumb she's almost a danger to herself on a daily basis. They'd realize how anxious Gretchen really is, how she focuses on maintaining her spot as #2 in the social hierarchy, the Brutus to Regina's Caesar, as she describes it in the film. They'd know how clueless Cady is about American teen life, how she lacks familiarity with the references that ultimately contribute to building cliques and social connections among her peers.

Cady's position as a Plastic keeps her from being fully revealed to others. But her anonymity—and her scheming—won't remain hidden much longer.


## DREAMS

I joined the Prom Committee because participating in things staved off my self-loathing, depression, anxiety, and internalized homophobia. The more I involved myself in a structured activity, the less I focused on what happened in my mind. The less my suicidal thoughts screamed. The less I thought about the urgent need for intimate friendships with specific boys at school.

Dana Delaney chaired the Prom Committee. We went to preschool together in the basement of a church in North Prairie. Her particular brand of popularity was effusive kindness, something that radiated from her more brightly the older we got. After our first year of college, we'd run into each other at a No Doubt show in Milwaukee and be genuinely glad to see each other, and we'd both clearly outgrown the shells of our high school lives by then. In high school I hadn't noticed how compassionately she treated everyone around her, but working with her to brainstorm the theme, design and construct the decorations, and plan the ticket sales was actually really fun. Her positivity kept everyone on the committee motivated and—dare I say it?—excited about doing the work for the dance.

The girls on Prom Court were all popular, with one exception. Like me, Chrissie Czerwinski, was an outlier. Chrissie also joined the Prom Committee and worked among us over those weeks. A night or two before the dance, Chrissie and I blew up balloons in Ms. Oliver's classroom. They'd end up attached to streamers or to carboard tubes painted black with metallic accents to approximate columns staggered throughout the dance floor. We talked as we worked. We kept half the fluorescent lights off, the stark shine from the hallway offering more than enough for us to see by. The votes for King and Queen had been cast, but the results were known only by Dana and Ms. Oliver until the day of the ceremony.

"I kind of can't believe we got on court," I said between balloon breaths.

She shook her head. "I know. It's a weird mix of people." She chuckled uncomfortably.

The room filled with the sound of our breath expanding the balloons in our hands. My head swam as they grew, and, track team or not, I needed to take breaks to catch my breath.

"I've been joking about winning," I said. Probably a hundred times by that point I'd asked people to come to the dance to see me win the crown. I lowered my half-inflated balloon into my lap and looked at her. "But let's be honest. You and I don't really have a chance. Not against these people."

"I think it's going to be Dana. Or Andie Price." Andie was tiny, cherubic, and blond. She always seemed to have a smile or a kind look for people at school. I didn't have a class with her at all throughout high school, but I saw her all the time because her locker was right outside the cafeteria, in a main thoroughfare we had to walk to get to class. The location made her seem like a minor celebrity. For much of our time in school, she dated Denver Preston, whom I later realized I had a wild crush on for most of the years I'd known him.

"They're both really nice. They've definitely got a good chance." I gave it some thought. "For King, probably Kevin Beauchamp? Jason Buettner might get it, too." Kevin had moved to our school during sophomore year and it was hard not to think of him as a new kid even though he'd been quickly absorbed into the popular group. He had a strong *Saved by the Bell* vibe mixed with a Luke Perry *90210* bad-boy cuteness that endeared him to every girl in our class. Jason, on the other hand, was a funny guy whose ruddy cheeks made him look like he'd just come in from an energetic recess. He fit in well with everyone and while he was also popular, he never seemed to wield that power over other people. We always referred to both of them by first and last name.

Chrissie tied off a balloon and set it aside with the others. "It's just going to be a fun night," she said, "no matter what happens."

I paused mid-balloon. "Yeah." I heard shouting and laughing from the gymnasium down the hall. Chrissie and I weren't the kind of people who belonged in the middle of the action. Moving from social pariah in freshman year to this moment, where I felt a skosh of acceptance, was enough for me. I thought ahead to college, to starting my life over on my own terms, and leaving behind the rough memories I had of this place as soon as I could. "It's going to be fun," I agreed. It was an honor just to be nominated.

That night when we did our run-through of the procession and the coronation, I didn't pay attention. I didn't need to take it seriously.

This wasn't a night for me. I wasn't part of my class's social elite and privileged kids. I was only a visitor.

## OCTOBER SURPRISE

Cady uses the Plastics' own tools and biases against them. She divides them. But Cady doesn't destroy the Plastics. Janis's plan doesn't upend the social order of the school. Instead, when Regina discovers Cady's treachery, she launches an act of mutually assured destruction: she releases the content of the Burn Book to the school. It reveals to each student what rumors have marginalized them, yes. But it also arms each student with ammunition against the others. The school erupts into violence as girls attack each other, accusatory, seeking accountability or explanations. Information meant to be kept secret isn't. Stories that should remain between friends are exposed. And everyone has something to lose.

Regina, a true evil queen, adds herself to the Burn Book to misdirect responsibility away from herself. It works. Cady, Gretchen, and Karen end up in the principal's office to account for the content of the book because they are the only three girls in the entire school not mentioned. "I don't think I should be in trouble because I'm well-liked," Gretchen tells the principal in her defense. Gretchen doesn't realize that not being maligned is not the same as being liked.

Ms. Norbury holds an assembly to quell the violence that erupts from the distribution of the Burn Book. She wants all the girls in the school to talk about their emotions and their issues with each other instead of letting these feelings seethe under the surface, where they destroy each girl from the inside out. Regina raises her hand and asks why she has to be there. "How many people here have felt personally attacked by Regina George?" Ms. Norbury asks. All the girls—and a few teachers—raise their hands.

Ms. Norbury has the girls apologize to people they've wronged and then stage-dive into the crowd as a trust exercise. When Janis takes the dais, she reveals their plot to destroy the Plastics, outing Cady as a liar and a fake. Janis, orchestrator of the plan, unmasks her own operative and in the process saves herself from retribution. Janis reveals herself as the most treacherous girl in the film. The least loyal. Possibly even the meanest. Despite this, she skates away from the assembly unscathed.

Cady loses everything—her Plastic friends, Janis and Damien, and even the respect and support of Ms. Norbury. And so Cady ends up right where she was at the beginning of the film: socially isolated, eating lunch in a bathroom stall, hated by everyone, whether she ever interacted with them or not.

## WILD NIGHT

I asked Grace Florkowski to be my date for Prom. She was my wildest and most unlikely friend. Whereas I was the serious academic, she blew off school. Where I followed the rules, she bent them. She was creative and marched to the beat of her own drum. She claimed to do all sorts of drugs from weed to opium, and once, at my urging, she tucked a book of Allen Ginsburg's poetry into the waistband of her pants at a Barnes and Noble and carried it outside for me. She dressed outlandishly compared to everyone around her, with ironic vintage store tees and sweaters, swishy wide-legged jeans. Her family moved to our little town from Milwaukee, a radical and shocking cultural change I couldn't begin to imagine. I think she loved the freedom the move offered her. This tiny new school in rural Wisconsin where supervision of kids was lackadaisical at best. I was in awe of her, maybe because the freedom she commanded to live her life on her terms was exactly the kind of power I wanted for myself. Asking her to be my date felt as transgressive as the footwear I bought to wear with my tux: a pair of black Nikes with white accents. My parents threw up their hands when I ignored their pleas to act like an adult, that my fashion choices would only embarrass me. I told them I was seventeen, old enough to do what I wanted, one of the most seventeen-year-old things ever said.

The night of the dance, we drove thirty-five minutes to the outer-outer ring Milwaukee suburb Waukesha, a bustling metropolis compared to our dusty town, and ate dinner in a restaurant built inside an old train car. We were rowdy, rambunctious. Grace, wearing a vintage 20s dress with kinetic fringe, drew the irritated attention of the diners around us. I knew we were supposed to act better, to be better. But I also knew in that moment we were kids. That this was one of our last chances to be horrible and selfish and irresponsible. Soon my friends would start hitting their eighteenth birthdays. We'd be moving out of our dead-end town. There was a brighter future waiting for us somewhere else.

Back at the high school, the dance was thumping in the gym. A DJ set up shop on stage and spun the biggest pop hits of the mid-90s. Kids danced in awkward groups around the floor, the stripes of the basketball court tangled under their feet. I couldn't believe it, but I was having fun. Fun with Grace. Fun with my friends. Fun letting go. For a night, I got to forget about the self-consciousness that terrorized my mind, not worrying about whether I seemed gay. I didn't worry about who was in the room. I didn't worry about what someone was going to say to me. I got to be myself—completely, totally myself with people I loved and who loved me.

At 9:45 pm, the Emcees, Carrie Sorensen and Scooter Hofstetter, gathered up the members of court from the floor and ushered us out into the hallway to line up for the processional. Freshman year, Carrie had been part of the advanced English class that saved my life, and in the years since then had fallen in with a group of kids everyone called the burnouts. They wore flannels every day, smoked during lunch out on the lawn, and ditched classes. She would be dead in less than a year, one of four victims in a late-night car accident on a meandering country road. Scooter perched at the top of our class academically and wore the thick glasses, unstyled hair, and unmatched clothes to go with the honor. School bored him, and the ease with which he completed his classwork made him bitter and acerbic. We often sat at the same lunch table and I'd hear him ripping apart any number of other students and teachers. But now he and Carrie stood on the stage with mics, calling the names of the girls on court and the names of their escorts.

I walked in with Chrissie on my arm. We paused on a dais as our names were read, and then walked to the risers where other members of court lined up. Girls in the front row, boys in the back. The tallest, I ended up in the middle of the risers.

I felt good. I looked out at the room of my classmates, kids from other years, parents. I thought about how I'd spent weeks telling anyone who'd listen they should be here now to see me get crowned king. What a ridiculous thought that was. Even as I said it, I believed it couldn't be true. But I tried to seem serious, to make it funnier somehow that I might actually believe I could win.

"The 1994 Prom King is," Carrie said, opening an envelope on stage. "Charlie Jensen?" Her voice turned up at the end. A question.

I froze.

I know what happened next because my dad was in the audience holding a camcorder. But this is the only reason I had any idea, because the very minute I thought I heard my name, my mind floated up and out of my body like it were filled with helium. It dabbed against the ceiling of the gym, while my body stood immobile on the risers.

First, there was applause. It filled the room. My face, though, was slack. My jaw dropped.

Brice Sheafer, standing next to me, jabbed me in the ribs with his elbow. "Go!" he hissed.

I paused a moment longer, desperately trying to reel my thoughts back into my head. What was I supposed to do? Why had I goofed off at rehearsal? Why had I run all over this school telling people I was going to be crowned Prom King?

I stepped down the risers like scaling an uneven hiking path, sure my legs would give out under me at any moment. I stepped onto the floor. Last year's Prom King, Charles Williams, placed the white crown on my head. Behind me, seven boys shrugged at each other.

I looked around the room at the parents, students, teachers, gathered at the dance. I was a tremendous asshole. How else to explain what I'd done and said for weeks, and this result that I was certain, at the core of my being, was impossible.

Scooter announced the name of the Queen. "Chrissie Czerwinski!"

Chrissie moved forward, overwhelmed, and sat in the chair next to me. Shannon Frederick, the prior queen, placed a tiara on Chrissie's head. We stayed there for a while as the audience clapped and cheered for us, and then the DJ started the music to indicate we should recess out of the room. Chrissie and I, the royals, led the court back across the gym, up onto the dais, and out into the hallway.

I looked at Chrissie. "What the fuck just happened?"


## IT IS DOUBLE PLEASURE TO DECEIVE THE DECEIVER

Damien, Janis, and Cady planned to turn Regina's minions against her through the race for the Spring Fling Queen, but when Cady's elected to the court on her own accord, it sets off the chain reaction of events that lead both to Cady's final transformation into a Plastic and the endgame of the film. Cady, grounded by her parents for hosting a party, sneaks out to participate in the climactic Mathletes competition against a rival school, answering the game-winning question, and afterward sneaking into the dance, where she's crowned queen, having won the election through no rigging or politicking, just being herself— the Plastic version of herself, at least.

There's a long speech where Cady rejects the honor. She snaps the plastic crown into bits and uses each shard to honor another girl at the dance, girls from cliques of all kinds. Girls who, like her, had just been yearning for attention, to be seen by their peers. And that's the moral of *Mean Girls*, if there is one—that cliques and the fervent social sorting of our high school years, rather than helping us band together with like-minded friends, actually obscure us to those around us.

The most significant symptom of Cady's Plastic transformation is summed up in the shot when she gazes into her compact while Janis tells her about an art show she's going to be in. Cady mumbles some listening noises and then bolts from the conversation, signing off with a Plastic-trademarked farewell "Love ya." But Cady has no idea she's become Plastic. She thinks she's just fitting in, that she's made all the right choices to land at the top of the social ladder. Privilege like this always feels earned, and people who wield it don't perceive it as anything other than the reward for hard work. Cady hasn't earned anything, not really. She gained power by being invited into proximity to it, an opportunity she had in part by being born white and upper middle class. It isn't until the illicit party she hosts—when she throws up all over Aaron Samuels's (Jonathan Bennett) shoes, alienates Janis and Damien by skipping Janis's art show, and enrages Regina—that Cady realizes she's made a terrible mistake trying to be someone she's not.

The dismantling of the Plastics—Janis's initial goal—and the subsequent annihilation of every girl-girl friendship in the school caused by the release of the Burn Book has a liberating effect on the students in their senior year. We see the rigid cliques from the early cafeteria monologue now intermixing, with friendships struck up between people who never before cared for one another. The Burn Book revealed to the girls that social divisions hurt all of them, that the most radical act they could give each other was the chance to be seen.

## I CAN SEE CLEARLY NOW

School returned to normal the Monday after Prom. No magical relaxing of the social order occurred based on Chrissie and me walking out of the gymnasium with crowns on our heads. In fact, we sat together still, at a lunch table in the middle of the cafeteria, surrounded by the same groups who always sat in the same places. Prom King didn't make me the most popular kid in school, and it didn't suggest I already was.

Even though things were the same, I felt different. I felt for the first time like people in this school actually liked me for who I was, and that maybe I could trust people not to hurt me. Maybe.

Scooter, the Prom Night emcee, sitting a few seats down, was talking. It took me a minute, but I realized he was complaining about the outcome of the Prom King election. "They split the vote," he said, as if he were a political commentator on a cable news show discussing the outcome of a national election. His voice was fired up and blustery. It was hard not to hear him. "The whole court was made up of popular people, and then Charlie. So all the popular people split up their votes between the popular people, and Charlie got elected by a majority of who was left." He meant the unpopular kids. He meant the kids who were sitting around him. But he didn't mean himself.

I looked around the cafeteria. Sure, maybe only half the kids in my class were eligible to vote in the end. Fifty people in all. If the other votes were distributed relatively evenly among the other court members, it meant I only needed about seven votes total to have the highest vote count. It wasn't likely that's how it went down, but it was possible that seven classmates, maybe even the people sitting next to me, elevated me to the crown.

I knew Scooter's grapes were a little sour. He would without a doubt graduate at the top of our class without breaking a sweat. He would get into the college of his choice, and if it were a state school, he'd receive a full scholarship. Chances were good he'd marry his high school girlfriend, start a family. He'd probably even go on to have a good job and make a good living. He'd never leave a 100-mile radius of the town where he grew up. That was the kind of guy he was going to be. And even though he was well-liked, he never got to breathe the rarified air of the popular kids' table. He was stuck sitting with us.

There was another path for me. I was only beginning to wake up to what it was, but I knew the first step was putting this town in my rearview mirror. I'd leave behind petty rivalries like this one. But I'd never have to leave behind the memory of that night, of feeling that despite everything I had experienced, I was going to be okay. And something better than this was waiting for me. I had to believe in it. I had nothing left to lose.

# COMING-OF-AGE

## DIAGNOSTIC I

"It's easier to read your pulse here," the doctor said. His hand snaked beneath the hospital blanket, under my gown. A brown beard hooked over his ears, the rest of his head shaved almost to skin.

Black and white cartoon animals tumbled across sunny wallpaper in the pediatric ward. My trachea savaged by little rips in the tissue that shrieked with pain each time I took a breath. My six-foot-two body stretched to the edge of the bed, built for much younger patients. Several days' patchy whiskers speckled my cheeks.

His fingers were warm, a surprise on my skin. Tracing up my thigh. The untouched part of me.

He looked at me through his dark eyes, smooth and brown. His gaze had a weight I could feel cover me. I couldn't look away.

The scent of musk bloomed between us when I started to sweat.

His fingers pressed into the rhythm beneath my skin. His body heat against my balls. I hitched a breath. I knew this wasn't right. My heart thumped so hard it rattled its flimsy cage of ribs. I was afraid of what he was doing. I was afraid of what it meant.

I was afraid, and I wanted this. His touch. His eyes on me. Whatever came next.

I was seventeen. It was August. On the precipice of senior year, the future beyond yet unknown.

## A LITTLE RESPECT

*Were the World Mine* begins with a familiar teenage trope: a game of dodgeball. Teens identified by classmates as queer know this special torture. A change in targeting. Not just being identified, but being hunted. Queer boys want to be to object of another boy's desire. To be in his line of sight. But not like this. The pack of Morgan Hill Academy rugby boys seem only too eager to destroy, their weapons all trained on seventeen-year-old Timothy (Tanner Cohen). He takes a shot to the face, cuing the twilight of a bruise where it hits.

He's last to the locker room. Like jackals, the bullies lounge on benches, lean against lockers. They call him faggot; he says, for the millionth time, "My name is Timothy." The bully who hit him drapes over a locker door like a wet towel and whispers in a stereotypical lisp, "My name is Timothy too." Jonathon (Nathaniel David Becker), the object of Timothy's desire and the last of the jocks to leave, asks him if he needs ice for his face. But Timothy—unable to differentiate between boys who offer cruelty and boys who offer kindness—brushes this off, preferring to remain isolated. Safe.

## WE KNOW WHAT WE ARE, BUT KNOW NOT WHAT WE MAY BE

Having graduated from my small town's only school, a K-6, I was bussed to Palmyra, Wisconsin to join a double-sized middle school class there. We regarded each other with suspicion those first days: who was cool? Who would become nerds? And who might kiss me?

Cautious friendships took root. I met Russ and Evie, fraternal twins, that first week. Evie had a crush on me, and Russ was an easygoing guy who never seemed to care too much about anything but being happy. I felt something fidget in my gut when I was around them. I assumed it meant I had a crush on Evie, but I always wanted to talk to Russ, to be around Russ, to make Russ smile. I wanted to be his best friend. He didn't seem to mind. A few weeks into the year, Russ told me he and Evie were moving. The feeling in my gut hardened, became an anchor I felt plummet without ever hitting the ground.

A few weeks later I ended up in the crosshairs of some mean eighth graders. They called me *faggot* and pushed me into lockers. At the fall dance, they surrounded me on the gym floor and separated me from my friends, pushing me and taunting me. Telling me who I was. What I was.

My mom knew something was wrong when I got home. It was like my lights had been knocked right out of their sockets. She found me crying on my bed and asked what happened. But I couldn't tell her—my mouth filled with shame. She put an arm around me, as if she could still protect me. "I think I know what's going on." Her voice calm and sweet and loving. My lights sparked, trying to come back to life. "They're making fun of your body, right? In the locker room? Boys are jerks. Don't listen to them. You'll be fine." Her reassurance fell flat in my mind. I wasn't worried about how I looked, or whether my body kept up with the grotesque renovations of puberty. I worried about what was happening inside me—the way I was becoming unlike everyone else around me.

The light sputtered out for good. She held me a while longer and said more, but I wasn't listening. I knew I was going to be alone. And in some way, I knew—deep in the depths of my mind—that these boys were right.

## DIAGNOSTIC II

████████████████████████ the doctor ████████ snaked
████████████████████████████████████████████
over ████████████████████████ skin.
████████████████████████████████████
████████████ My ████████████ little rips ████████

▮ shrieked ▮▮▮▮▮▮▮

▮▮▮▮ to the edge of ▮▮▮▮▮▮

▮▮▮▮▮ my ▮▮

▮▮▮▮ surprise ▮▮▮▮

▮▮▮

▮▮▮▮▮

▮▮▮ I ▮▮▮▮

▮▮▮▮▮

▮▮ pressed into ▮▮▮▮

▮▮▮▮ a ▮

▮▮▮▮ cage ▮▮

▮▮▮▮▮

▮▮▮ I wanted ▮ His touch. ▮▮

Whatever came next.

▮▮▮▮▮

▮▮▮

## IT'S RAINING MEN

Queerness is central to Timothy's life because he's the only queer person he knows he knows. No one lets him forget he's alone. They paint his locker with the word *faggot*. When it gets cleaned off, they put it back. He's tired of being ostracized for desire. Studying his lines for the school's production of *A Midsummer Night's Dream*, he intuits the recipe to make Puck's secret elixir, the one that makes people (and fairies) fall in love with the first person they see. He even rigs a plastic pansy bloom to serve as the method of delivery: just a spritz from the flower's pistil and *bam!* They're in love. At rehearsal the next day, he sprays it in Jonathon's face and—yes—Timothy's beloved looks at him with joy in his eyes, places a hand at his cheek, and gives him a kiss.

When another boy in the play reacts to this, Timothy sprays him. Then all the other cast members. They see each other—for the first time, as queer boys—and kiss passionately on stage.

The film's big metaphor appropriates the old chestnut that one queer person—a pansy—can pollinate a whole community, will recruit others into the "lifestyle." Timothy's powerful queer magic has done just that, turning the jocks of his school's rugby team into the background extras of an episode of *Queer as Folk*. He doesn't want to be alone anymore.

The parents of the town want the school principal to do something. No one among them has realized straight couples are the single most significant source of queer people. We don't make us. They do.


## WHAT IS PAST IS PROLOGUE

At thirteen, a doctor diagnosed me with asthma. Her clinic occupied a single room in the community center, barely larger than a custodial closet. One-room library down the hall. Gymnasium past that.

Her pageboy haircut lay flat and unwashed against her head. Her face as rumpled as a well-slept-in bed.

An inhaler, a regimen of pills, no explanation why I had attacks when visiting my parents' favorite vacation spot. Meds helped, but shortness of breath was always waiting for me when we arrived.

I would never learn why, on that trip four years later, a serious of rips split my windpipe. Why, back home, sweating in my bed, struggling to breathe, I wondered if I was going to die.

My mom stared into me as though she had X-ray vision. One of the few times I saw through her resilience to the scared and vulnerable part of her. Or maybe I was old enough to know that part could exist. "I think I need to go to the hospital," I told her.

I was seventeen. It was August. On the precipice of senior year, the future beyond unknown.

## DIAGNOSTIC III

████████████ pulse ████████████████████

████████████████████████████████████████

████████████████████████████████████

████████████████████████████████████████

in ██████████████ My ████████████████████

████████████████████████████████████████

body ██████████████████ built for ██████████

████████████████████████

His fingers ████████████████ on ██████████████ my thigh.

██████████████████████

████████████████████████████████████████

████████ a weight ████████████ I couldn't ██████████

████████████████████████████████████ sweat.

████████████████████████████████████████

████████████████ a breath ████████████████

████████████████████████████████████████

████████████████████ of ████████████████

████████████████████████████████████████

Whatever ████████████████

████████████████████████████████████████

future beyond ██████████████

## TAKE YOUR MAMA

Timothy has a fraught relationship with his mother (Judy McLane). After her first day at a difficult new job, she sits in her parked car, coming to terms with the uphill climb ahead of her. Timothy slides in next to her. As they talk, it becomes clear Timothy's dad is out of the picture because of his son's sexuality, and even as Timothy tries to assert his identity in the conversation, his mother spits back, "Every single day I have to come out of the closet, just like you." But it's not just like Timothy. Her closet is her own.

The mother of a queer son is no longer just a mother. Timothy's coming out shifts a new slate of considerations into her lap. She fears for his safety. She worries he will always be lonely. But it's the failure of her imagination that limits her the most. Her son will not live a life that looked like hers at all. It will be his own, and she'll have to learn how to live queerly through him. Having a queer son means she'll also face bigotry and scrutiny from other parents. They'll wonder what she did wrong, how she and Timothy ended up like this. They'll treat her like an error.

When Timothy's magic makes nearly the entire town queer, that's the closest his mother will come to understanding his current loneliness. She's one of the few people who doesn't fall under the spell. She finds herself alone.

## THERE SCATTERS DANGERS, DOUBTS

How many times did they call me *faggot* in those years? The whispered voices from the row behind me: *buttfucker, cocksucker.* This was how I learned how two men have sex.

I tried to remain invisible, but at a height well above most classmates, I literally stuck out in any room I entered. I marked the safe rooms on a map in my mind. The music room. The English teacher's room. That was all I had. I was so worried about getting trapped by bullies that I avoided using the boys' restroom at all during school.

I woke up every school morning knowing my day would be a series of calculated risks and evasions. Today, we would call it *anxiety.* Dread was the word for what I felt every day at the prospect of going to class. I kept a ledger in my head of the people I could trust and the people who would be only too eager to sell me out in order to climb a rung or two higher on the social ladder. More than a few times, I judged them wrongly, and their words became a target I wore on my chest.

I knew the only way to lose it was to leave.

## DIAGNOSTIC IV

████████████████████████████████████████

████████████ under my ████████████

████████████████████████████████

████████████████████████████████████████

████████████████████████████████████████

████████████████████████████████████████

████████████████████████████████████████

████████████████████████████

████████████████████ skin ████████

The untouched part of me.

████████████████████████████████████████

████████████████████████████████████

████████████ bloomed ████████████████████

████

████████████ into the ████████████████

heat ████████████████████████████████████

████████████████████████████████████████ of

████████████████████████████████████

████████████████████ His  touch. ████████

████████████████████

████████████████████████████████████████

████████████████████████

## BETTER OFF ALONE

Timothy's only friends are Max (Ricky Goldman), a boy of color, and Frankie (Zelda Williams), who self-identifies as "heteroflexible," defined by her as "I'm straight, but shit happens." Like Timothy, Max and Frankie are outcasts in the otherwise white suburban township they call home. Max's racial difference makes him unique among the town's residents we see, and Frankie's assumed feminism isolates her from the conservative community. On top of his queerness, Timothy—and, we suspect, Max and Frankie too—is of a lower class than his peers and most other people we see in town.

His mother cuts up her wedding dress to craft the fairy wings Timothy will wear as Puck, a final recognition her marriage is over. That she's chosen her son over her husband. And that choice has led them to dire financial straits.

Despite friendships with Max and Frankie, Timothy's sadness is a shackle. He knows no one can return his affection. Jonathan falling under Timothy's spell doesn't change anything. Timothy still feels alone because he knows Jonathan's feelings are not authentic. His feelings are just magic. Jonathon didn't choose to love him, Timothy realizes. Timothy isn't better off than he was before the play, the potion, the pandemonium.

## THE ROSE OF YOUTH

Hospital days crawled by, punctuated only by visits from the nursing staff and, occasionally, a doctor. Checking vitals. Pulse, heartbeat, temperature, breathing. My parents and brother visited during open hours, but huge swaths of the day were closed to everyone but patients and staff. No friends came by; no one knew I was there. Daytime television a torture of its own. The animals swirled in a tempest on the walls. Did the wallpaper lift the spirits of the young kids forced to stay here? Or was it for them like it was for me—a reminder of youth, immaturity. A clear expression we had growing to do.

Because of the IV in my arm, I wasn't allowed to shower. It didn't take long for me to ripen. My mom bought me deodorant from the hospital gift shop to stem the catastrophe of my body. The only scent they had was musk, so these memories soaked up that deep, complex scent—syrupy and sharp—and, because of what happened: masculine, sexual.

## I FEEL LOVE

It is Timothy's English teacher Ms. Tebbit (Wendy Robie) who chooses *A Midsummer Night's Dream* for the spring play at Morgan Hill Academy; she who stands up to the anti-queer bigotry in town even as the parents call for her dismissal for mounting the play and—apparently—making all their children gay. And it is she who tells Timothy that, though he's had his fun, he must restore the world back to what it was, even though it means losing Jonathon's companionship. He must return to isolation.

Everyone falls back in love with their old partners. Timothy expects Jonathon to return to his girlfriend, resigns himself to his fate. After the climactic performance of the play, Jonathon finds Timothy removing his Puck makeup at the school theater. Timothy anticipates cruelty, but Jonathon kisses him—and reveals he's been closeted this entire time.

When we look back at their interactions, we see Jonathon holding space for Timothy, offering, whenever possible, his small, private kindnesses.

It reframes the moment when Timothy, irate over finding *faggot* painted on his locker again, confronts the rugby team and tries to start a fight. He's tackled to the ground almost immediately. Jonathon pulls the boy off Timothy and barks at Timothy to "get out of here." In that moment, we think Jonathon is just one of them. But this is how Jonathon protected him.

## DIAGNOSTIC V

▮▮▮▮▮▮▮▮▮▮▮▮▮▮▮▮▮▮▮▮

▮▮▮▮▮▮▮▮▮▮▮▮▮▮▮▮▮▮▮▮

▮▮▮▮▮▮▮▮▮▮▮▮▮▮ skin.

▮▮▮▮▮▮▮▮▮▮▮▮▮▮▮▮▮▮

▮▮▮▮▮▮▮▮▮▮▮▮▮▮▮▮▮▮▮▮

▮▮▮▮▮▮▮▮▮▮▮▮▮▮▮▮▮▮▮▮

▮▮▮▮▮▮▮▮▮▮▮▮▮▮▮▮▮▮▮▮

▮▮▮▮▮▮▮▮▮▮▮▮

▮▮▮▮▮▮▮ on my skin. ▮▮▮▮▮

▮▮▮▮▮▮

▮▮▮▮▮▮▮▮▮▮▮▮▮▮▮▮

▮▮▮▮▮▮▮▮▮▮▮▮▮▮ .

▮▮▮▮▮▮▮▮▮▮▮▮▮▮▮▮

▮▮▮▮▮▮▮▮▮▮▮▮▮▮▮▮

▮▮▮▮▮▮▮▮▮▮▮ this ▮▮▮▮

▮▮▮▮▮▮▮▮▮▮▮▮▮▮

▮▮▮▮▮▮▮▮▮▮

▮ was ▮▮▮▮▮▮▮▮▮▮▮▮

▮▮▮▮▮

▮▮▮▮▮▮▮▮▮▮▮▮▮▮ the future ▮▮▮▮▮▮

## TRUE COLORS

*Were the World Mine* was fanciful in 2008, but rewatching it over a decade later, the concepts feel in conflict with a society opening its eyes to sexual violence, sexual harassment, and the kinds of manipulation men have been known to use to get sexual satisfaction from those around them. Jonathon's queerness saves Timothy from being viewed as a sexual predator—and true, we don't see them do more than cuddle and kiss. But still. The intent.

His effort to turn the entire town queer, even if just for a moment, is exactly the kind of manipulation that trounces their agency and makes them unwitting—if not otherwise unwilling—participants in someone else's desire.

Even the title feels like a gross artifact—then, it suggested a fever dream of a world in which queer people were safe from harm when expressing desire, a world some of us are closer to occupying than ever before. But now the title smacks of the kinds of power and greed that fuels toxic masculinity in its work to subjugate women and queer folks.

Queer acts have been punishable by death, castration, imprisonment, ridicule, ostracization, familial disowning, and other physical and emotional abuses. For its time, the film offered a salve. What if we, suddenly, were the norm?

## WHAT DREAMS MAY COME

After the hospital, something awoke in me.

I told no one. I was waiting. To get out, to get free, to get away. Somewhere I could build up a new version of myself. Senior year, these plans flowed under my skin.

A closet: a space for all the desires I couldn't talk about. And, even then, I didn't understand how fundamental they were to making me. I learned later how many boys my age were exploring each other's bodies, learning. I was too afraid to try in the conditions I was in. I wanted to live. More than anything. I couldn't risk harm, not when I was so close to getting out.

The closet offers protection—a perceived invisibility. But it harms as much as it harbors. Part of the harm is convincing occupants they are alone. I certainly felt alone. Like I was the only one—though I knew, deep down, I couldn't possibly be. That I would find others.

# SEXUAL THRILLER

## ACT ONE: THEY MEET (CUTE)

I walked into my college's campus bookstore before the rush of procrastinating students made the textbook checkout lines unbearable. After nine quarters and a summer session of this, I knew the bookstore's layout, relying less on the dot matrix printer labels on the shelves and more on muscle memory.

Steps through the door, I caught the gaze of a handsome middle-aged man chatting with a bookstore employee. His eyes sized me up from head to toe. At six-four, I didn't enter spaces as much as I disrupted them. His look lingered longer than a glance at movement flashing on the periphery. His look hungered.

The man was short. Pomade and a prayer held in place a head of dark brown waves. A scarf, looped around his neck several times, dangled its fringed ends near his knees. He wore a timeless camel coat. His dark eyes and olive complexion stood out among the apricot-skinned Abercrombie and Fitch models of the Midwest university's student body. He kept a grizzled stubble. He smirked at me when our eyes met. I gave him nothing but a glance, my intentions unknown.

The texts for Intro to Meaning sat in the section for CLit, the unfortunate abbreviation used for cultural literature courses. I pulled each book from the list as I found it. The man with the scarf and the bookstore kid pulled up next to me. "This is where they'd be," the kid said.

The man half-glanced at the shelves. "So you have the Barthes, then."

"Yeah." The kid pulled a copy off the shelf and handed it to him. I held the same Barthes in my hand.

He listed off another name, and then another, each book he requested already cradled in my arms. It hit me. I blurted, "Are you my professor?"

"Ted Strange." He held out his hand. "You are?"

His grip was warm and firm. I melted a little inside as I introduced myself.

"These are the rest," the kid told him, handing him a stack of the books I still needed to grab.

Ted thanked him for his help as the kid wandered off, leaving the two of us in the CLit aisle. Anxiety sweats dampened my armpits, a frequent side effect of talking to strangers. Even worse when they were handsome. Even worse when they were handsome and giving me the look Ted was giving me. "Well," Ted said, shaking the stack of books in his arms. "I suppose I'll be seeing you soon, won't I?"

My face reddened like a time-lapse sunset. "Yes," I stammered. Common words of my native language felt new to my tongue. My body flushed. I started sweating again. He took a few steps backward, still looking, still smirking, and then turned on his heels. He vanished around the corner, leaving me holding the keys to everything he was about to teach me.

## DON'T YOU KNOW THAT HE'S TOXIC

Dan (Michael Douglas) is the villain of *Fatal Attraction*.

The film doesn't want us to think so. It advocates for us to hate and fear Alex Forrest (Glenn Close) for her relentless pursuit of a man she knows she can't have. We start with a glimpse into Dan's idyllic life with his wife Beth (Anne Archer) as they rush to get dressed for an upscale work event. What a great guy he is, stumbling around the kitchen in his half-buttoned white shirt, his underpants, tending to the dog while Beth scolds their daughter Ellen (Ellen Hamilton Latzen) for playing with her lipstick. They could be any upwardly mobile white couple in New York City and, by extension, perhaps any married white couple in America, whose intimacy has evolved into the kind of cozy familiarity that means home.

Alex, alone at the party, drinks at the bar. We'll learn later she's new to the city, but in this moment—Dan next to her as he orders a drink, greets her, asks her how her evening is—she's the kind of predatory woman the culture has mythologized into being. The lone wolf. Dan doesn't impress her, but he keeps engaging. When Alex asks if he's alone too, he confesses he's with his wife. Dan lingers. His attraction is clear to Alex and to us.

Alex radiates a confidence uncommon to representations of single women in their thirties in this decade. No baby mania. No kooky character flaws Dan would have to overlook to love her. Alex's honesty about what she wants disarms Dan—she knows he's married and a colleague, so what's the use of pretending this could be anything but a friendly flirtation? When they end up in bed, it's because this is what Dan wants. What he lets Alex have. Alex owes nothing to anyone. She can have sex with whomever she likes, whenever she likes. She hasn't taken vows. And within the first thirty minutes of us knowing Dan, we know he is a liar, a manipulator, and a selfish asshole. He'd be the obvious villain of any number of other films. But because we're in Dan's point of view for almost the entire film, we're convinced to look past his shitty deeds.

How he becomes perceived as the victim of this film is peak male fuckery.


## ACT TWO: TEACHER'S PET

Though the course had introduction in the title, I studied alongside the program's graduate students. You could easily tell us apart in the classroom. The undergrads wore thick woolen sweaters that threatened to drown their wearers and sensible shoes for walking. The graduate students appeared to be recently necromanced, preferring to wear all black, their hair dyed either black or platinum, every outfit accessorized with silver jewelry or swing set chains or both. We all smelled like cigarettes.

Ted's resonant classroom baritone had the academic affect you'd expect to come from someone educated in the Ivy League, clipped in pronunciations and bloated with the arrogance of the rich and privileged. It was like a drug to me, all of it, even his stereotypical tweed jackets with elbow patches. It was only about fifteen minutes into his discussion of the syllabus that I decided we could be in love.

Operation Hot for Teacher, named after the Van Halen song, was essentially my evolving wardrobe concept focused solely on Tuesdays and Thursdays when Ted's class met. Some days this meant I returned to my dorm before class to slip into something more fetching, whether it was the signature thin-wale corduroy overalls that emphasized all the inches of my body, or an oversized flannel shirt layered over a long-sleeve tee.

Beyond dressing for success, I wasn't sure what seduction really entailed. I hoped showing up would be enough. I took cues from two reliable sources of mentorship: Cher from *Clueless* ("Anything you can do to draw attention to your mouth is good") and Jordan Catalano from *My So-Called Life* (say as little as possible and look tortured).

Ted's class was impossibly hard, so looking tortured required no additional effort. We read J. L. Austin's *How to Do Things with Words*, a deceptive title that made it sound like a children's primer but instead dove deep into the philosophical underpinnings of language itself. I was out of my depth. The graduate students knew so much, had read everything and could cite it at will. An undergraduate woman and I ended up huddling in desks next to each other, as if our shared body heat would stave off the chill of our academic shortcomings.

Despite my foundering, I enjoyed the learning. I much preferred being the smartest one in class, but if I couldn't be that, perhaps I could be the cutest. Maybe even the teacher's favorite.

## YOU'RE TOO GOOD TO BE TRUE

A *Madame Butterfly* motif recurs throughout *Fatal Attraction*. The two tales have much in common. In the iconic Puccini opera, a young Japanese woman, known only as Butterfly, falls under the spell of a white businessman from America. He marries her, gets her pregnant, and leaves the country, promising to return. Years pass and Butterfly holds onto hope. When the businessman returns, now married to an American woman, Butterfly realizes he only wants to take her child and raise it in his new family. Like many heroines of opera, Butterfly kills herself because—the opera suggests—she has no reason to live.

Dan and Alex listen to the opera as they cook dinner in her apartment. Alex is a contemporary Butterfly, seduced by Dan into believing what to him is a convenient marital pit stop is something more meaningful. They aren't just fucking. They're connecting. As a single woman in her thirties, this is what Alex has sought in 1980s New York City, when glass ceilings reveal the footfalls of the men walking above her and sexual harassment is part of her job description. Dan feels like an answer to prayers. Dan feels like a real chance.

## ACT THREE: YOU ARE CORDIALLY INVITED

Halfway through the term I was sure my seduction plan was failing. Ted barely looked at me during class, and his comments on my work kept pressing me to think harder, to read more deeply, to reflect on my assumptions until they broke.

Our class gathered one afternoon at a popular lunch spot near campus where students could grab smoothies, falafel, an overstuffed sub sandwich, or what passed for tacos in the Midwest. There were just a handful of us. We talked through our final projects. The graduate students sounded like they'd be writing work that would undermine capitalist society and destroy the concept of marriage. I had a plan, something that might feed into a longer paper about how cinema operates as its own discrete language system. Ferdinand de Saussure's ideas in *Course in General Linguistics* had influenced me, once I understood it. Saussure suggested we use language to describe our world, but once we learn to speak it, language actually structures the world within our brains. He also theorized that, within conversation, two people can use the same words (which he called "signs") but that the actual meaning, the impression of those words in the brain, never fully matches. I started making notes toward identifying film as a language system with a common grammar and structure that allowed viewers to follow the story as they watch.

Ted joined us, sitting reverse-cowgirl on a chair, one forearm placed over the backrest. He seemed as if he were contemplating a career in piracy. It was a practiced, studied effort to be cool, seamless when set against our ragtag group of goths and undergrads. He laughed and joked with us, speaking to us like we were his colleagues—and I suppose in some ways the graduate students were. People like me were just kids overhearing the adults speaking after dinner.

I sensed he was getting ready to head back to wherever professors went when they weren't teaching. "Ted," I said, speaking his name out loud to him for the first time. When he turned to me, the Hot for Teacher fire rekindled anew. His eyes, studying my face, bored through whatever façade I'd created and touched the real part of me, the scared part of me that didn't even know who I was.

"Yes, Charlie."

Everyone else stopped talking and followed Ted's gaze, half a dozen paste-white faces glinting in the fluorescent light. I cleared my throat. "Do you have a doctorate?"

He smirked, glancing down at the floor. A soft snicker tumbled out of him. "Yes. I have several."

I paused. "So why don't you go by Dr. Strange?"

Perhaps only a second passed. But for me, each second divided and divided like the cells of a zygote, extending the lifespan of a minute into an unending pause. I focused on Ted's face, his eyes, avoiding the curious or scolding glares of the grad students. I had a lifetime to consider the choice.

At last, he chuckled. The tension cracked and turned to dust. "Dr. Strange is my father." His voice was light, as if everyone's father, too, was a doctor, and perhaps he was saving them both from a lot of *Freaky Friday*-style hijinks by establishing a different identity.

The graduate students laughed. I smiled and prayed to melt into my shoes.

Ted stood up, swirled the chair back around to face the proper way. "Before I go," he said to the group, "I'm having a holiday party at my place in a few weeks. I'd love you all to join me for drinks and snacks."

His eyes locked onto mine. I knew this meant I was especially invited.

## IT WASN'T ME

Dan doesn't want to be held accountable for his choices or his actions. He hides the reality of the weekend from Beth, feeding the dog the plate of dinner she'd saved for him in the refrigerator since men are incapable of taking care of themselves. He leans on Alex in those days for survival. She meets all his wifely needs, tending to his many appetites, gassing him up with her attention and desire. There's a famous scene when Dan and Alex tear each other apart in the industrial elevator of her apartment building. It feels like Dan views Alex as some kind of reward—for being a good husband, maybe, or for making all the right choices for his family. The privilege is deeply ironic.

This privilege convinces Dan he doesn't have to offer Alex any closure. Alex becomes the face of 80s horror from this point forward. She refuses to fade back into the rain. The confidence that made her so beguiling in those first scenes flips into an insistence that terrorizes Dan. As she says, in an iconic moment from the film, "I won't be ignored, Dan." She evolves into a Freddy Kruger figure, stepping out of Dan's dream and into the nightmare his reality will become.

She calls his office but he won't take her calls. She calls his home in the middle of the night, the only time and place, she says, she knows without a doubt where he will be. When she tracks him down in person, in the city, and confronts him about his responsibility to her, she reveals she's pregnant. She's in her mid-thirties. She believes she might not have another chance to have a child. By our contemporary standards, this feels like her valid choice to make. But the film wants us to believe that she's not only insane, she's robbed Dan of his DNA.

We never find out if Alex really is pregnant. She insists over and over again that she is, but Dan—and by extension, the film—wants us to believe this is her big manipulative gambit. A pregnant mistress cannot be ignored, Dan. The evidence of his crime grows inside her, and she plans to release it into the world whether he likes it or not.

Alex demands recognition from Dan. He refuses whenever that recognition does not take the form of Alex satisfying his needs.

## ACT FOUR: AN UNEXPECTED GUEST

Dr. Date authored an advice column in the university's daily paper. Sex-positive, inclusive of all genders and sexualities, he was progressive for his time and popular among students. That November, Dr. Date threw a singles mixer at the university's art museum, a mini Frank Gehry monstrosity we referred to, somewhat lovingly, as "the TV dinner" for the steel panel façade's resemblance to a Swanson's frozen entree.

The museum clung to the cliff along the river literal steps from my dorm, and I decided to go with my friends. It was time for me to be open to love's possibilities again. I'd spent my sophomore year hopelessly in love with a guy who lived two doors down from me, while he, in turn, mooned over my roommate. Despite the crush that blossomed into a heartbreaking love for this guy, I tried dating a Brad, and then another Brad, over the course of the year, only for my neighbor-crush to appear at my door. Each time he expressed interest in me, and then, when I dumped the Brad, scurried off and left me high and dry. It sent me into depression, and when I returned to campus the following fall, I moved to a different dorm, toward a life I was building for myself.

At the entrance to the mixer, we were required to put on a nametag. If we were interested in meeting men, we wore red tags. Women, green tags. And if we were interested in both, we wore gold. I put on my red tag, marked "Charlie" across it with a black Sharpie, and wandered into the museum.

I milled around with my friends, falling in and out of love with passersby. I didn't know what I was looking for. I didn't know *who* I was looking for. I waited for someone to pluck me out of the crowd, kiss me, and marry me. I spotted a hot guy wearing a tight gray t-shirt that clung to his chest and biceps. I did the only thing I knew how to do: I looked at him. I looked at him over and over again. Through the side of my eye, dead on, with my head cocked coyly at an angle, even turning around to seem surprised he might be looking at me. Nothing worked. I was going to be alone forever. Or in a sexual relationship with someone who would ultimately decide if I graduated from college. It was complicated.

Mikhail, one of the baby gays who lived on the floor where I served as RA, stopped me to say hi. As much as I was sexually naïve and not fully at peace with my sexuality, Mikhail was self-possessed and unabashed in his. We chatted and he asked if I'd had any luck. "I saw this one guy," I said, looking around to find him, "but I'm too shy to say hi."

"Who?" Mikhail asked for a description. But then I saw the guy in the next room.

"Him." I pointed. "Gray shirt."

"Torry?" He asked like I would know. I shrugged. "That's Torry." He grabbed my hand and dragged me like a mule. "Come on." He put one hand on Torry's back and the other on mine. "Talk," he said, maybe a little annoyed.

"Hi." Torry held out his hand. I gave it a quick pump. He had strong hands, thick. My heart fluttered.

Torry was from a small town in Minnesota. He was a few years older than me, a little behind on his degree because he was paying for it himself. He had spiked brown hair shaved close on the sides, and at 5'8" came up to my shoulders. He was muscled and manly, but with a boyish face and nervous smile.

I was sure he wouldn't be into me. I was too tall, too thin, gangly, even. My hair unruly. My skin too oily. My clothes never seemed to fit right. I felt self-conscious about everything.

Torry suggested we walk to grab a coffee, and I offered my favorite campus hangout two blocks down the street. The black sky, the dramatic lighting against the campus buildings—it felt like the backdrop to a movie. Conversation flowed, and we laughed at each other's attempts at humor. On the walk back to my dorm, Torry led me up onto a ledge in front of the union. He got on his tiptoes and kissed me. Two people leaving the mixer cheered for us as they walked by. I'd won!

He wanted to come up to my room, but I suggested we meet again another time, a proper date. We parted ways at the front door. My guts danced like they hadn't since I met the sophomore year guy. The beginning of something real.

## ALL BY MYSELF

Dan is one of the most exceptional assholes in cinema history. Even with the escalations following his indiscretion, he doesn't tell Beth a single thing about what he's done, keeping her in the kind of innocent darkness that makes her, like Alex, a Butterfly figure. Alex makes an effort to reconcile with him over what's happened. She invites him to see *Butterfly* with her at the Met, but he refuses. Dan believes he's entitled to return to his life as if none of this ever happened. Alex can never have that option. The sincerity and vulnerability in her dialogue positions her as a character who asserts what she wants and needs, but because the film does so much work advocating that Dan is the victim, she sounds, even in her most valid moments, like a nutcase, like *she's* the one who misread the situation and now lives in a fantasy world Dan had no part in creating.

Meanwhile, Dan does everything he can to construct a new world with Beth in Bedford, Connecticut. If Dan sees Beth as the princess who needs protecting, then Alex is the crone who wants to destroy and replace her. What Alex does next is an example of the psychoanalytic concept of *passage a l'acte*, which describes the moment a violent thought morphs into action. Jacques Lacan, an explicator of Freud, identified this moment as "an act that approximates speech," or a way for someone to deliver a message without words. At its core, Lacan wrote, this is a person's demand for recognition from someone who holds power over them. The "social bond" of society—a general agreement to abide by laws and standards, such as not harming another person—is the guardrail against violent ideas becoming action. *Passage a l'acte* is the force that busts through that internal guardrail and unleashes violent acts. Alex's *passage a l'acte* is an unforgettable message: she cooks their family's pet rabbit in a pot on the stove. The film shows us the dual discovery in a series of parallel edits: Ellen as she runs to her pet's hutch in the backyard, and Beth as she investigates what's cooking on the stove. Dan finally confesses to Beth and she throws him out. Poor Dan. Living the life of so many philandering men, occupying a hotel room and phoning his daughter to tell her that he loves her, but doesn't love her enough to make better choices with his body.

Alex picks up their daughter from school and takes her to ride a rickety rollercoaster on the boardwalk (picture the words "metaphor" in flashing red lights). In Alex's mind, this is not an act of violence. She's bonding with Dan's child, trying to step into the maternal role she felt Dan promised her. Beth thinks her daughter has been kidnapped. She scours the town for Ellen, stopping only when she rear-ends another car and winds up in the hospital. We don't know how Ellen gets to the hospital, but she's there and she's safe. Beth needs Dan back in the house because of her injuries, and so he gets to move home. He could thank Alex for that. Instead, he buys a gun.

## ACT FIVE: GHOSTING

I didn't attend Ted's holiday party. In the weeks following the Dr. Date mixer, I spent all my free time with Torry, living the dream of having an on-campus boyfriend who loved crashing with me in my single room. We ate together in the dorm, studied in the coffee shop, and saw movies, grabbed dinner, and danced our asses off at the Gay 90s and the Saloon downtown.

Operation Hot for Teacher came to a halt. I was falling for Torry, feeling so lucky to have a man with an incredible physique express any kind of interest in me. It quieted insecurities about my own body to be seen as beautiful by him.

When I wasn't investing my time and energy in him, I researched, wrote, and edited the final paper I thought I might expand into my honors thesis for the CSCL program. "The Language of Film Is Universal: Cinema as a Language System" felt like a crowning academic achievement, something I could have written only under Ted's tutelage and with the tentative confidence I'd built over the weeks of flailing in his course and receiving his praise and encouragement. I always performed near the top of my class, but for the first time in my college career, I wasn't just memorizing facts and regurgitating formulas on tests. I felt like I could think for myself. I created something; I grew into the student Ted believed I could be.

## PICTURE TO BURN

People don't like to mention that Dan tries to kill Alex.

In the aftermath of her trespass into his home, he confronts her at her apartment. Before he says a word, he busts the door open, knocking Alex backward. He chases her through the apartment. It's a long, drawn out fight. Alex won't give up—she's a survivor. But Dan manages to get on top of Alex, squeezing her throat with his hands. The look on his face is empty. No humanity exists behind it. He stops before she dies, but then he sees a knife. He hesitates only long enough to consider the impact of his action on himself. He has no interest in Alex's life. It has no value to him. Not even her "child," real or imagined, is worth saving. In the end, though, he leaves her beaten, gasping on the floor. Dan hopes his assault sends a clear warning to Alex. But Dan has tried to kill her. Dan poses an existential threat to Alex. Alex cannot believe she will ever be safe.

This is why Alex is such a strongly crafted character. Her motivations are clear, her communication is direct. She acts in her own interest, and she reacts authentically to Dan's abuse. She defies the male expectation to submit and in that way is an important feminist icon of the era.

After all the violence and extensive gaslighting Dan puts her through, Alex shows up at their country home with a knife, slashing at her own leg in what we now recognize as cutting, a form of self-mutilation used to relive stress and anxiety by people with mental health issues. She presents a greater danger to herself than anyone else. Beth tries to reason with her, but Alex can't hear her. She's been pushed too far. She's been used. Abused.

Tossed away. Beaten, nearly killed. Erased. She has nothing left to lose.

That's why *Fatal Attraction* is really Alex's story. It's she who goes through the dramatic arc. This is her climactic final gambit, her last chance to capture her want and, in the process, fulfill her dramatic need to be loved, seen, and valued.

Dan drowns her in the tub, "saving" Beth in the process. It's a violent, prolonged act. Alex's eyes, wide open in the water, stare off into the infinite dark beyond this world. For Dan, order is restored. He kills the beast who threatened his family. In many ways, his arc echoes Hansel, who eats from the witch's house and, rather than suffer the consequences, kills her and escapes.

Adrian Lyne reshot the original ending. In the first version, Alex kills herself and frames Dan for murdering her. Audiences didn't like it, even though Dan still wriggled his way out of accountability and went free. That ending more closely resembles *Madame Butterfly*, but improves on the narrative by attempting to make the abusive man face consequences. In the reshoot, after Dan leaves her body in the tub, she leaps up, laughably reanimated, but before she can strike with the knife she (somehow) still wields, Beth—here comes the metaphor—shoots her in the heart. Dan escapes accountability *and* responsibility. And what began as one man's transgression against two women ends as a life-or-death conflict between those women. Patriarchy's most enduring tool to maintain power and authority is to convince those it oppresses that they're in conflict with one another.

## ACT SIX: UNMASKED

In the middle of Operation Hot for Teacher, when I was deep in the academic mire of my project, I asked Ted if he would be willing to do an independent study with me in the Winter Quarter, helping me refine these ideas in preparation for the Senior Project Seminar in my final term. He agreed and, prior to falling for Torry, I was thrilled about the opportunity to learn from him, and maybe kiss his face.

But after Torry, I worried about how my Fall Quarter choices might come looking for their logical end. That Ted might expect things from me now, things I didn't want to do, things I'd rather pretend were an accident or inconsequential.

I decided to call him and back out of the arrangement. I picked a time I thought he wouldn't be there, preferring to leave a message.

"This is Ted," he said, answering the phone. My stomach twisted into knots.

"It's Charlie," I said, "from Meaning."

"Yes, Charlie." His tone warmed like sugar into caramel. "How are you?"

"Listen, about the independent study thing." A silence opened between us. I tried to dive through the phone to picture what was happening on his end—sitting in his chair. Was he looking out the window? Was he smiling? Was he fidgeting with something on his desk? What was he thinking about me? "Turns out I can't do it this quarter. My schedule." Like it was an explanation.

"Oh, I understand."

"I'm sorry."

"Not at all." He took a breath. "Does this mean I won't be seeing you again?"

I didn't know what to say. The answer to that was clearly no. Could I just say no? "I don't know," I said.

He was quiet again for a second. "Is this the moment where you sever all your connections to me and vanish from my life?" His voice had become very small, thin—uncharacteristic of the charismatic man who dazzled us at the front of his classroom. This was the Ted beneath the Ted. The vulnerable, emotional part of him.

I knew this was the moment our connection would be severed. He knew this was that moment.

But I had never told someone that moment had arrived. I didn't know how. I was stupid enough to believe that showing up to class and flouncing around in my cutest outfits to get the attention of an older man wouldn't have consequences for me, not if I didn't want them, but not for one second had I considered what kind of consequences I was tossing in someone else's face when I did that. Of course, sexual accountability is complex and nuanced. I never consented to any activity. I removed myself from the one event—his house party—when that could have been a construed outcome. But I knew what my intention was. It was safe to say he did too. And now his intentions with me were also clear. But it sounded like he never saw it as a sexual affair. It sounded like he truly liked me. Something I wasn't even sure I could say about myself.

"No, no, of course not." I wanted to offer him something. A consolation prize. But I only sought exoneration from the guilt of knowing I'd hurt someone, reckless and foolish. I consoled no one. Ted knew I was lying.

"Well. Then I look forward to our paths crossing again." His office chair shrieked, the way a mouse might as he rolled across it.

I told him I was sure we'd see each other on campus. I pictured that recklessly long scarf flapping in the wind, the way I'd watched him on campus weeks before during a particularly blustery day. He hadn't known I was watching. He carried an armful of papers down the main quad, that scarf reaching into the sky like a hand grasping at something just out of reach. His hair riffled on his head and the bottom of his coat blew open behind him. The way the sun lit him, the expression on his face—some kind of bliss, like he was in the right place doing the right thing. At the time I thought it beautiful, and now I envied that confidence. I had none. In six months, nothing about my life would bear resemblance to where I was during that last phone call, the last time I spoke to Ted. The last time I was naïve enough to believe getting what I wanted and getting what I needed were the same thing.

I was the villain of this story.

# POSTMODERN PASTICHE

## JUNE 1999

I strode into the classroom with a VHS copy of *Scream*, some notes, and all the academic bravery I could muster. My classmates in the senior seminar came to this room from every corner of the program, each with their own focus, obsession, or interest. But none of them I recognized. None shared a classroom with me these past four years. I didn't even know their names.

To complete my film studies program, I'd written a long paper on powerful feminist women characters in Alfred Hitchcock's work. This senior project—a paper and presentation—was to satisfy my degree requirements for cultural literature, a program in which we read Freud, Lacan, Irigaray, Mulvey, Foucault, Žižek; discussed the male gaze in cinema, and deconstructed contemporary magazine advertisements to determine their subtext and subliminal messages.

Over the course of the program, I wrote psychoanalytic readings of the films *Heavenly Creatures* and *The House of Yes*, watched and loved *Paris Is Burning*, read and deconstructed Art Spiegelman's *Maus* books. My senior project was supposed to demonstrate not only my mastery of the techniques I'd learned from these explorations, but self-directed inquiry on a subject that intrigued me.

I chose horror. I chose *Scream*. Even then, three years after its release, it was still a watershed moment in horror cinema.

My presentation offered evidence that Billy and Stu were queer and closeted. With my tape cued up to the climactic scene of the film, I slid it into the VCR and adjusted the volume. With a grand gesture, I spun the television around on its casters so that no one in the room could see the screen.

They were not supposed to look. They were supposed to listen.

## NOVEMBER 1995

I sat on the edge of Christopher's bed. He sat across from me, on his roommate's bed. My hands fidgeted in my lap. My heart beat in a series of quick, powerful *thunks*. As we spoke, he scooched toward me, a couple inches at a time, slowly enough he hoped I wouldn't notice.

I noticed. I knew where this was going. I kept looking at the door. What if his roommate walked in?

When he crossed from bed to bed, we kissed. Not my first kiss— I'd kissed plenty of girls all the way back to Jill Bonnett in seventh grade. But it was first time I kissed a man. The first kiss I felt run all the way through me. In all the other kissing I'd done in my life, it never felt like this. It never felt so alive. The way his whiskers stung my chin and cheeks sent a tingle through me from scalp to toes.

Christopher was kind, cautious. He asked if I felt okay. I didn't know how to put into words how I could feel the phantom of his lips on mine, that I wanted more. I kissed him again. More intently. More intensely. More me.

I walked into his room unsure of who I was. Now I was certain I was gay.

The first step out of the closet was this realization, the one I accepted of myself. There would be hundreds of steps that followed this moment as I told the people in my inner circle. There were other gay people on our floor and in the building. One neighbor, with his henna-dyed hair and rainbow charm necklaces, was so adamantly gay that I felt threatened just being near him. How could he put himself at risk that way? Opening himself up to mockery, even violence. I should have envied him, but I didn't. I avoided him, worried even being seen with him would encourage assumptions about me.

It would take time for me to learn how to be a member of the queer community, part of that largely unseen web of interconnections we acknowledged to one another with a knowing glance, a subtle grin. It would be a blossoming, me opening myself up to the world around me in a way I never had before. Even if that world felt at times like it wanted to harm me, hide me, or see me dead.

## REBEL WITHOUT A CAUSE

Billy spends most of the first act of the film trying to have sex with Sidney. He's perfected the toxic male performance of acting like he doesn't want it too much, but making it clear that he does, in fact, really want it, but only if she's ready—and if that turned out to be now, that would be great.

Billy pops up through her second-story window, like Romeo played by James Dean. She puts off his pressure to have sex. Randy will assure us later, when he reads the rules of a horror film, that you should, under no circumstances, have sex. Before Billy climbs back down, Sidney flashes her breasts at him, as if to show him she's trying.

Late in the film, after they've had sex and Billy steps out as one of the two killers in the Ghostface costume, he tells Sidney she was bad in bed.

What he means is, *You didn't please me.*

What he suggests is, *I couldn't be pleased by you.*

What he reveals is, *I want something else.*

## OCTOBER 1996

Students gawked at the pedestrian bridge that crossed the river between the East and West Bank campuses of the university. In the night, a group of activists wheatpasted 18" x 24" sheets of paper to the bridge. Each one with the photo of a notable figure from history with three words describing their legacy, ending, every time, with the word "Queer":

JAMES BALDWIN
AMERICAN NOVELIST
ACTIVIST
QUEER

Straight students were outraged by this display. Some stuck their chewed gum to the faces of the writers, actors, politicians. Some just blacked out the word *queer*. I walked and looked at them, taking it all in, each Xeroxed page washed gold in sunrise. Though I had to keep my queerness a secret from most of the people around me, I felt in that moment like I was plugged into something bigger—something unseen that was tired of living in shadows.

I asked around among my queer friends about who might have done it. It was still a small and tightly networked group, despite the university's size, and it didn't take long to find out who had organized the displays. I learned several of the students were connected with my campus's LGBT office, though the office itself had no knowledge of their activity.

The LGBT student center was in the process of organizing a speakers' bureau of students who could visit campus groups, dorms, and offices to talk about their experiences being part of our community. There were about twenty of us attending a preliminary meeting of the bureau, a mix of folks from across the acronym. The facilitator welcomed us. "The purpose of this group is to build understanding between our communities and theirs," he explained. Part of the problem was that straight people, due to the politics of the closet and their own ignorance, either didn't know queer people or didn't know they knew queer people, and that lack of contact was preventing progress on queer political issues. As members of the bureau, we prepared a version of our coming out story—whatever that meant to us—to share in front of an audience, and then to answer their questions.

We broke up into pairs. I spoke with a shy trans woman and we each shared our stories. She was the first trans person I'd known I'd met, and I listened to her story, her challenges, her hopes. I shared my own story, which at the time was still developing. I had come out to my parents and siblings over the prior six months—far too soon. Before I was ready. Before I understood myself and my identity. My first year of college, my dorm was home to the only other person from my hometown who attended my school. There were no secrets in dorms, and soon I heard news about my sexuality was circulating through my high school. I was worried more than anything that my parents would hear something—and probably something cruel—from someone in town before they heard it from me.

Being part of the speakers bureau pushed me to embrace a new level of visibility as a queer person. But I wasn't alone. One of my assignments took to me to a neighboring Lutheran college, where I spoke with three other panelists about our experiences being queer. I knew we were doing important work, but at the same time I couldn't shake the feeling that I was in the zoo, on the opposite side of the bars, with straight people marveling at the wonder of my existence. Even though these conversations were for their benefit, each event I did for the speakers bureau somehow made me *more me*. As I embraced the vulnerability of visibility, the door to the closet drifted farther away.

Coming out wasn't an event. It launched a lifelong commitment to being the fullest version of myself. I was still coming out, daily, to people I'd just met and people I'd known for years.

For a long time, these people would confide in me that I was the first gay person they knew. "That you know you know," I'd say.

## THE WAY WE WERE

In the moments leading up to the climax, Billy and Stu reveal to Sidney they are the killers. They explain to Sidney that they're going to ask her a series of questions and, no matter her answers, she's going to die. Stu sidles up behind Billy and places his head on Billy's shoulder. It's intimate, capturing them in a two-shot in this tender pose, even as they're covered in blood.

They look like they could be in love.

## JANUARY 1997

Sexual Health Awareness and Disease Education was housed in the School of Public Health and led by Dave, a tall guy with wild graying hair who radiated positivity and support. At my friend Lori's encouragement, I received special permission to join the group in the second quarter even though I had not taken the required public health course on STIs. I learned the scripts for various presentations we gave on campus and in the community, teaching consent, good sexual health practices, and providing the most up-to-date information to other students.

The AIDS pandemic continued to ravage the gay community in the mid-90s, but infections had moved into the general population. This stoked and deepened anti-gay sentiments and anti-gay violence across the United States. My high school health class had mentioned AIDS exactly once when my teacher told us, "If you have gay sex, you *will* get AIDS and die." Though I knew intellectually how to protect myself— condoms were then the most reliable method of prevention and also freely available almost everywhere, especially on a college campus—the lack of research and public information made it a challenge to believe in any idea of safety.

It was difficult in those years for someone to disclose their HIV status. The stigma was too strong. There was too much at stake. Any number of devastating actions could be taken against them—they could be fired, they cold lose their housing—but disclosure meant facing stigma from within the queer community as well. As a public health crisis, those fighting to stop the spread of AIDS took drastic measures to change sexual behavior, sometimes seeming to echo the words of my health teacher. The Red Cross banned sexually active gay men from giving blood, a prohibition that continued without exception until 2023, even when there was so much more reliable information about transmission, detectability, treatment, and prevention.

For me, and for some members of my microgeneration of gay men who came out after the crisis began but before accurate information was widely available, AIDS was terrifying. We knew of thousands of men who died slow, difficult deaths in the 80s and 90s. I did not want to be among them. When I came out to my parents, they told me they were afraid I would die of the disease. Many other gay men heard the same thing.

Layered beneath these fears were my own deep-seated issues about sex and sexuality. I wanted to have sex, but I had a weird Puritan streak in my brain about it. Walking through a gay bar and feeling someone grab my ass or slide a hand down my back made me uncomfortable. If I complained, I was told to "lighten up" and "enjoy it." Even by my own friends. Worse, I didn't feel a connection to my own body. Insecurities plagued my brain. All of it made me feel even more isolated in the soup of my conflicted feelings.

Members of SHADE marched in the Homecoming Parade the next year, and I wore the comical full-body condom costume for the event: a long, gauzy tube with a cut out for my face and a rubber hat shaped like a receptacle tip. I handed out condoms along the parade route as others marched with our banner and handed out handbills about our work.

SHADE undid some of the shame and discomfort I felt around sexuality. I was forced to talk about it, publicly, and to help people make safer choices. By extension, I took better responsibility for myself. It would be more than a decade before I felt fully connected to my own sexuality, my own body, my own desires, but all of that work started here, with a gesture toward learning to talk frankly and openly about sex.

## EYES WITHOUT A FACE

Billy is the moody, over-sensitive boy who doesn't say much—his social dysfunction is charitably interpreted as normal masculinity. He exudes a dangerous kind of confidence throughout the film—a toxic masculinity—whether he's crawling up into Sidney's second-floor bedroom or, you know, murdering classmates.

Ghostface—the black-clad killer with a mask inspired by painter Edvard Munch's tormented figure in The Scream—calls Sidney up to ask her what's her favorite scary movie, but she laughs it off. "What's the point? They're all the same. Some stupid killer stalking some big-breasted girl who can't act who is always running up the stairs when she should be running out the front door." Sidney's indictment of the genre's heroines almost immediately comes back to haunt her when Ghostface appears at her house. Sidney—against her own advice—runs up the stairs to her bedroom, where the doors to her bedroom and her closet nest in such a way that neither can be fully opened. Despite her haughty hot take on horror movie heroines, she's no different in the heat of the moment.

Billy crawls through her window a second time—a horribly-timed romantic gesture that scares her. But when a cell phone drops out of his pocket, Sidney leaps to suspect Billy of being the killer. More than that, she trusts in her own belief. She gets him arrested, and continues to avoid him once he's been released.

When Sidney later goes to the party at Stu's (Matthew Lillard) house, Billy shows up against her wishes. "Dude," Stu says, winking at Billy. "What are you doing here?" The wink is a double-edged gesture: it means both "we're in cahoots" and "I'm flirting with you." Here, knowing what we know by the end of the film, this wink is among the most meaning-laden winks of all time.

## OCTOBER 1996

Dance music thumped through the door of the house, the windows chattering like teeth. The queer fraternity was an anchor of the queer social scene. Though I wasn't a member, I was a fan of their parties. Their house stood at the end of fraternity row, tucked around a corner as if seeking just a bit more privacy than the other houses, as if they were more modest, more conservative. Inside the house, where the couches and side tables crouched along the walls and the spinning strobes and colored lights flashed while insistent beats played, the opposite was true. Everyone was more themselves there, as though passing through the threshold meant taking off or putting on one's public costume. I loved these parties in part because it was easy to get booze, and booze quieted my anxieties and insecurities. I feared and hated myself less when I was drunk.

My queerness felt like a train passing me in the night, cars I could look into as the windows flashed by, but something I didn't occupy. Something that wasn't carrying me. I was afraid of having sex and I was afraid of never having sex. Afraid of being left alone and of being fully myself.

I stood against the wall in the basement of the campus's gay fraternity, near the bar, nursing my cup of party punch and trying not to make eye contact with anyone, even as I gazed with longing at any number of men who passed by me. What did I want? To be seen, touched, loved. But not acknowledged, understood, known.

My friend Karen walked up and introduced me to a man I'd never seen before. He had short dark hair with bangs swept away from his face, five o'clock shadow working overtime. He had a kind face. He was older—mid-twenties maybe. He wasn't in school. Karen hovered for a few minutes but then excused herself to let us talk.

I don't remember what the man and I talked about, but I know he asked me if I wanted to go home with him. I was outside my body talking to him. I heard myself say, *Sure*. I was drunk, or drunk enough, which was my goal. In the car to his place, it took five minutes for me to lose our location. I vanished into the city with him. I was nineteen.

I fumbled out of my clothes at his apartment. I kissed him. I felt his body over me. He asked if he could fuck me but I demurred. Then he fell asleep.

In the morning, he offered me breakfast. I said no. I wanted to go home. Was I sure? He could whip something up, or we could go out. No, I said. I pulled myself into my coat to armor me. He tried to make conversation on the way home, but I couldn't. I must have seemed like a miserable person. He dropped me at the door of my dorm and I never saw him again.

"Good thing he didn't murder you," a friend said at breakfast when I told her what had happened. She was half-joking. I hadn't considered my safety in all this—a privilege of being born white and male. The next summer, a young gay man launched a killing spree from Minneapolis, traveling down the continent to Miami where he shot Versace on the front steps of his mansion. I watched it unfold on the news. I considered myself, somehow, lucky.

## A KISS BEFORE DYING

In the psychoanalytic film analysis framework, stabbings are representations of male sexual violence, with knives standing in for the penis-phallus. Male victims largely outnumber the women in *Scream*; only Casey (Drew Barrymore) and Tatum (Rose McGowan) fall victim to Ghostface. On the other hand, Casey's boyfriend Steve Orth (Kevin Patrick Walls) is stabbed in front of her, Principal Himbry (Henry Winkler) is stabbed in his office, Kenny (W. Earl Brown) the cameraman gets his throat slashed, and Dewey (David Arquette) is stabbed in the back. Of the male victims, only Randy (Jamie Kennedy) is injured by other means, shot by Billy. It must be assumed that a killer whose knife is an ever-present accessory would prefer to kill with it. Ghostface, to put it plainly, seems really into penetrating male bodies.

Casey and Tatum are notable victims because they each fail to confirm Stu's heterosexuality. Casey, we learn, dumps Stu to be with the more stereotypically masculine jock Steve, and Tatum, the "cool girl," embarrasses him in front of his friends. Neither of these girls appears to die of stabbing—Casey gets strung up in a tree, and an automatic garage door crushes Tatum as she tries to escape Ghostface.

And Randy does get stabbed, eventually—in the second film, in a van parked at a curb. We the audience know what's going on inside, having seen him swept into the arms of Ghostface lying in wait. But from the outside, maybe it's just two folks having some very vigorous sex in that van.

## FALL 1996

I met Mike my second year of college through a rudimentary chat service I accessed from my roommate's computer using the black-and-green display of a Telnet window. IRC, Internet Relay Chat, was where I found a community of queer men facing the same issues, questions, and desires I faced. Mike was among them, though I didn't know his name was Mike at first. Everyone had a handle that afforded them anonymity.

With IRC, I was free to be myself but not necessarily vulnerable, like I would be in the real world. It was the best I could do then. Because the community was relatively small—or close-knit—it wasn't long before my IRC connections began linking up in real life. At bars, at parties we'd meet each other and at some point, one of us would tentatively ask, "Are you _____ on IRC?"

Mike was tall and pale with dark hair. His quiet demeanor made him a cutting observer of the world around him. He had an intuitive sense of what everyone was like on the inside, no matter what face they presented to the world. When he spoke, he'd say something sharply funny or acerbic, then take a long drag off his cigarette to emphasize his inner darkness. He didn't go to the university. He lived with his family in the suburb New Hope, a place he preferred to call "No Hope." We shared a taste in music and movies. We started hanging out more regularly. Mike and I also both really liked horror movies, and we saw *Scream* together at the Mall of America.

The mall was a four-story monstrosity where each level's circular layout was a half-mile around. It featured everything from staples like Gap and Old Navy to Minnesota oddities, like a cheese store specializing in curds. It sincerely sought to up the interactivity of the mall experience by adding theme restaurants in the vein of the Rainforest Café, where it rained hourly (near but not on diners), and a Knott's theme park in the center, complete with a couple mild roller coasters.

The movie theater occupied a big swath of the top floor, and its lobby gave a panoramic view of the theme park and rings of stores below. Mike and I arrived to find a crowd of people, some there to see *Scream*, yes, but also to see everything the giant multiplex offered. I was swept up in the excitement of the night and the stress of navigating so many people waiting for snacks, buying tickets, and moving to their seats. We showed up early to make sure we'd get a ticket, then rushed in to find two seats together.

For months after, Mike spun the *Scream* soundtrack in his car: Moby's light electronica, the alt-country of Nick Cave's "Red Right Hand," and Gus Black's plaintive slowing down of "Don't Fear the Reaper."

*Scream*'s mix of humor, winking at the audience, and genuine chills was revelatory at the time, unlike anything I'd seen. Sidney was a vulnerable final girl, affected by the chaos around her, wanting to withdraw, but instead forcing herself to act and save the day.

## A HISTORY OF VIOLENCE

If Billy and Stu read as closeted (murderous) lovers, they are echoes of the spirit of Leopold and Loeb, killers who strived to commit the perfect murder in Chicago in 1924, and whose stories were adapted over and over again for the cinema, including *Rope*, *Compulsion*, and *Swoon*, the last of which most clearly casts the two as a romantic couple. Their crime and its trial were a sensation, and Leopold and Loeb's story attracted the attention of celebrity attorney Clarence Darrow, who defended them at trial. Billy and Stu also believe they have stumbled on the perfect crime, and an alibi that will cast them as victims and survivors rather than perpetrators. Leopold and Loeb, too, were late teenagers at the time of their crime, just a couple years older than *Scream*'s murderous duo.

Ghostface's trademark is asking his victims about their favorite scary movies, and this suggests Billy and Stu are well-versed in the cinema of the horrific—which would include, of course, these representations of Leopold and Loeb and the subtle queer coding directors used when repurposing their story. But Billy's fixation on his mother cribs right from Norman Bates in *Psycho*, and his echoing of Norman's classic line, "We all go a little mad sometimes," affirms the connection. When Sidney asks Billy for a motive, he replies, "Did Norman Bates have a motive?" Both Norman and Billy kill with knives and do it in costume, and both seem to imply that an overidentification with an absent mother figure turns boys and young men into sissies and mama's boys.

This, in turn, causes young men to make poor life choices: disobedience, homosexuality, murder.

We learn at the end of the film that Billy and Stu killed Sidney's mother out of revenge for an affair she had with Billy's father, which caused Billy's mom to leave his family, and that they've set up the new murders to look like Sidney's father did it all. But the deeper you look into all of this, the less you find: at the end, you just have Billy and Stu, who have murdered all the people who, in some way, kept the two of them from being together.

## JUNE 1999

My senior project on *Scream* was an earnest attempt to make sense of the film's metaphors and insinuations. Horror and thriller genres up until that time were notoriously and often straightforwardly homophobic and transphobic—from Anthony Perkins's mother-loving motelier in *Psycho* to the cross-dressing killer of *Dressed to Kill* to the possibly trans-identified killer of *The Silence of the Lambs*. Even *A Nightmare on Elm Street's* Freddy Krueger, a child-killer, can be viewed as queer coded (and without argument in the homoerotic *A Nightmare on Elm Street 2*), as he was developed in an era when homosexual men were generally feared by straight people to be violent pedophiles.

Though I enjoyed *Scream* a great deal and, as a fan of horror films, wanted it to be taken seriously, I was troubled as a queer viewer. Was the film suggesting something about homosexuality?

I wanted the presentation to offer evidence. Here's what my classmates heard as the video played:

BILLY: (to Sidney) Watch this. (to Stu) Are you ready?
STU: Yeah. Yeah. I'm ready baby. Hit it! Get it up! Get up! Hit it!
*stabbing sound*

STU whimpers. Then: Jesus, man. Oh, shit. My turn.

BILLY: Don't forget. Stay to the side and don't go too deep.

STU: Okay, I'll remember.

BILLY: Ah, fuck! Fuck! God damn it, Stu.

STU: Sorry, Billy. I guess I got a little too zealous, huh?

BILLY: Gimme the knife.

STU: No.

BILLY: Give me the knife. Now!

STU: You see, Sidney, everybody dies but us. Everybody dies but us. We're gonna carry on and plan the sequel because let's face it baby, these days you have to have a sequel.

SIDNEY: You sick fucks. You've seen too many movies.

STU: Don't you blame the movies. Movies don't make psychos, movies make psychos more creative.

*sounds of the knife puncturing flesh, scraping bone*

STU: Stop it, Billy, I can't take anymore. I'm feeling woozy.

With the television turned around, the images hidden from my classmates and professor, the scene sounded like gay porn. Like Billy and Stu were taking turns fucking each other.

And, with the knife standing in as the metaphorical dicks they couldn't shove into each other, they kind of were.


## NOW

Twenty years later, I still love *Scream*. I drafted this essay over a long stretch of months from late summer 2018-spring 2020. In that time, I moved twice, boxing and unboxing my life each time, trying to make the hard decisions about what to keep, what to donate, what to throw away. In the process, I stumbled upon hard copies of my college coursework, from my earliest short stories and poems to the academic papers I mentioned above.

Among them, of course, was an early proposal for the *Scream* presentation, which referenced the concept of the "closet of connotation" outlined in the book *Monsters in the Closet: Homosexuality and the Horror Film* by Harry Benshoff. The closet of connotation is the system of symbols, signs, and codes that suggested queerness before queerness itself could be present, for better and for worse. Though I'd forgotten a lot of the details, some of which I reincorporated here as I revised, I have never forgotten how it felt to walk into my senior presentation with that worn VHS tape in my hands to talk about queer coding and how it influences audience perceptions of good and evil. How I felt so seen and so vulnerable in that moment.

# ACT II

# FILM NOIR

**MINNEAPOLIS, MINNESOTA | JULY 25, 2000 | EVENING**

An ambulance wailed on Portland Avenue, zipping to the hospital down the street. Seven stories up, my boyfriend Torry and I draped ourselves over our couch and love seat. We smoked our after-dinner Kamel Red cigarettes, waiting for *Popular* to begin. The overhyped fanfare of the Minneapolis local news knuckled into the living room with us, followed by the blather of its anchors. "An update now, in an eight-year-old murder investigation," the anchor said, our attention half his and half our own. "Police have arrested this man for the 1992 murder of Linda Jensen." A photo of the suspect flashed on the screen.

We recognized the face. It was Torry's Uncle Kent.

Our heads spun and our eyes locked together from our separate roosts. Neither of us could believe what we saw. We needed confirmation from each other it was real.

Torry shouted at the anchor. His confusion reacted with anxiety in a complex alchemy in his voice. Adrenaline exploded into my bloodstream and the cigarette trembled in my fingers. I stamped it out in the ashtray. How was this possible?

The report didn't offer details. Torry jumped from the couch and snatched the phone, punching a number into it before holding it to his ear. We waited.

**FADE IN ON:**

Uncle Charlie (Joseph Cotton) looks dead, flat and stiff on a Newark flophouse bed. In his expensive, well-tailored suit, in this dark room, he evokes the vampiric legacy of Bram Stoker's blood-thirsty count: pale, his features so still they appear to be wax. Outside, drifters tear apart day-old bread on the waterfront. The rusted fossil of an old jalopy sinks into the earth next to a sign that reads *No Dumping*. The city's slow ruin reflects the moral decay of the man who lies before us. Despite the poverty below, a pile of money spreads over the nightstand, tossed there in haste, even if its owner now seems unrushed. The police have connected the dots. They know who he is. How he got this money. How he can afford to dress so well. And why, despite these factors, he holed up in a run-down residential hotel with daily and weekly rates. What he really needs is to vanish. To get as far away from Newark as he possibly can. To go west.

## BECKER, MINNESOTA | SPRING 1999 | DAY

Boisterous and charismatic, mid-section thick with middle age, Uncle Kent's blond hair darkened to brown as it reached down into his full beard. He laughed loudly, and often, and loved to spin yarns you knew probably weren't true but may have been inspired by truths, the way a pearl, at its core, is just a grain of sand. He made a good living working as a car salesman in St. Cloud, and that unique salesman brand of kindness and coercion radiated off him. I couldn't help but be charmed.

Uncle Kent, his wife Debbie, and their four children lived in a typical split-level home in Becker, Minnesota, population 2,730. Aunt Debbie was also typical: strong Minnesota accent, short hair, kind, soft-spoken. Their oldest son was close to graduating high school. He planned to attend a small college for Christian men, where he'd consider joining the ministry and devoting his life to the Lord. Their twin daughters, both eighth graders, were identical neither in looks nor personality; in fact, they were merely sisters born together. One was quiet, neat, studious. The other wore thick make-up, talked about boys, and struggled in school. They, too, held their faith close to them and had plans to attend the sister institution of their brother's college, where they'd get a liberal arts education in a faith-based community of learners. Their youngest son was like a miniature version of his brother but ten years younger, still carefree and full of energy.

Generous lawns skirted the houses in Kent's neighborhood. The homes featured two-car garages, backyard decks with unobstructed views of the distant horizon. It was the kind of town where you'd want to raise a family, where you'd trust your neighbors to keep an eye on all the kids playing outside, riding bikes, wandering the unpainted roads until well after dusk. It was a community where murder existed only in television and movies. Killers were fiction. Safety was reality.

The first time I walked into their home, a menagerie of crosses, hand-stitched proverbs in frames, and decorative psalms accused me of sins from walls, side tables, and throw pillows. I wrapped my arms around myself for most of that visit, worried that even though they knew Torry and I were in a committed gay relationship, they would reject us. Reject *me* as the living embodiment of his transgression against the natural order. After a couple hours, my arms fell to my sides. Uncle Kent and Aunt Debbie were among the first devoutly Christian people I met who knew I was gay and treated me with kindness and dignity. Their small, basic kindness would bias me to believe their lies, even when the simple truth made more sense.


**MATCH DISSOLVE TO:**


Young Charlie (Theresa Wright) reclines on her bed in a casual dress, but like a child has her shoed feet on the comforter. Her dark hair erupts into fluffy curls at her ears. This first scene in Santa Rosa echoes our introduction to Uncle Charlie, establishing an emotional parallel between the two characters right down to the lighting and set design, though this room is no flophouse; it's a comfortable middle-class home. Young Charlie doesn't appear dead, but she does seem burdened with a distinctly late-adolescent ennui—so much of this shows us she hovers between the worlds of children and adults, belonging fully to neither one.

Santa Rosa, as revealed in a series of establishing shots: enormous trees shade houses and streets, downtown bustling with townspeople while cars swim in their lanes. Even the sunny California weather, which surely never changes, makes it a kind of heaven on Earth—the "America" Americans sold to the rest of the world.

Uncle Charlie steps off a Santa Rosa streetcar. Gone is the dour man we saw on the Newark bed. This Uncle Charlie is charming, sincere, loving. He gulps down the affection his sister's family lavishes upon him.

Thornton Wilder, playwright of *Our Town*, wrote the script for *Shadow of a Doubt*. You can see his signature in the way it idealizes small town life, the stability of the nuclear family. Before Uncle Charlie's arrival, everything is perfect. Mother, Father, and Young Charlie's brother and sister—everyone is happy. Uncle Charlie's rupture of the nuclear family will ultimately turn the entire town upside down. Unmarried in middle age, urban, learned, cultured, refined, dapperly dressed, Uncle Charlie—while wearing the mask of the heterosexual—is wrapped in the trappings of cinematic queer coding used throughout the era of the Hays Code, when filmmakers were prohibited from representing queerness directly on screen. To work around it, they used innuendo, tropes, and symbols like striking fashion sense (*Suddenly, Last Summer*), overidentification with a mother figure (Hitchcock's *Psycho*), and sexual dysfunction, abuse, or violence (*M*). Uncle Charlie embodies what this era believed threatened the tranquility of the American family.

## BIG LAKE TOWNSHIP, MINNESOTA | FEBRUARY 24, 1992 | AFTERNOON

Linda Jensen was part of Uncle Kent and Aunt Debbie's neighborhood, someone they said they knew but didn't know well—the kind of person they'd wave to if they saw her out jogging, or would offer a smile at the grocery store.

When Linda's husband arrived home that Monday, he found his wife stabbed to death in their bedroom, their nine-month-old daughter crying in a playpen. A comforter covered Linda's body, a knife plunged into her chest to fasten it to her. The bed sheets were missing, never to be recovered. The autopsy revealed Linda had been raped. She was thirty-nine years old.

A photo of Linda accompanied reports of her death. She wears a simple cream turtleneck, dark curls falling to her shoulders, a deep red lip, her teeth electric white in her broad smile.

Murder investigations work like a nautilus shell, beginning with those closest to the victim and working outward as each suspect is eliminated. Due to the nature of the crime, the way the body had been left by the killer, the initial investigation centered on the person closest to Linda, the one with the greatest means and most likely motive to do her harm: the husband.

His name was Charlie Jensen.

## CLOSE UP:

Young Charlie idolizes her suave and cultured uncle. He loves this reflection of his influence, a power he holds both over his sister and his niece. To stoke her adoration, Uncle Charlie gives his namesake an emerald ring, something far too precious to entrust to a teen. For Young Charlie, the ring means someone she loves finally regards her as an adult, someone worthy of adult things. She feels seen, loved.

The ring is the connection to this film's "MacGuffin," a Hitchcock signature. The MacGuffin is often some kind of closely-held secret or resource upon which the future hinges. Ultimately, it's just something sought by the characters to advance the plot, or a physical representation of the story's primary conflict. In *Notorious*, it's uranium hidden behind a locked door, the key to which the protagonists must steal. In *The Birds*, it's Melanie's practical joke on Mitch, represented by the two caged love birds. These objects resonate with their own energy and hold our focus. Ultimately, they're just plot devices. The characters' focus on obtaining the thing informs their narrative choices. Getting it results in unexpected knowledge that twists or changes the conflict of the film.

Examining the ring, Young Charlie finds an engraving, and this feature—and Charlie's desire to decode it—will put her on the path direct to the climax of the film. When she can't get a waltz out of her head at dinner and asks everyone to help her remember the name, Uncle Charlie gives her the wrong answer. The waltz on her mind was the *Merry Widow Waltz*. And her uncle, she's about to discover, is the Merry Widow Killer.

## ZIMMERMAN, MINNESOTA | VARIOUS DATES AND TIMES, 1999-2000

Torry's grandparents Richard and Joan didn't answer his phone call. Of course they wouldn't. They weren't home. They'd rushed to wherever Uncle Kent was being held to see what they could do. Or if they were home, they were avoiding reporters. They'd circled the wagons, brought family over to talk through what was happening and how they would help. Torry tried his mom. She lived in Duluth and was recently remarried for the third or fourth time. No response there, either. We had to wait.

Torry and I often dropped in to see Richard and Joan. Their home clutched the edge of Lake Fremont, a typical Minnesotan body of water, a place they'd occupied for so long that every inch of wall and floor space was covered by some kind of décor. Two birds sang together in a cage in the living room, and a cocker spaniel wandered through the house, greeting anyone who would give her the time of day. By the time I knew them, they were in their early 70s. They accepted me into their home and treated me with the same affection they showed Torry. I was grateful for it. My own parents were back in Wisconsin. I had one brother in Phoenix and another married to his work in the Minneapolis suburbs, and the rest of my extended family I rarely saw. Torry's family wasn't my own, but I felt included by them, cared for by them. For better or worse, I was part of their response to Uncle Kent's arrest.

There are stages of acceptance to an arrest like this, just as there is with death. The first stage, where Torry and I stood together the night we saw the news report, was denial. Neither of us could believe it. There had been a mistake. They arrested the wrong man. Uncle Kent couldn't have killed anyone. He was Uncle Kent. He had a family, he had kids, he had everything going for him. Before it was all over, there would be many stages, but the rest we'd experience on our own, in our own minds, in the silence we found there.

## TRACKING SHOTS

Young Charlie's unfettered love for her uncle doesn't waver until she meets Jack (Macdonald Carey). Like Uncle Charlie, Jack pretends to be someone he's not in order to get close to a woman who has what he wants. But this undercover cop kills the last thing keeping Young Charlie in that in-between realm separating childhood naïveté from the adult awareness of the world. The arrival of evil in the form of her uncle sets off a chain of events that won't let her stay in the soup of her innocence much longer.

Jack tells her Uncle Charlie murders rich widows to inherit their money. She doesn't want to believe it. She thinks it's ridiculous. But Jack's clues stick with her. Uncle Charlie's flashy wealth. The ring engraved with unfamiliar initials.

Uncle Charlie opines one night at dinner that rich "useless" widows live lives of leisure, hemorrhaging the money their dead husbands worked so hard to earn. The monologue seems to go on without end. It's a savage takedown steeped in misogyny. What irony there is in this Lothario dragging "faded, fat, greedy women," as if their bodies are symbols of the excess that makes him ill, even as he plots to kill them and inherit their estates. His argument strives to justify his crimes by restoring this wealth to the realm of the masculine. But he's not a crusader. He's a parasite.

"But they're alive!" Young Charlie protests. "They're human beings."

Uncle Charlie, in extreme close up, turns to look at his niece. At this shot distance, in this lighting, he appears inhuman. Just a geography of shiny and shadowy features. Only his eyes—dark, hooded—reveal any intent. "Are they?" His voice is flat. Emotionless. Lethal.


## CENTRAL MINNESOTA | AUGUST 2000 | DAY


Uncle Kent was held in a high security jail following his arrest. Torry and I met his grandparents and traveled there to see him. We cleared the security checkpoints, driving through multiple chain link fence gates toward the building. Once inside, we registered with the visitor's desk, consented to a security screening that included a metal detector and a possible frisk, even though we wouldn't be in the same room as Uncle Kent at any point during our visit. The precautions felt extreme, and they told me a lot about the crimes connected to the men in this jail.

Guards moved us into a bland room where corporate cubicle partitions carved up the space into little pods. Each pod had a monitor with two chairs facing it. We were the only visitors, giving the room an eerie, extinct vibe. Square windows let sunlight in to cheer up the ghastly fluorescent bulbs plugged into the ceiling, but rather than making the room feel warm or inviting, it just felt like jail.

Torry and I dragged over chairs from a nearby pod as his grandparents sat down. A guard explained Kent was moving from his cell to the communication room. We had no idea how far this was from where we sat, and that was part of the security protocol. The waiting was unbearable. Richard, usually the stoic type, hunched forward in his chair. His shoulders slanted sharply toward the floor. Joan fidgeted with the handbag in her lap. Torry drew circles on her back with his palm, comforting her and burning off his own nervous energy.

The monitor flashed on, quick as an eye blinking open. Uncle Kent sat in a small square room with concrete block walls painted dark blue. The camera shot him from above eye level, forcing him to gaze up at us. His bright orange jumpsuit vibrated in stark relief to the rich wall color, and he looked tan with it on, almost healthy.

He greeted us with a huge smile. "Hey, folks!" He sounded as upbeat as a game show host. We asked how he was doing and he assured us everything was fine. "This is all a big mistake. They're going to figure it out soon enough and I'll be home before you know it." I knew he was putting on a show for his parents. He didn't want them to worry. He'd never tell us what was really going on outside that room, or how scared he was. His training as a car salesman had never been this useful. He went on to talk about his meetings with his defense team, the initial strategies to get the case dismissed at arraignment, and his assurance he'd be out in just a few weeks. Torry's grandparents were eager to believe it. I wanted to, too.

After, Torry and I stopped by Aunt Debbie's house to check in on her and the kids. The kids were shell shocked, hollowed out versions of themselves. While Uncle Kent sat behind bars, the rest of them had to carry on with their lives—school, work, shopping—with full knowledge of the allegations against Uncle Kent in a case that touched the lives of almost every person in the region. In a small community like theirs, anonymity didn't exist. Everyone knew them. Everyone knew about this.

Standing in the kitchen like she had all those months ago, Aunt Debbie looked at me. She said something about the murdered woman, her family. "Her husband's name is Charlie," she said. "The Jensens."

A shudder ran through me.

But Aunt Debbie was still looking at me. "Are you—" She paused. "Related?"

The way she looked at me. The tone. She wasn't just asking about my family tree. She was asking if, somehow, I was responsible for her husband's arrest. If I was some kind of genealogical vigilante who had skulked around their family looking for evidence the police could use. If I was a family member of a murdered woman who would stop at nothing to get justice.

"No," I said. "Only my immediate family lives here, and everyone else is in Denmark."

Jensen is one of the most common Danish surnames.

Charles is a generic boys' name with steady popularity over the last century.

And now there were two Charlie Jensens, standing in different families whose stories intersected at the moment of a murder.


**MONTAGE:**


Young Charlie confirms the ring belonged to one of the Merry Widow Killer's victims. The game of cat and mouse begins. But which is which? Now we see Uncle Charlie with his veneer peeled away—the charm dissolves, the practiced praise vanishes. Even his face when he looks at Young Charlie has a sinister glow to it. He feels more alive than ever. He's found his first worthy adversary, the only woman who ever challenged him.

Young Charlie emerges as his only nemesis because that thing they share, the unshakable connection? It's primal. The film shows us again and again these two are two sides of the same coin. Or perhaps the moon is a better metaphor: one side light, the other dark. Young Charlie wants to expose him for what he is, bring his crimes out into the light, while Uncle Charlie makes efforts to keep Young Charlie trapped in the dark. He rigs a stair to give way under her step, but she catches herself before falling. He lures her into the garage, where the running car has clogged the air with carbon monoxide. It almost works, but she's dragged, unconscious, onto the driveway when a curious neighbor (Hume Cronyn) hears the engine. As she comes to, Young Charlie and Uncle Charlie look into each other's eyes. The only thing they see is death.

## ST. CLOUD, MINNESOTA | FEBRUARY 2000 | DAY

About six months before his arrest, Uncle Kent squired us around the car lot where he worked in St. Cloud, a small city nestled in the necklace of forgettable towns that ringed it. I had a modest down payment to put toward a purchase, and a stomach full of angry bees. Torry insisted the car have leather interior and I wanted a moon roof. I imagined summer nights driving through Minneapolis with that top open, feeling the cool night breeze in my hair. I also wanted a CD player to give that vision a soundtrack.

All the options started to add up. Before I knew it, I was sitting across from the finance guy at Kent's dealership, my entire life's history under review and evaluation. There were six of us in that little office, glass windows looking out onto the showroom floor where new cars begged me to drive them away. The finance guy looked middle aged and tired, the kind of tired that came from looking at numbers day in and day out. Most of what he said to me went over my head. Interest rates, principal, loan periods, APR. He threw so many scenarios at me I wasn't sure which way was up. Meanwhile, Uncle Kent and three of his colleagues stood around and watched. I could tell these were the ones who worked with people. They reeked of charisma. Uncle Kent offered me a kind word here and there, gripping my shoulders in his hands, and he felt like my only ally in the room.

The car, purchased and registered in my name, would become the longest and most enduring link I shared with Torry, tethering us for years after our relationship ended. And in that way, Uncle Kent too remained part of my life for the ten years I drove the Altima. When I bought it, the car felt like a kind of gift. But some gifts have consequences.

## ZOOM FROM LONG SHOT TO EXTREME CLOSE UP:

Young Charlie glides down the stairs, her face resolute. Her hand, draped over the banister, displays the ring in its full glory. She's just liberated the MacGuffin from Uncle Charlie's room, where he's squirreled it away to hide the evidence of his crime. Uncle Charlie raises his glass to toast his niece. But then the camera, acting as Uncle Charlie's eye, zooms in on the ring from Uncle Charlie's perspective until we're in extreme close up, a technique we'll see Hitchcock use again in three years in *Notorious*. The zoom reminds us no one else in this house knows what's happening except the two Charlies and the audience. It puts us in an anxious state. Uncle Charlie's smile falls away, but he regains his composure. "Charlie," he says, his voice as light as the bubbles in his champagne glass. "You're just in time for a farewell toast." The gauntlet is thrown.

Uncle Charlie's next target, a local widow, bats her eyelashes at him, waiting for her inevitable seduction. But now, Uncle Charlie's too distracted to work. He needs to survive. For a parasite, it means restoring anonymity. He needs to run, or he needs stay and fight.

## BIG LAKE TOWNSHIP, MINNESOTA | SUMMER 2000 | DAY

Months before the arrest, Torry and I sat on barstools at the counter in Uncle Kent and Aunt Debbie's kitchen while she cleaned up and loaded the dishwasher. Debbie mentioned something about an injury that sent her to the hospital for stitches. I asked her what happened. She nodded at the machine. "Oh, just being clumsy. I was loading dishes and slipped on some water on the floor." Dishes clanked against each other as she talked. She didn't look at us. "I fell onto a knife in the dishwasher and it stabbed me in the stomach."

She went on to say Uncle Kent had taken her to the emergency room and might have even saved her life. I believed what Aunt Debbie told me. That it was an accident, that it could happen to anyone. But after Uncle Kent's arrest, this memory sounded different in my head. It *may* have been an accident. In going back through news articles and court records from this time to help jog my memory, I learned something I didn't know then: in 1995, Uncle Kent was arrested and convicted of domestic abuse. He may have stabbed her, and then, feeling guilty, helped her recover from the wound. Maybe he apologized to her. Maybe he promised never to hurt her again. Maybe they prayed together. Only Aunt Debbie and Uncle Kent know what really happened. Aunt Debbie did not have to testify. In the initial investigation, she told investigators Uncle Kent had been with her the day of the murder, giving him an alibi.

Victims of domestic violence often cover for their abusers. They want to believe he's sorry, that he'll change, that the trouble is over. They're reluctant to press charges. In less than a year, on the witness stand, Uncle Kent testified he engaged in a consensual affair with Linda.

Aunt Debbie wrapped up the story with a moral. "Now I always put the knives into the dishwasher blades down. Just in case."

## REAR PROJECTION

The family wishes Uncle Charlie well at the train station. Young Charlie stays behind in the car to confront her uncle face-to-face. Two Charlies—light and dark, good and evil, young and old. Young Charlie is no longer the naïf. But before she knows it, Uncle Charlie has her in his grasp near an open door, ready to throw her out. A terrible accident. And when they struggle, the two Charlies, in each other's grip, he almost manages to get the upper hand. But there's a twist, a reversal of fortune, and it's Uncle Charlie who loses his balance, swan dives out the door to his death.

It's hard not to think back to his widow monologue. The hatred he feels for these women. He describes them like a cancer feeding off the economy men built in life. They serve no use, and in that way Uncle Charlie acts as a cleanser, a healer, repairing the world and restoring the patriarchy. Young Charlie occupies a unique middle ground. She's a grown woman. She embodies all the optimism and enthusiasm we'd expect to see in a young person for whom the world is an oyster opening to reveal the pearl within. But by sharing Uncle Charlie's name, Young Charlie commands enough patriarchal power to destroy its angel of death.

Santa Rosa itself is not changed by the events of the film. It remains sun-dappled and idyllic—the quintessential American small town, here standing in to remind us that community and interconnectedness is a real form of safety, while the anonymity of the city empowers criminals to victimize the strangers around them. Sunlight draws shadows on the ground, though. Now Young Charlie knows what lurks within them. The young woman we first met has vanished like one of Uncle Charlie's victims. What remains is a wiser woman, one who has peered into the ugliness of the world and survived. She'll live her whole life and never escape the weight of her uncle's evil deeds.

After Uncle Charlie's death, there's no need for her to be known as Young Charlie. From then on, she's just Charlie. The only Charlie.

## LOS ANGELES, CALIFORNIA | MARCH 2020 | NIGHT

Kent's case was tried twice. He was convicted the first time, but it was overturned on appeal due to a technicality. The second conviction was automatically appealed to the Minnesota Supreme Court—as all capital murder cases are in that state—but the verdict was upheld. For a while, the Innocence Project worked with Kent, but they, too, abandoned the case. Now Kent remains in prison, required to serve at least twenty-five years of his sentence before he can be considered for parole.

I used to feel foolish for questioning his guilt. Two trials, an extensive investigation spanning years, DNA evidence linking him to the victim. This case requires me to believe that every interaction I had with Uncle Kent was phony. That he was a sociopath.

In the wake of the additional research I did to write this, I learned more about Uncle Kent's other run-ins with the law, his history of violence. In addition to his prior domestic abuse change, in 1996 he was convicted of insurance fraud. In 2018, the *Washington Post* published the results of a study that declared past or current intimate partners were responsible for forty-six percent of homicides against women in the previous decade. Of these killers, one-third were known to be dangerous, either because women held restraining orders against them or because the men had been arrested for or convicted of domestic violence before committing the murder. A woman who dies by stabbing is twice as likely to have been the victim of domestic violence. The statistics, deeply troubling, suggest Linda Jensen was a victim of intimate partner violence. And Kent, with his history of fraud, domestic violence, and his admitted consensual extramarital affair with Linda, is the most likely perpetrator.

Linda's daughter will be thirty-nine years old in 2030, the first year Kent will be eligible for parole, the same age her mother was at the time of her murder. Linda's murder was violent and vicious, and it took place while her daughter sat in a playpen. I look into that photograph of Linda, the only available artifact left of her from this pre-Internet crime, and I know there's a different painful truth I must accept on her behalf, her husband's behalf, her daughter's behalf. The longer I've resisted acknowledging Kent's responsibility for this crime, the longer I've participated in a system that witholds justice from her and her family. The longer I've been the wrong kind of Charlie in this story. The longer I've stood willingly in the dark.

# COMEDY OF MANNERS

## LOS ANGELES, 2016

The package arrived on a weeknight, dropped without ceremony beneath my apartment complex's mailboxes. My dad's left-handed cursive mumbled across the label, making its accurate arrival at my address a special kind of miracle. It felt too light, almost empty when I picked it up, but I already knew what was inside: the entirety of my childhood as captured through the lens of a 16 mm camera and a VHS camcorder.

My dad entered the twenty-first century on his own terms and at his own pace. An extensive collection of vinyl records and cassette tapes grew into towers of compact discs. The stacks and stacks of Beta and VHS tapes he'd amassed since the advent of the VCR gathered dust as DVDs found their way onto his shelves. Having grown tired of the fuss involved in dragging out the old projector, setting up the screen, and threading the narrow strip of film into the complicated switchbacks of the projector's gears and pulleys, he had them digitized. It was the only way I'd revisit familiar moments from my own childhood, or, in the wake of my mom's death five years earlier, see her move through the world again.

The box contained the DVD versions of these film strips, along with transfers of the VHS camcorder tapes from the 90s—my high school years. Those cassettes included essential documentation of my school musical performances (all featuring the added soundtrack of his muffled chuckles), my unexpected coronation as Prom King, and the errant track meet or two.

I opened the box at the dining table. I gasped when I saw what I had. Something I'd forgotten. A treasure.

My roommate Serena perched on the sofa. Her petite frame took up barely a single cushion, and her short red hair, curled into her trademark mini-tentacles, reached around her face. As she gazed lovingly into her iPhone, she asked for an explanation for my reaction to the box.

I withheld information, preferring her to see it without preamble. "We have to watch this." I dropped one of the DVDs into the player and turned on the TV. Moments later, the fuzzy, washed-out images of my hometown appeared through the lens of my dad's camcorder. My best friend Kevin appeared in the driver's seat of his late-80s Corolla. His chin-length hair, parted in the middle, cradled his extra dark sunglasses. He wore a long-sleeved tee and banged-up khakis. A lit cigarette hung from his lip. We were two years apart in school, which meant he was stuck at home while I was off sowing oats in Minneapolis. When I came home to visit, we filmed this, a travelogue of the tiny town, narrating it with our commentary.

There wasn't much to do in in Eagle. As an aspiring filmmaker, I loved to swipe my dad's camera from the house and took it with my friends and me when we ventured to the outer ring Milwaukee suburbs of Waukesha and Brookfield. One such series of videos we made, "Documentary of a Stranger," involved Kevin, our friend Lisa, and I approaching an unsuspecting Barnes & Noble patron and asking if we could interview them. Sometimes it was for my college sociology thesis (I was not in college). Sometimes it was for a high school psychology project (I hadn't taken psychology). We only offered the explanations needed, and nothing more. We'd ask them as many questions as they'd let us, everything from what pain reliever they'd prefer if they were trapped on a desert island to any "stupid human tricks" they were willing to perform for us. People were surprisingly cool at first, right up until they weren't. Sadly, that video had been lost, the victim of frequent college-era relocations. But what I had was maybe even better.

"Who is that?" Serena asked.

"That's Kevin." Serena had heard me talk about him in the lead up to his wedding the year before.

"No, *speaking*."

I was behind the camera, unseen, but talking. "That's me," I said. But it didn't sound like me. Not at all.

Serena burst out laughing. "What is going on with your voice?"

I had no idea what to tell her. In this moment I suddenly realized how thick and rural my accent had been growing up. I pronounced words in ways that now sounded foreign and weird to my ears, fourteen years removed from the Midwest.

I listened to that eighteen-year-old version of me like an archeologist of my own life. Who was he? On top of the wild pronunciation, there was something strange in the sound. A tightness. A constricting of the throat around my air. The way it seemed like I spoke only from the back of my throat, choking the words out. And the false depth I tried to create then—maybe to sound more masculine, to fit in. I sat in that apartment watching myself across decades, now a stranger to my own youth.

## RESCUE ME

*She's All That* opens on Laney (Rachael Leigh Cook) working on an abstract multimedia collage project while the opening credits roll by. We know right off the bat she's not the vain type: her unkempt hair explodes from a loose bun on top of her head. She wears well-worn clothes with a shapeless industrial apron over them. She later takes breakfast to her brother's room, acting as both surrogate mother (offering a meal) and typical sister (threatening to spit in his juice if he doesn't wake up). In the next shot, her dad, driving the family's run-down pick up, drops her and the painting off at school. We've learned a lot about Laney in these scant two minutes: she's poor, her mother has left or died, and she's the weird arty girl who doesn't fit in.

A big Jeep with the license plate "Mr. Prez" cuts in front of us and pulls into a reserved parking space. A strapping senior boy in a letterman's jacket strolls into school, pauses to admire a framed photograph of himself, then calls a classmate by the wrong name, delighting her because he's spoken to her, even if he thought she was someone else. This is Zack (Freddie Prinze Jr), a boy almost genetically engineered to float right to the top of the social ladder. He's handsome, athletic, and—as we'll learn in a few scenes when he confronts the stack of acceptance letters from every Ivy League school with a postage stamp—smart.

In high school terms, both Laney and Zack are untouchable, but for opposite reasons. Laney is beneath the notice of most of her peers. They don't get her. She makes no attempts to be anyone other than herself, even if that person doesn't connect with anyone but the overweight and possibly-gay kid in her class. Zack, on the other hand, is like an untouchable god. Only a select few get to share his rarified air.

If the trope sounds familiar, it's because *She's All That* cribs directly from *Pygmalion*, which in turn begat *My Fair Lady, Educating Rita,* and even *Pretty Woman.* One critical component in all of these works is class distinction. The woman is poor or working class, while the man who makes her over into a "lady" is a member of a wealthy or privileged class (in *Rita*'s version, he holds a doctorate). The power dynamic is bloated with aggression; these films collectively suggest that economic divisions drill down so deeply into our lives that they even affect notions of gender identity and expression, and that these women, who are mainly busy living their own lives by their own rules, need to be rescued and repaired by wealth and masculinity. They also suggest that men are the best evaluators of what proper feminine identity entails, and that they are—wait for it—qualified to teach it to people who have been women for literally their entire lives.

Possibly the most realistic application of these tropes happens in *She's All That*. Resetting the story in high school layers in the tremendous social pressure women face during that period. Boys apply pressure on them to appear a certain way, behave a certain way, and there are subsets of girls who, in turn, enforce these expectations upon one another. That Laney at the beginning of the movie gets to exist outside of these expectations, even at the loss of a stereotypical teen social life, is actually something to celebrate. But the film, like society, suggests she's merely not reaching her potential.

## RURAL WISCONSIN, 1977-1995

My hometown could be described, in the most generous terms, as a place where two two-lane highways meet. Highway 59 and Highway 67 cross at the foot of the town's highest elevation, a formation known as Diamond Hill after a farmer found a 16-carat gemstone in the dirt when digging his well in 1867. Thinking it was only a topaz, he sold what was then worth $850 ($15,000 in 2021) for just $1 ($17 today). Diamond Hill was home to Eagle's only distinctive architectural feature: a bright yellow water tower of the kind common to these rural towns. Unlike most places, where the town's name was painted across the top of the tower, Eagle's featured a single visual statement: a smiley face.

By description alone, Eagle might conjure up the fuzzy feelings offered by the beloved fictional towns of television, like Mayberry and Stars Hollow with their quirky and memorable denizens. Throughout the month of December, St. Theresa's Catholic Church amplified Christmas carols from speakers within its steeple, blanketing snow-covered homes with another layer of holiday cheer. The Krestan family worked together at their eponymous corner grocery store, where Bill was the butcher and Ann rang up customers in the front. Jim and Kathy ran the Variety, the local drug store where they brewed homemade root beer, sold nickel candies, and kept a menagerie of inexpensive jewelry and glass figurines in a sales case that stretched along one wall. Mealy

Furniture, a one-room showroom of basic home items, stood one block away from the Mealy Funeral Home, the kind of commercial cousins whose lineage stretched all the way to the time when carpenters built both chairs and coffins. Alice Baker Library occupied an old white Victorian-style home on Main Street, and Eagle Elementary, the only educational facility in the whole town, perched on top of Diamond Hill's sister elevation across the train tracks, a solid brick building where cinderblocks were thick and shiny with decades of glossy paint.

For a small number of residents, Eagle served as a bedroom community for Milwaukee commuters. For most families, though, Eagle was the only option. The community felt resolutely blue collar. Economic development of any kind was rare, and the local economy hinged on two bars. In the mid-90s, an intrepid chef from out of town opened a fine dining establishment in the hollowed-out shell of our closed bank. Camille's Fattoria offered delicious takes on Italian food, but at prices too high for most residents to afford. It closed in less than two years.

My dad worked remotely from his sales job, managing a territory that included Wisconsin, Minnesota, and the Dakotas. He spent one week a month in Minneapolis making calls to his customers, and for most of my childhood spent the other three weeks working out of an office in our home. While I didn't know specifics, I knew I grew up with nicer things than most of my classmates and neighbors. When I was five, my parents added an in-ground pool to the yard. Meanwhile, one of my best childhood friends lived catty corner from me in a rental house with peeling paint, a cracked foundation, and an orchard where worms occupied every apple. I always had clothes and shoes for school. Nothing wore out before I outgrew it, and hand me downs—in part because my brothers were eight and eleven years older than me—were rare. Despite my dad's success, my mom strived to live pretty frugally. She pinched every penny while my dad tried to wrench them from her fingers. When my mom died in 2011, we discovered the monthly allowance she and my dad budgeted for themselves saved in a bank account over twelve years, leaving behind enough money for us to establish a scholarship in her memory at the community college she attended in her fifties.

The rural transpositions of the Wisconsin accent are many, and they likely have their roots in the foreign tongues spoken by the immigrants who settled in these villages far from urban centers. We pronounce "creek" as "crick," while the Os in "roof" sound like "rook." Though it's not pronunciation-based, the greater Milwaukee area calls water fountains "bubblers," a term used only here and, for some unknown reason, in little pockets of New England.

## EVERYBODY COMES TO HOLLYWOOD

*She's All That* takes place in the Los Angeles area. When Laney and Zack leave a performance art show at a theater, they amble down a sidewalk bedazzled with stars on Hollywood's Walk of Fame. Zack's blond beefcake friend Dean, played by the late Paul Walker, speaks with the stereotypical SoCal accent, most noticeable in how he pronounces his long O vowel sounds. They're not lengthened and flattened the way they are in the Midwest. Instead, they're almost more rounded, a little clipped, the way someone surprised by a result might flinch and say, "Aoh!" Dean is the worst-case scenario jock in the film: it's he who dares Zack to prove the power of his influence and popularity by turning one of the school's unfortunates into the Prom Queen. This places Laney in direct competition with Taylor (Jodi Lyn O'Keefe), the girl who just dumped Zack for a *Real World* cast member based on Puck, played unnervingly well by Matthew Lillard. Zack spends the movie in search of his own authenticity, while Dean seems unburdened by the concept. Instead, Dean forges himself as whomever the people around him expect him and want him to be, whether that's the incorrigible asshole or, later, the sweet and misunderstood popular guy trapped in a prison of social expectation.

The most jarring aspect of the film is Laney's accent. Though she spends much of the film in full California sunshine, wearing spring and summer fashions, and walking among palm trees, her accent is her tell. She's not at all from Southern California. Her vowels are long and wide, and they sound much different from anyone else's. It's not clear how intentional this is. On the one hand, it further ostracizes her from the other characters in the film. While her social standing doesn't match theirs, neither does her speech pattern. It underscores the way she's an outsider at her high school, even an outsider among the outsiders in her art class, where she finds herself the butt of jokes from students who are richer and more privileged than she is, and who speak with the neutral resonance of the region. It also subtly reinforces the perception that Laney is naïve, innocent—childish, even. She's never been kissed, and probably never even been on a date. She lives in a tower of her own design, in the basement of her house where she works on painting after painting, searching for who she is even as she's in the midst of covering over that identity with paint.

Rachael Leigh Cook was born in Minneapolis, Minnesota.

## MINNEAPOLIS, 1995

When kids in high school bullied me for seeming gay, the thing they always focused on was my voice. For years I heard people using a stereotypical gay lisp to ridicule me. If I "sounded gay," it was because I didn't approximate the kind of hypermasculine speech patterns of other boys in school, who in turned learned them from their largely blue collar dads, uncles, and brothers. Speaking in a tone more intelligible than a grunt was suspect. Boys often forced their voices as deep as they would go, trying so hard to fit this weird macho ideal they foisted upon each other.

When I got to college in Minnesota, I gave myself permission not to care. About any of it. About my voice. About whether or not people thought I was gay. I was just going to be myself, and I was going to be cool with that. The rare opportunity to start over with a completely new social structure was a gift, I knew, and I wanted to capitalize on it as much as I could. And that was when the way I spoke started to change. My voice started to change. My accent migrated west toward how Minnesotans spoke, slowly and surely. People still assumed or suspected I was gay, sure. This wasn't an issue of closeting myself further. But I did notice fewer and fewer people asked or made comments, and people were more accepting of me and kinder to me as a result.

I joined a film club on campus that showed cult films on 35 mm on Friday and Saturday nights at the mostly-deserted student union. The group was varied but arched toward nerd, as if every high school clique had nominated its own Quentin Tarantino to attend this meeting. The standard-issue nerd with rumpled clothes, thick glasses, and unkempt hair. The jock nerd whose camouflage made it easy for him to blend in with the fraternity crowd. The queer nerd (me). Then there was Janice, the goth nerd. She had short dyed-black hair, like Nancy in *The Craft*, and dressed almost exclusively in black layers, with maxi skirts, long beaded jewelry, and spiked collars. She had a nervousness about her, as if always ready to be startled by a flash of movement on the periphery. Although I dressed like I was somewhere between a Nirvana video and a dancing Gap khakis ad, I sensed Janice was an outsider too, the way I'd felt my whole adolescence.

She walked me back to my dorm after that first meeting and we got to know each other better. "Your accent is really cute," she told me.

"My what?"

"Your accent. The way you talk."

I gave her an incredulous look. I had no accent. "What are you talking about? You're the one with the accent!" I laughed, then mimicked the sound of a shocked Minnesotan: "Ohhhh mieeeee Gaaaaahd."

She gave me a puzzled look, but didn't say anything more.

## JUSTIFY MY LOVE

What's curious about *She's All That* is how little Laney actually changes. She receives from Zack's sister (Anna Paquin) what amounts to an overdue haircut and quick makeup tutorial before attending her first high school party. In the iconic scene, "Kiss Me" by Sixpence None the Richer plays as Laney descends the stairs in a chunky heel and silk dress, her frumpy hair shorn to frame her face in a long bob. Just as she nears the last step, she stumbles in the heels and falls into Zack's embrace. At the party, she's bullied just like she always was. The mean art girl (Clea Duvall) gloats about how little she's worked to get into the best art school while Laney might not even afford to go to college at all. Taylor pours her cocktail down the front of Laney's dress. This confirms everything Laney ever believed about them, but it doesn't say anything to her about herself. There's nothing wrong with Laney apart from the fact that she knew better than to try doing something new.

Of course, a physical makeover isn't really enough to buy admission to the popular crowd. Aside from Taylor, Dean, and the art school girl, most of the kids in Laney's school are pretty benign. They strive not to upset the social order by keeping with their own groups, but several of them are nice, but several of them are nice to Laney, even downright supportive, as the film goes on. This is really because they gave themselves an opportunity to know Laney—or, to put it more clearly, they were given permission to know Laney. And they like her, especially once they realize how much Laney's personality puts Taylor's narcissism and selfishness in stark relief.

It wouldn't be a high school film if it didn't ultimately hinge on Taylor and Laney striving for Prom Queen. Like a U.S. general election, it all comes down to deep-seated political beliefs. Republicans would vote for Taylor, upholding the idea that wealth should be preserved within family lines and that the meritocracy hinges primarily on the opportunities afforded to us by our social position and family name.

Laney, on the other hand, represents the Democratic perception that anyone can rise into the echelon of success when power structures close opportunity gaps and level the playing field. The school faces an austere ideological choice in their voting.

Despite the fact that he and Dean made the bet about making a girl over and turning her into the Prom Queen, Zack undergoes the most significant change. Unlike Laney, he doesn't need a makeover. One of the reasons he's so popular despite being fourth in their class academically is that he's a) gorgeous and b) an athletic powerhouse on the soccer field. He's also, generally speaking, a kind person, despite the spirit of the bet he's made. Of course, that bet reveals that within Zack blooms the same narcissism as in Taylor, and Dean, and the art school girl, and any number of other privileged kids. Zack knows his interest in someone elevates them from untouchable to royalty. But through his relationship with Laney, as he comes to understand the economic challenges her family faces and the emotional devastation of losing her mother so young, Zack grows. It's not as clearly presented to us as a makeover reveal with a 90s manic pixie dream girl song playing behind it, but it does show. He rejects his friend's dominant belief that girls are objects to be possessed and used. He rejects the pressure from his father to make a decision based on family legacy and prominence. He seeks the kind of authenticity Laney's always had within her. The movie tricks us into believing that we're going to watch Zack rescue Laney, but the opposite happens. Laney rescues herself, over and over, from any number of painful social situations sprouting from Zack's bet, and she teaches Zack, in the end, how to be a human being.


## TEMPE, 2003

I pursued a master's degree in creative writing at Arizona State, a tightly-woven campus in suburban Tempe. The campus architecture, all Brutalist concrete structures with narrow windows to keep out the blazing sun, seemed to huddle together under a slip of shade only they could see. I worked with people from across the United States in my program. Josh, a poet from Michigan, spoke with the familiar elongated vowels of my childhood, but with the regional difference that makes a Michigander a Michigander. Caroline had a velvety drawl from her native South Carolina. I worked as a graduate hall director with an entirely different cohort of graduate students from the higher education program, and they, too, brought with them a slew of other manners of speaking.

The creative writing program awarded me a teaching fellowship in my third year. In the semester-long class I took on pedagogy with the other new teaching assistants, I co-presented on multiliteracy pedagogy, which acknowledges every student's experience in the classroom as part of the course's text, empowering each voice in the classroom to present a perspective for discussion and deconstruction. As part of that presentation, I facilitated a game of Cross the Line to highlight how invisibly diverse every classroom—even a room full of almost exclusively white graduate student teachers—could be. As I read each statement aloud, students moved to one side of the room or other to indicate whether the statement applied to them or did not. One of the last ones I read was, "I am the first person in my family to pursue an advanced degree." Only two students did not cross the room, indicating the statement accurately described both of them. They were my co-presenter Carol, from the Philippines, and me.

The shock of self-consciousness struck me over the head. Suddenly I didn't feel like part of this group, this cohort of aspiring teachers. I really was an outsider, maybe even a trespasser in academia. It underscored the urgency of not sounding like a backwoods hick from rural Wisconsin when I taught, when I read from my work, when I gave interviews, when I presented in front of groups. I feared I was more likely to be perceived as stupid if I sounded like the people from my region of birth, where the opportunities to pursue higher education were blocked by poverty, family responsibilities, the demands of blue collar work, and the emotional support required to succeed at the college level. But more than that, the sounds of those words meant pain to me. The sounds of my shamers and tormentors. The evidence of my own failure to fit in and belong.

## OPEN YOUR HEART

By the climax of the film, Zack's metamorphosis is almost complete. He tries unsuccessfully to get Laney to go to Prom with him, and learns too late she's gone with Dean. For his part, Dean's been playing the hurt puppy card to Laney, hoping to make her believe that beneath his crude and cruel exterior is a Wounded Boy Who Just Needs to Be Loved. Zack does the most uncool thing possible, taking his sister as his date, and commits to having the best time possible.

After one of film history's most outrageous and unbelievable choreographed group dance sequences, Zack's crowned King, surprising no one, and the film stretches out the Prom Queen announcement, pouring silence into the moment so that we can focus on Taylor and Laney's expressions. Taylor is confident, but under that she's a little worried Laney might win. And Laney's face tells us she does want this after all. That the social acceptance of her peers does mean something.

She doesn't win. Taylor takes the crown, her birthright. This will probably be Taylor's most significant life moment. She's gotten everything she wanted: fame, in the form of knowing she's the most popular, most envied, and most powerful girl in school.

Dean takes Laney to a hotel room after the dance. He tries to get sexual with her, removing his Wounded Boy costume. She blows an air horn in his ear. When she gets home, she finds Zack has been waiting to speak with her, still in his tuxedo. He has a lot of apologizing to do, and we know he'll mean it because, through knowing Laney, he's discovered who he really is. What Zack needed most at the start of the film was to break through the layers of pressure and expectation placed upon him by parents, coaches, teachers, and peers. Laney teaches him about his privilege, his achievements, and about taking risks both to express himself and to see himself the way other people do.

In that moment, Laney sees him and realizes he's all that.

## LOS ANGELES, PRESENT DAY

Scrubbing my accent didn't take long. It took attention and practice. Minding my vowels. Enunciating my ds and ts so that they sounded different from one another. The rural tics were gone before I received my MFA, but more than that, they were forgotten. So much so that when I did finally encounter it again—my own voice, my original accent—it sounded like a stranger. And by then, in a lot of ways, that's who that kid had become.

My mom walked this path, involuntarily. Though she was a naturalized citizen from Belgium, she wasn't often told to go back where she came from the way immigrants of color are. She was white and she spoke like an Upper Midwesterner. The cost of this safety was devastating. Her first American teacher made her speak with marbles in her mouth as she learned English to remove any trace of a foreign accent. Unlike some first-generation children, I didn't grow up bilingual. In fact, when I asked, she refused to teach me to speak Flemish because it was "useless." I was young at the time—maybe eight—and her words stung enough that I never forgot them. As I got older, the pain in those words became clear to me. Not only had my mother lost her accent and eventually her fluency, her culture had been cut away from her.

Seventy years after my mom lost her accent, I wrote this essay from a desk in California. I'm confident the accent of my youth has almost entirely disappeared. It reappears on occasion—for instance, I'll never be able to pronounce the word *bagel* without sounding like Jerry Lundegaard from *Fargo*—but both the effort I've put in and the nearly twenty-five years since I left the Midwest have opened the space in my mouth to bland, regionless elocution. I ask myself now what else I've lost. Whatever tethered me back to those painful years is gone. I move forward with the voice of someone who's never known social isolation. Someone whose voice isn't afraid to be heard.

# SURVIVAL HORROR

**JUNE 6, 2005 | 8:30 A.M.**

My cell phone buzzed from its roost on the desk. My ex-boyfriend Torry's name flashed on the caller ID. Calling this early, it could only be bad news. He wanted money, or for me to bail him out of some problem. I debated picking up.

The desert outside was bright, sunshine undeterred as it sliced into the room through half-open blinds. The office was a converted bedroom in the old College President's cottage. Over its years of use as a residence, it hosted celebrities as varied as Robert Frost and Ronald Reagan. Today, I was the first and only person at work. I drank coffee. I checked email. I was there early for exactly this reason: to work without disruption. Leave it to Torry to sabotage that plan when I'd least expect him.

Against my better judgment, I answered the call. It would last two minutes and thirty-five seconds.

"Is this Charlie?"

It wasn't Torry. "Yes." Cautious. Torry's bill collectors would sometimes call me up when they couldn't find him, demand money from me to cover his debts. I'd learned to kill these conversations. We weren't legally bound to one another and I owed nothing. But they didn't call me Charlie, a name I only used face-to-face with people. Bill collectors and other strangers called me Charles. And they didn't call me from Torry's number.

"This is Jason, Torry's ex. I don't know if you remember me."

I'd met him just once, years ago. After we split, Torry took the car because he needed it commute to his job, while I lived, worked, and went to classes on a dense campus where I could easily ride my bike or walk as needed. But Torry wasn't good at holding down jobs, so when a lien holder called up looking for Charles, demanding several back payments on the car, I insisted Torry return my keys. Jason was with Torry when we made the trade. They were dating then. Apparently not anymore. I attempted kindness. "Oh, hi."

"Are you alone?"

"I'm at work."

"Can you go to a private place?"

I knew folks would be showing up and mounting the stairs to their own offices. Their steps creaking on the stairs making the whole house seem to groan. "Hold on." I went downstairs and stepped onto the porch of the cottage. A handful of students walked the paths toward their nine o'clock classes. Anyone arriving at work I'd see coming. "Okay."

Jason paused. "I'm sorry to tell you this. Torry took his own life yesterday."

The moment that followed had a shape.

It grew like a bulb of blown glass, hot and molten and unstoppable.

I took in air. My chest clenched like a fist.

The moment cooled and hardened around me.

"What?" The word burst. Insistent. Explosive.

I started sweating.

I glanced at objects, hoping they'd be an anchor to keep me from floating away.

Paint chips curling off the columns on the porch.

Cracks in zigzag over the otherwise smooth concrete.

Specks of dust churning like a nebula in the air around me.

Jason recounted the weekend: they went out Friday and partied all night. Saturday they played phone tag. When he couldn't reach Torry on Sunday, he went to Torry's house. Torry didn't answer. Jason called the police. They found Torry's body.

Jason said there'd be a memorial. Details were coming. He said he had a lot to do—people to call, arrangements to make. He promised he'd call me. He'd keep me in the loop.

I snapped the phone shut in my palm. It felt like a brick.

## DEATH

Most films begin in the ordinary world, the status quo, the familiar. Whatever event sets off the main character's journey will upend this world and plunge her into its opposite. *The Descent* begins in sunshine, in friendship, and in joy. Sarah (Shauna Macdonald) and her friends Beth (Alex Reid) and Juno (Natalie Mendoza) swoop across the frothing rapids of a river, howling and laughing as they go. At the end of the run, her husband Paul (Oliver Milburn) and their daughter Jessica (Molly Kayll) perch on a rock, clapping and whoohooing their congratulations. Juno and Paul share a moment, the kind of loaded film event that tells us they have a secret. They're fucking. Sarah doesn't know. Beth picks up on it, but says nothing.

Paul and Sarah drive down a two-lane road, Jessica in the backseat entertaining herself as the two adults try to connect. Sarah asks Paul, "Are you okay? You seem distant." He tries—too hard, it turns out—to convince her he's fine. "I'm fine," he says. We watch from the backseat as he holds her gaze too long. Their car drifts across the center line as a small truck approaches. They collide head on. Tires shriek. Pipes tied to the truck's roof launch into Sarah's car on impact, cratering the windshield. One pipe impales Paul. Another strikes Jessica. They die instantly. Only Sarah survives.

Sarah wakes up in the hospital. She tugs the IV from her arm, wanders into the empty hall, the light from overhead bulbs green and sickly. She doesn't understand where she is, or why. The lights thud off behind her, one set at a time, approaching her. She runs, calling for her daughter, realizing now what's happened. The darkness overtakes her in a foreshadowing of her next life-or-death crisis.

The familiar world has vanished. It will become its opposite.

## JUNE 6, 2005 | 9 A.M.

I was alone in my office. I sat at my desk, palming it. I took breaths.

My coworkers would arrive soon, rousing the office to life. I didn't want to explain the sweat stains in my armpits, on my back. Why my voice trembled. My eyes, red, stocked with precarious tears, would tell no lies.

I had to keep this truth inside my body somehow, out of view. If nobody knew, it wasn't real. I'd imagined it. A dream.

I couldn't be there. I grabbed my bag and dashed down the stairs two at a time.

I ran into my colleague Paul, just arriving, at the foot of the stairs. He said good morning, or something. I told him I had to leave.

His face, pale, kind of blank, eyes curious. "Everything okay?"

I choked on a sentence. I tried again and got it out. "Somebody died."

There was no turning back.


## DEPRESSION

*The Descent* features a cast of primarily women. Horror and thriller films victimize their characters with relentless violence and fear before they die. There is almost always a survivor, usually a woman. She's a trope commonly known as the "Final Girl." The cost of her survival is trauma. It lives on within her, and she'll never be the same. Even if the cause of the horror dies at her hand, she'll embody the story. She'll never be free of her torment. The horror in this film is distinctly emotional. Sarah suffers a nightmarish loss, the kind of event that usually signals an ending and not a beginning. With Sarah deeply in her grief mindset, we've entered the wild terrain of North Carolina, its misty, shadowy mountains stippled with forest, far from civilization as we know it. Things will only get worse.

It's a year since Sarah's accident. She drives with Beth to meet Juno and Juno's new thrill-seeking friend Holly (Nora-Jane Noone), as well as sisters Rebecca (Saskia Mulder) and Sam (MyAnna Buring). All adventurers. They're going spelunking, the next logical escalation from white water rafting. Sarah does not know of Juno's affair with her husband.

They spend a raucous night in a secluded cabin in the woods, the kind of horror trope we expect of slasher films or monster films. This film will be both. But the woods, against expectations, are the safe place. The women celebrate with beer, reconnecting their friendships across the gap of the prior year. Juno pulls out an old photo of Sarah, Beth, and Juno happy in the beforetimes. Sarah smiles, but a shroud falls over her. "Love each day," she says. "That's just something Paul used to say."

Juno shares her name with the queen of the Roman gods, a figure associated with war, protection of the community, and fertility. It fits that our Juno is sleek, athletic, beautiful, and kind of a jerk even when she's trying to keep the group working together. It's a complex theological alchemy that seems at odds with itself: war, and the people it kills, embodied with fertility and birth. Perhaps there's a metaphor about survival here. Juno is the opposite of Sarah, who is meek, emotionally distant, and alone.

Sarah wakes in the night, approaches the window to look at the moon. The peace shatters in an instant when a metal pipe strikes through the glass, killing her. She wakes with a start in her bed. She's not safe from her grief anywhere. Not even in her dreams.

When the women arrive at the cave entrance, Juno slips the map and guidebook into the glovebox, wanting to have a "real adventure" with the group. She hopes it will bring them back together, heal the rifts and fractures widening since the rafting trip. Her intent isn't to sabotage, and she can't know the outcome of her choice will be an epic battle and rebirth.

It starts innocently enough. Big girls'-trip vibes. They explore grand caverns, lit only by their headlamps and red flares. The rocky landscape is slick with water, stalagmites and stalactites protruding around them. After a quick lunch, Sarah breaks off from the group and calls that she's found the next passage. Each woman shimmies through on her belly, one at a time, until Sarah brings up the rear with their bag of ropes. She gets wedged in tight. Beth works with Sarah to calm her down, ease her panic, until behind them, the rumble of bad news: a collapse. Sarah pushes through and flops onto the ground just as the path behind them seals with debris.

The only way out is through.


## JUNE 6, 2005 | 9:30 A.M. ON


A suicide is an act that becomes a presence.

It comes home with you. It stands beside you. It lives with you. You wear it like clothing. You speak to it, but it doesn't answer. It doesn't acknowledge questions. It towers over you. It's what you stand on. It's what you breathe.

The desert sun forced its authority on every inch of landscape. Fiery warmth pushed down from the sky, absorbed by concrete and radiated back up. In my house, I kept every blind and curtain drawn to resist this light and heat. The house entombed my cold grief, and I filled it several times over.

The first day I cried until I was out of breath. I cried until, exhausted, I fell asleep. Torry was in my dreams. I walked downtown Tempe, en route to somewhere urgent in the dream. I ran into him on the street. He smiled at the sight of me. "I just wanted to say goodbye," he said, and hugged me. I asked him where he was going. Why he was leaving. He laughed. I was struck by how happy he seemed. How unburdened. Wherever he was going, either the decision or the destination suited him.

I wanted to talk about it. Everything. All the thoughts in my head needed to spill out, if only someone were there to listen. When someone called me on the phone, I couldn't bear to speak. Instead of words, I just cried. Body-wracking sobs. I didn't know where the feelings sprung from. It felt like the core of my being had cracked open, allowing misery to sprout where once the light of the world couldn't reach. In the end, all I could do was listen to the platitudes other people offered me—*He's in a better place. His pain is over. He's with his maker. The angels have welcomed him. He's swaddled in the light of heaven. He's found peace.*—which felt cruel in their banality. Their lack of specificity. I told Paul that first morning "Somebody died," but it wasn't the whole story. *Torry* died, and that meant something to me it didn't and couldn't mean to any other person on this earth.

It went this way all day. The blackout drapes in the bedroom made a false night all afternoon. When the actual night fell, I didn't notice. I'd brought the darkness indoors with me.

The physical feeling was the worst part. A tightening of the world I could feel against my skin. Torry's absence in the world was as real to me as a firm hug squeezing me. It was not the embrace of a loved one, but instead a kind of binding. The corkscrewed clench of a boa constrictor.

The only way out was through.


## DENIAL

The caves in *The Descent* are a metaphor for Sarah's subconscious mind. Like her grief, the passages are never-ending, and she and her friends get lost in them, then trapped in them. More, something in them wants to hurt her, the same way her grief won't let her rest. Like her mind in sleep, the caves hold something in their darkness, something Sarah wants to escape. But it's important to note that the group only moves *deeper* into the caves, the same way Sarah has moved so much into her grief she appears just a shell of the vibrant, athletic woman we saw in the opening shots. The women are pushed there first by the physical dangers—collapsing passages that block their exit—and soon by another more sinister force altogether.

This deep, the caves have no natural light—only what the women brought in with them. Battery operated helmet lamps. Battery operated flash lights. Glow sticks. Flares. It ratchets up the claustrophobia, the darkness, limited vision. It's hard for the women to grasp the whole picture of what's around them. Holly dashes off when she thinks she sees daylight, but falls through a hole, breaking her leg on the way down. The women rush to her.

In the chaos, Sarah thinks she sees a flash—a man—but in her state of mind, she doesn't trust her eyes. Then it happens again. There's no mistaking the figure crouched in the beam of her flashlight, the way it studies her before crawling away into the black.

It's not a human. Or maybe it was once, centuries ago. Isolation and necessity evolved these creatures to live in full darkness. Their eyes, clouded over, see nothing. Their noses have flattened against their face. They make clicking sounds as they move, indicating they've learned to rely on echolocation to navigate and hunt. Their claws and muscular limbs scale the walls and ceilings of these caves. Their skin a sickly gray.

By the time the women have noticed them, it's too late. They've been hunted this whole time. Now, more than halfway through the film, with Holly's injury making her an easy target in this herd of prey, they act.

The women run, but they're no match for the home team advantage. They end up right in the creatures' feeding ground, littered with the bones of humans and animals. Juno, true to her name, emerges as a warrior whose instincts are as vicious as the creatures. It makes sense. She's the most selfish person in the group. Her instinct to survive trumps all others. But the same impulsiveness that inspired her to leave the maps behind, the same singular focus and determination, causes her to mistake Beth for one of the creatures. Juno stabs her in the throat before she realizes what she's done. This is the most important character moment for Juno, someone we already don't trust because she's recklessly endangered the group and because we suspect she's no one's friend. She looks into Beth's eyes. Juno realizes she'll have to answer for this if Beth survives. Juno leaves her to die.

The only way out is through.

## JUNE 7-8, 2005 | NOVEMBER 2001

The next day I couldn't get out of bed.

If I moved, I cried. If I thought about Torry, I cried. If my phone rang, I cried. So I gave in. I stayed home, stayed in that darkness, the bedroom drawn black against daylight.

The day after that, my tears vanished into the shower's streaming water. But I pulled myself together and, optimistic, I went back to work. I sat alone in the office, the silence of the cottage an invitation for me to fill it. It wanted activity, but I gave it my grief. I couldn't stay focused on work. My attention kept turning to Torry. The quiet let my untethered thoughts reach a gallop. In minutes I was crying, then crying uncontrollably. I called my boyfriend Geoff and asked him to come get me. We had a meeting spot on campus for pick-ups, a place where a little street pushed into the tight-knit buildings. A roundabout there allowed easy access back to University Avenue. It was a short walk from my office. I cried as I gathered up my things. I cried down the stairs and out into the hot morning air. I cried walking the paths in front of Old Main. Even in this moment, this devastating grief, my instincts were to stop myself from crying and prevent anyone from seeing me. An emotional person in public is distressing, but I was hard pressed to recall a time when I had even seen a man crying in a public place. But I couldn't stop the avalanche of sadness tumbling out of me. I cried across the main walk that led students to the center of campus. I cried passing between buildings. I cried waiting for Geoff's Corolla to appear. And when it did, when I was safely inside of it, I released the full torrent of my misery.

"Thank you," I told Geoff as he turned left onto University Avenue. I choked on sobs. "This is just so hard."

He watched the road, cars passing us. His face blank. He seemed to take care choosing what to say. "I'm confused. I thought you didn't even like Torry."

The words shot through me like a spike. They were accurate, and that's why they hurt. My relationship with Torry was a mess. Most of the time he was not a good partner and sometimes not even a good person. Despite this, our break up had been devastating for me. My first heartbreak. Now my first real grief.

Torry kept coming over after we split. His credit card bills, insurance bills, the random magazine or mailer kept coming to my address. Over time these visits grew from angering to annoying. After about a month of this, he asked me if I wanted to see a movie.

No hesitation. "No."

"Oh." He sounded surprised. He lingered in the living room fanning his mail in between his hands. "Okay. I guess I'll go."

Seconds after I'd pressed the door closed behind him, there was a knock.

I cracked the door. I looked through two inches between the wood. "What?"

"Can I come in?" Tears drove down his cheeks.

I rolled my eyes but moved aside.

Now he was sobbing. "I'm sorry," he said.

His words ricocheted off me. "What for?"

He blubbered. He explained he didn't want to break up. He'd been frustrated. He'd told me I wasn't supporting "his dream," a multilevel marketing scheme with a husband and wife who'd convinced him he could make six figures in just three months if he followed their system. Meanwhile he'd been sinking what little money he—and we—had into buying product to sell, but with both of us new to the city, he had no one to sell to. He'd been flyering cars around Tempe at night, hoping someone, anyone would reach out to him to buy. Torry was right—I wasn't supporting this dream. I was telling him to get a job. He lived rent-free in the apartment that came with my residence hall director job. I had a meal plan that fed him. He needed to do his part. Instead, he packed up his things and left.

He took a breath. He shrugged as if giving up. "I just wanted to teach you a lesson."

I watched him cry. I wondered if the tears were real. "I guess I'm not the one who needed a lesson," I said.

This memory knocked back and forth in my head like the tongue of a bell. Though I had wished over and over again for Torry to *go away forever*, I hadn't meant death. I hadn't meant suicide. I couldn't help imagining his last day. What clothes he'd put on. How he'd watched the clock as the minutes ticked away, welcoming the sunset and his final moments in his bed. Did he think of me? Did he regret me? Did he, like I did now, wish that everything had somehow been different— that we had been different? I didn't want him to be alone. But that was how he'd died. That was how he chose to die. This knowledge I'd carry for the rest of my life. He taught me the lesson after all: grudges are a luxury reserved for the living.

## BARGAINING

Sarah's separation from the group is a physical representation of her emotional distance. Once she's lost in the caves on her own, it's like she's achieved the full potential of her grief. Although it comes to us through others, there's something inherently selfish about grief. The way it turns focus inward. How it forces us to study our own wound over and over until we memorize the jagged topography of its scars. Until we recognize the absence that sparked it as a new, permanent part of us. The mind's relationship to grief is like the tongue's insistence on exploring the place where a tooth's been lost. The constant touching of the emptiness teaches the mind to revise itself. It's how we adapt.

Beth served as Sarah's last human connection in this world. As her final act, Beth tells Sarah Juno did this to her. "Don't trust her. Find your own way out." Beth hands Sarah the pendant Juno has worn throughout the film: a golden feather with the words "Love Each Day" inscribed on the back. "It's from Paul," Beth rasps. Sarah reads the message, taking in its irony. She wants to rescue Beth, but Beth knows that will only put them both in danger. She begs Sarah to end her suffering. Sarah bludgeons her with a rock.

After Beth dies, Sarah is free—free of love, free of responsibility, free of fear. The husband she's mourned throughout the film wasn't the man she thought he was. Their life together was a lie. She has nothing left to lose. Juno has fulfilled the promise of her namesake: she has wrought death, brought war. Her affair with Paul brought about his death. And now, in the shadow of all of this, Sarah is reborn.

She makes quick work of two creatures that ambush her. A third, the first one we've seen with visible breasts—the first female creature— bows over the body of a fallen creature, whimpering. Mourning him. Sarah dashes away, but trips into a pool thick with the blood of the dead. Submerged, she is silent, waiting. She rises from the surface of the pool, her face coated red, almost glowing in the light of her torch. She becomes the hunter. She becomes death. When the female creature attacks her, Sarah mauls it with her bare hands, stabbing it in the eye with a bone. She no longer looks, acts, or sounds human. She is pure survival. Like the creatures hunting her, she has adapted to her circumstances.

She pushes deeper into the cave, confident she'll find the exit. She knows the only way out is through.

**JUNE 7, 2005 | 6:40 P.M.**

My mom called to check on me later that night. Before I could even speak, my face exploded in tears.

She wanted to help, to console me, to help me move through the pain, but I could tell she was confused by the wall of grief I pushed toward her. "It's okay for me to feel what I'm feeling," I insisted when she tried to calm me down. She said it had been years since Torry and I been together. Like Geoff, she didn't understand why I was in so much pain. I didn't know how to say it. I wasn't even sure why I was devastated. "This is about him as a person," I said. "Not our relationship." The more I realized no one understood what was happening within me, the more alone I felt. The deeper the grief took root.

While people I knew had died, and people I loved had died, Torry's death was so different from those. He was young, just a couple years older than me. He was the kind of person who was always *so alive*, vibrant and messy. And I knew him intimately. I knew his body. I knew him inside and out. For a while he'd been part of me. And when he died, I realized he still was.

I'd glimpse him out at a bar, hanging out with a group of people I'd never seen before. On one such occasion, he'd sent me a shot— Bailey's topped with whipped cream meant to be drunk without using the hands, known as "a cocksucker," a way of suggesting he, too, wasn't over what had happened.

I'd last spoken to Torry on my birthday that year, two months before he died. It was our first conversation in some time. Our relationship reached a point where our social connections were so thin I rarely heard what he was up to. I didn't even know where he lived. I'd been afforded the time and space to move on, and the healing softened me toward him. We spoke through the mist of our history, not in its mud. The chat was light. Surface. Casual. Kind. After, all that remained was what I felt: surprised. A little relieved.

My brother Gary called after my mom. She'd handed off the baton.

I was lost in a maze of my own thoughts, the same carousel of ideas turning in the same order. I presented these to Gary. "I don't understand why he didn't reach out to me," I said, "if he was this desperate, if he was ready to give up."

"He didn't contact you because he knew you would do everything you could to help him," Gary said, "and he didn't want any more help."

Some of the weirder thoughts I had were about the most ridiculous things about being alive. I was sad, for instance, that Torry could never shop at Target again. That he'd never have the chance to see the new Batman movie. Every time I thought something like this, my grief cracked open like a new pomegranate and everything I held inside flowed out. "Do you think he knew what he was giving up?"

"Of course he did. The fact that he knew and still went through with this tells you how much pain he was in."

It made sense. I hadn't thought of it that way, from Torry's perspective, but I was trapped in my perspective. My grief-gazing. Memorizing the shape of his absence.

My tears were losing steam. It was easier to breathe. "I just wonder if he thought about me before he did this."

Gary paused. "If he had thought about all the people who loved him," he said, "he wouldn't have been able to go through with it."

It was cold comfort. But comfort. The first comfort. My only comfort. I took it in.


## ANGER

If the cave is the subconscious and the creatures the way grief attacks us—won't let us rest—the way the women react to the experience is meaningful. When the creatures' ambush separates the women, sisters Sam and Rebecca cling to each other and work together to make their way out. Juno tracks them down and, as they try to find the way out, discovers a pack of creatures laying in wait. The trio runs until they reach a chasm. Rebecca tries to rig her way across, but a creature climbs the ceiling to her and rips out her throat. Rebecca stabs it, dropping it into deep water below. Another creature drags Sam away, disemboweling her in front of Juno. To escape, Juno jumps into the water.

Juno cares only about saving herself. Sarah has lost her humanity. The film comes down to the two of them, standing together in a rounded chamber. Sarah confronts Juno about her affair with Paul, dangling the necklace from the same hand now also holding Juno's climbing axe. The final indictment.

Juno, despite her savage bravery in battle, is a coward in life. She runs from the ruptures she creates, leaving others to do the emotional work of cleaning up after her. Was it Paul's distraction about Juno that led to his distance that day of the rafting trip, why he was so desperate to prove to Sarah that he loved her? Though the cave creatures present a lethal threat to Sarah, it's Juno's friendship that is actually her biggest existential crisis. Juno's choices, which have tried to place Juno at the center of these narratives, have forced Sarah to reassert narrative dominance in the film. Sarah takes back the power to tell her own story. She will become her own hero.

There's so much Juno should say, but won't—and they don't have time. With the thunder of creatures clamoring through the cave toward them, they stare at each other in a tense face off. Sarah looks inhuman, her skin enrobed in blood. In the same way Juno put her survival first, leaving behind the wounded, running on instinct, Sarah has become a survivalist. She isn't prioritizing herself over anyone else. There isn't anyone else. She's alone, here in the cave, and in her life.

She raises the climbing axe and plows it through Juno's calf. Juno, who took them to the unmapped caves. Who left Beth to die. Who, Sarah now knows, insinuated herself into Sarah's marriage and who, Sarah might believe, caused of the distraction that killed Paul and

Jessie. Juno shrieks. She pulls out the axe, but she's too injured. Sarah knows the injury will make Juno easy prey for the creatures bearing down on them. Sarah sprints away, deer-like, leaving Juno exactly the way she's lived: fending only for herself.

She's almost through. She's almost out.

## JUNE 25, 2005 | 7 P.M.

Each day in June felt expansive, almost endless. The hours stretched so far, became so thin, I worried they'd snap apart. I was aware each minute that passed carried me further and further from the last day Torry lived. A cruel injustice.

In the weeks after his death, I kept seeing Torry. In a crowded restaurant when two people deep in conversation leaned away from each other, his face appeared in the gap between them. Or passing a car on the freeway, his silhouette dark behind the wheel. Each vision jolted through me. My mind fought itself: *Torry's dead! No, he isn't!* I almost convinced myself Torry faked his own death, maybe to escape his creditors. Maybe to begin anew. I hadn't seen his body before it was ferried back to Minnesota and interred next to his sister Tracy, who'd died ten years prior. Maybe the obituaries I read online were an elaborate ruse.

I went to Jason's house for Torry's wake. Geoff came with me. I could tell he wasn't thrilled about it. Jason's house was part of a suburban-style development common to Phoenix, a cluster of similar-looking houses huddled along winding side streets to create the illusion of organic design. The homes could only have one of a limited number of exterior colors, the landscaping in front yards a different configuration of the same five elements. Inside, it was decorated in a bland-adjacent, contemporary style. Each room appeared purchased whole from a furniture showroom. Overstuffed couches. Wrought-iron fixtures. Wall-to-wall beige tile.

The house was full of people, mostly men. I didn't know anyone.

When Torry and I'd moved to Arizona, we only knew my coworkers. After our split, they supported me, stayed friends with me, tried to keep distance between him and them. Torry developed his own circle of friends, mostly from going out to bars I guessed. Every man in the room aside from Jason, Geoff, and me appeared to be cousins of one another, like a standard-issue homosexual you would see populating the bars and clubs of the city: all in their 20s and 30s, most of them white, all with similar fit frames and short, spiky haircuts. I didn't speak to anyone. I didn't know what to say. I wasn't sure what I wanted to hear. There was no easy way to get through this.

Jason swam toward us through the throng of men. "Come meet my boyfriend," he said, leading us to the kitchen. Steven was pulling hors d'oeuvres from the oven, replacing them with the unbaked tray sitting on the counter. He looked annoyed, more annoyed that he had to say hello to us. We left him to his baking.

Jason moved us to the couch in the main living area, out of earshot of the other mourners. Now I could hold the reality of Torry's death in my hands as though it were an object. A relic. It didn't attack me the way it once had. But this didn't mean I was settled with the idea. I struggled to accept it, to shrug off the heavy shawl of guilt, shame, anger, and despair I'd worn since Jason's first phone call to me. I needed details. At least, I needed different details.

Jason told me Torry had been diagnosed with MS about a year and a half ago, when they were still dating. "You may have seen some of the symptoms when you were together," he said.

"Like what?"

He rattled them off. "Mood swings." Torry was a hothead from the day I met him, the kind of outbursts I thought showed a kind of passion, but was just the echoes of the abuse he'd survived. This part of his personality was so essential to his own identity that it inspired his tattoo, a cartoon cat he joked was just like him: cute and cuddly until you pissed him off, and then he'd scratch you.

"Attention and memory issues." Torry could never focus on school. We took a class together, a survey of post-Freudian psychoanalytic theory. While I could buckle down and do the reading, write the eight-to-twelve page papers, he'd interrupt me, fidget, doodle at the coffee shop where I did my work. Getting Torry to admit he ever forgot something was a fool's errand. He preferred to insist he'd never known or been told, a subtle gaslighting that paved over the potholes in his recollection.

"Uncontrollable shaking." I flashed back to a night I'd woken up with Torry in my arms, his body shivering and violent. I asked what was wrong, but he couldn't answer. His teeth chattered. His skin felt cold to the touch. My own heart raced, afraid he was having some kind of breakdown. I wanted to call an ambulance. Before I could make the call, the tremors stopped. "I'm fine," he said. I asked him if that had ever happened before, if he knew what it was. "It's nothing. Come back to bed."

"Fainting." Here I had two memories. Once, early in dating him, he bent down to hug me when I sat in my desk chair, and seconds later went limp. I thought he was joking around, being silly or weird. He came to a few seconds later. Another time, maybe a year later, we walked home from work together in July or August. We talked about our days, and halfway into my telling I realized he wasn't next to me anymore. I looked back, and he'd fainted on the sidewalk, landing partly on the grassy area separating us from the street.

The real breaking point, Jason said, was the cancer diagnosis. Though it's rare for people Torry's age to develop pancreatic cancer, it's possible. But I had a hard time believing it, even as Jason recounted the doctor's appointment when Torry found out, the prognosis he was given, and the unlikely chance of survival even with treatment. What did ring true for me was Torry's rejection of even trying treatment. It was going to be costly and physically devastating, and he would lose weight, muscle, and hair and appear to be as sick as he really was. I could see him choosing his own terms.

And so there I sat, listening to Jason, half-believing him, interrogating Torry's ghost about what was true and what was a lie, just like I had done for all the years I'd known him.

## ACCEPTANCE

Running through the tunnel, Sarah trips on a pile of bones and seems to knock herself out upon impact. But a few seconds later, her eyes snap open. Light—natural light—washes her face clean in the darkness. She's so close.

With renewed strength, she crawls to her feet and scales the slope of bones leading toward the light.

Then, in our first shot from outside the cave since the women entered it so long ago, we see the natural world: trees, mountains, fog in the distance. And Sarah bursts into the shot from under the soil, gasping for cool, clean air. She pulls herself up through the gap she's made. The metaphor for rebirth can't be ignored. This Sarah—hunter, survivor—no longer resembles the meek, grieving Sarah who went into the cave with us. In a series of quick shots, Sarah dashes down to the forest floor, gets back to the parked car, yanks the keys from the visor, and drives off at top speed.

When she's sure she's safe, enough distance between her and the cave creatures, she pulls to the side of the road to breathe, to gather, to assess. She gulps air into her lungs between sobs of relief. When Sarah turns her head away from her window, that's when the final jump scare occurs: Juno, her face flat with anger, is sitting in the passenger seat, ready for revenge.

It's a dubious cliffhanger for an ending, from a narrative perspective, calling into question whether Sarah even really got out of the cave or if she still lies there, dreaming this wish fulfillment before the creatures locate and devour her. From a psychological angle, if we assume she escaped and drove away, then Juno's apparition is the unequivocal marker that Sarah will be haunted by a new trauma. No longer will she dream of the death of her husband and daughter; she'll be tormented by the friend she attacked and left to die. Like Sarah herself, Sarah's grief is a survivor. It's not ready to leave her whole. It wants her to remember.

There is no way out.

## AUGUST 15, 2005 | 4:45 P.M.

In the weeks following Torry's death, I coped the only way I knew how: I wrote. I journaled through my grief and confusion, documenting each limp I took away from the moment Jason told me he killed himself. At first, only fragments would emerge. Language could not wrangle my thoughts and feelings into coherency. The fractured gestures were flinching, erratic. As time moved forward, the words formed lines. Formed stanzas. Formed poems. I had no funeral to attend beyond the stilted memorial full of strangers at Jason's house. I never saw Torry's body. I never watched it lowered into the ground beside his sister's grave. The pieces I wrote performed these rituals for me, giving me space to shape my grief into short, austere poems.

Torry continued to assert himself into my waking life. Mail addressed to him arrived at the post office box we once shared. The most ironic was a magazine mailer shouting *TIME IS RUNNING OUT.* Beneath that: *Renew* Men's Health *today.*

Well into August, I heard a sound passing through the walls of my home. It was so faint. A wail of sorts. The sound would creep into the room with me, no matter where I was. Its devastation felt like the language I'd recently mastered.

It was too much a reflection of my state of mind to be something from the natural world and not just a manifestation of my subconscious, my grief, my guilt, my despair. When it continued first for hours and then days, I tracked it through the house, thinking it could lead me somewhere, to something, to a message from Torry or some kind of artifact he wanted me to find among the storage bins and closets and boxes of my past.

That the sound articulated itself into the mewling of a cat, too, felt apt. Torry's love of cats was part of the reason he got his tattoo. It made sense to me that Torry would take the form of a cat to visit me. It made the only sense I had left.

I looked everywhere for the source of the cries: cupboards where I kept the pots and pans Torry and I bought together. Closets that held a couple hand-me-down shirts and sweaters he'd given me. Out on the patio where the landscaping had grown wild, the vined plants wrapping their tendrils around an old wooden bench like a squid tangling its prey. In the laundry closet in the car port, a jumble of half-used detergents and stain removers scattered on the shelves. That's where it felt closest, loudest, most urgent. But there was no creature in the laundry closet. After hours of more searching, I'd return to this spot and—I didn't even know why. Because of an instinct, maybe, or a hunch—I popped the hood of my car, the car Torry and I shared for those years. It had remained idle here since the day I first learned of Torry's death.

There, on the engine block, I found a kitten perched, as if she'd been waiting for me for some time.

The kitten and I regarded each other, neither of us moving. I wasn't even sure how she'd managed to get in there in the first place. My instinct was to rescue her, worried the machinery of the car might kill her. I reached out to pick her up. If I touched her, I could be sure of why she found me.

Before my fingers even brushed her fur, she flinched, dropped down into the engine's tangled guts. She vanished into the day, into the desert. Into a future that didn't include me.

# BUDDY COMEDY

## FRIDAY, NOVEMBER 16, 2007

My uncle, my father, and I approached the U.S./Canada border checkpoint at Blue Water Bridge in my uncle's SUV. The sky spread above us unbroken in its grayness, uniting Port Huron, Michigan, and Sarnia, Ontario under the same religion. We shuffled forward in a line of cars waiting to take the bridge over the St. Clair River.

My uncle's audible breathing—wheezing, sniffling, interrupted only by the fleshy rupture of phlegm when he cleared his throat—broke the silence in the car.

A Canadian Border Patrol agent approached us, peering through windows, beginning with the passenger side. As he moved around the van, I could feel him approaching my window in the backseat.

I tried to seem casual—like the old blanket thrown across my lap didn't conceal human remains.

## JUST SAY YES

Aaron Green (Jonah Hill) has one job: get Aldous Snow (Russell Brand) from London to Los Angeles for a concert at the Greek Theater, with a quick layover in New York for an appearance on the *Today* show. It sounds easy enough, except that Aldous Snow, sitting at the bottom of multiple addictions and the most devastating artistic low of his career, is a walking, uncooperative id. This is the fundamental problem of *Get Him to the Greek*.

Aaron, a huge fan of Snow and his band Infant Sorrow, is over the moon to meet and spend time with his idol, until he's spent literally one minute with the man. Aaron realizes anything that goes wrong, even direct results of Aldous's decisions and actions, will be Aaron's fault and that Aldous will not only not listen to Aaron's instructions, he will often do the opposite.

## TUESDAY, NOVEMBER 13, 2007

We met my uncle for breakfast the morning after we arrived in Port Huron. He was impossible to ignore. At 6'5" with a thick frame, he entered any room like a planet, complete with his own gravitational pull. He stood with stooped shoulders, his blond hair flecked with orange. His speaking voice usually rasped with a whiskey huskiness to it, though he was prone to raising his voice into a boom that got everyone's attention. Like my dad, he cleared his throat constantly, and any time he moved his joints, he would groan, or mutter, "Jesus Christ." The last time I'd seen him in person was his wedding when I was 12 years old. When we reunited in Port Huron, I was 30 and gay; he was divorced and living in an enormous house in Sarnia that was as cold and empty as his life.

He took us to the hospital. My grandmother Edith, or "Dee" as she liked us to call her, lay propped up in bed in intensive care, a breathing tube shoved down her throat. Fluorescent lights washed the room with sharp shrieking. Though it'd only been a couple years since I'd seen her, she looked unlike the woman I remembered. Her hair, which for the entirety of my life had gathered in a *Bride of Frankenstein* mass of gray curls on her head, was now completely silver, flat, and unwashed. Her face drooped. Her eyelids sagged, half-closed.

I sat down in the molded plastic chair set next to the bed. I said hello and placed my hand on hers. She responded with a weak nodding of her head, a faint squeeze of her hand. She could hear me, maybe see me. She knew I was there.

Edith was the only child of Danish immigrants, and while she'd been born in the United States, her family moved right back to Denmark after she was born. Her parents Oscar and Thea, both orphans, gave her the middle name "Lykke," or Lucky, because she had two parents. Four years later, they were back in America, settling among other émigrés from their homeland in a rural area outside Detroit. Edith married a Danish immigrant named Svend, and for the first few years of their marriage, they lived with Oscar and Thea. This was where my father and brother were born. Later, the family settled into a spacious four-bedroom home in Southfield, a white suburb of the segregated metropolitan area. My grandfather died of emphysema in his mid-60s. After a career spent working as a tool and dye maker for the automotive industry, years of inhaling smoke and fumes wrecked his lungs. That same year, Oscar died at 92. Thea moved into the home in Southfield until she became too frail to be cared for, and died in a nursing home at 100.

My grandmother lost everyone over those last years. Gus, her friend and constant companion. Her cousin Valerie. Her best friend Carole. One by one her circle dwindled. The house was sold and she moved into a small apartment. Just two days before she went to the hospital, my uncle had finished moving her into an assisted living facility an hour north in Port Huron, where she'd be just a short drive over the international bridge from Sarnia. But almost as quickly as she arrived there, she ended up in this hospital in severe respiratory distress, perched on the edge of life.

My dad and uncle spoke with the hospital staff. My uncle was convinced she had a good chance of a miraculous recovery. The nurse explained that was less and less likely with each minute that passed. Rather than improving, she merely held steady. The nurse doubted she could breathe on her own, but this would be the only way to know if her condition would improve.

In the quiet that followed: the beeps of my grandmother's pulse through the monitor. The ventilator's flex and whoosh. Footfalls tapping against tile. Everything felt bare and wounded and vacant. Or maybe it was just me.

## GANG OF LUST

We first meet Aldous at his London flat, overlooking the Thames and Parliament. He's a mercurial brat. When Aaron explains he's arrived to take Aldous to the concert at the Greek, Aldous insists the event was scheduled for two months later and that Aaron himself has changed the date without telling him. Aldous's mother (Dinah Stabb), a quiet, birdlike woman, chirps back whatever Aldous tells her. *Yes, it's in two months. Yes, they changed it. Yes, you've been inconvenienced.* Aldous's brother echoes her. It's clear they both exist in Aldous's world to reinforce his delusions and enable his bad behavior.

That night Aldous takes Aaron on a trip through a drug-fueled Wonderland. When they finally leave for New York at the very last second, Aaron spends the entire journey to the *Today* show playing interference between Aldous and the substances he conjures almost out of thin air. Aldous's impulsive behavior, though, is the opposite of what it seems. He doesn't want to lose control. He wants to wrangle the misery of his broken life by corralling it within a blissful high. What Aldous doesn't realize is that the lows continue to find him because he falsifies the highs. He can't have one without the other.

Aaron's stress level about being late for the *Today* show is a third character in these scenes. Aldous's narcissism prevents Aldous from caring, convinced (and confirmed through lived experience) that nothing can begin without him. These characters, living at opposite ends of the economic spectrum of the same industry, stand in for something larger than themselves. Aldous's wealth and privileges mean he never faces consequences, partly because he does not acknowledge they can exist. All Aaron sees are consequences: what failure now will mean for his idol's career, what getting fired will mean for him financially, for his own future.

## TUESDAY, NOVEMBER 13, 2007, CONT.

We got the call that my grandmother was in her final hour while we ate dinner at a Chinese restaurant in Sarnia. We rushed back to the hospital to be with her, and I sat by the bed holding her cool hand in mine. Her skin was thin and pale as airmail paper, bluish and translucent. She labored to pull each shallow breath into her body. I was there when she took her last.

My dad went quiet. My uncle paced like a caged lion. "C'mon, Ma!" he yelled at her. "Wake up!" He huffed and moaned and sighed as he stomped around the room. I sat by the bed, the only one in the room shedding tears. I dared not make a sound while my uncle was in his agitated state, not wanting to draw his attention. "Wake up, Ma!" he yelled again. I half-expected him to leap onto the hospital bed, to administer CPR, or, I don't know, shake her lifeless body until it worked again. I didn't understand the reaction and I didn't want to be part of it. I wanted him to shut up. I wanted him to calm down. I wanted a moment of peace to let my own grief escape my body.

His shouts alerted the nurse, who swept through the curtain like a breeze. "Why don't you give me a few moments to get her ready," she suggested, her tone practiced. We moved into the hallway to wait. My uncle, raging now in silence, radiated beams of energy that electrified the entire ward.

When the nurse rejoined us in the hallway, she explained a funeral home was en route to collect my grandmother and prepare her for what was ahead. Her demeanor was so kind and loving. What would it be like to work this way, family after family mourning a loved one? I appreciated her even as I shrank from my embarrassment of my uncle's performance of grief. His words and actions rang false to me somehow, like he was acting out a performance he'd seen modeled on television. Did he feel anything—anything authentic—at all?

There was nothing more for us to do that night, but we waited for the death workers to arrive. My dad and uncle watched them put the body into their car. My grandmother had requested this act of her children. She always said morticians were scam artists.

## THE CLAP

Aldous makes it to the studio with mere minutes to spare, completing his interview with Meredith Viera as Aaron scrambles to find a sheet of lyrics to the singer's disastrous, career-ruining single "African Child," whose words and music video seem to lampoon war, famine, poverty, and racism, often in the same breath. The song, which we hear in the very first moments of the film, encapsulates Aldous's brand of white cis-male privilege: that deigning to extend his attention to a marginalized population is a form of activism, despite having regressive, harmful, and tokenizing approaches to understanding that population's experiences. Aldous never considered that his perspective on "Africa" wasn't necessary; in fact, he assumed it was. At the last second, Aldous embraces a moment of clarity and performs his classic cut "The Clap," announcing the anniversary concert at the Greek before he rushes off stage. Aaron still needs to get them to LA.

The next sequence firms up *Get Him to the Greek's* unexpected thematic undertone: family ties. At the airport, Aldous throws another curve ball. He's taking them to Las Vegas to visit his father and former manager (Colm Meaney), whom he hasn't seen in years. Aldous is estranged from nearly every family member who doesn't suck at the teat of his success.

For his part, Aaron, too, is staring down familial issues. Shortly before departing on his odyssey, Aaron's girlfriend Daphne (Elisabeth Moss), deep in the sleepless throes of a medical internship, tells him she's gotten a once-in-a-lifetime residency opportunity in Seattle. They live together in Los Angeles, making this kind of change a make-or-break relationship moment. But instead of acknowledging her, Aaron pulls focus back to himself. The conversation becomes an argument, and it feels like they've broken up. Aaron has no other personal relationship in the film. This rupture leaves him adrift just as he inserts himself into Aldous's orbit.

## THROUGH WEDNESDAY, NOVEMBER 14, 2007

At the funeral home, we watched the undertakers put my grandmother's body in the hearse, per her instructions.

We followed the hearse out of town, into a woodsy area of winding two-lane roads. No other cars.

The crematorium appeared in the middle of nowhere, a dirty steel industrial building passersby would assume was set free against the ravages of time. Corrugated metal roof. Ominous smoke stacks. Huge doors wide enough to accept an automobile. We watched them pull her body from the hearse, carry it to the rolling track that led into the oven, and we waited as she made this final journey toward the fire. The door to the oven opened. The unremarkable box that held her body traveled by conveyer inside with painstaking slowness. No one spoke. The quiet allowed the chipper sounds of the natural world to creep into the crematorium—birds, insects, the breeze tousling the trees. It seemed an apt soundtrack to my grandmother's return to dust. At last the casket cleared the door. It slid down behind her. "Okay, she's in," my dad said. He turned to leave.

We drove to the bank, closed her accounts, which had already been placed into a trust.

We wrote and sent an obituary to the newspapers.

At her assisted living facility, we packed up all the loose items we could: artwork, clothing. The remaining pieces of her Danish porcelain figurine collection. I gathered her coats from the closet, each one black with faux fur necklines, oversized buttons. We moved everything into my uncle's SUV. It only took one trip.

We took her things to his house overlooking Lake Huron. A warehouse where he ran his business loomed behind the house, somehow even bigger and more ominous—I didn't know what he did, but the warehouse was packed to the gills with junk. Junk on shelves. Junk on walls. Junk in piled up boxes. Nothing had a function in the space aside from rows of large metal racks holding it all. Danish pride was everywhere. Danish flags, renderings of Viking ships in red and white. This was a space most people who knew my uncle would never enter. I couldn't help feeling all of it—the volume of stuff, the Danish regalia—were only there for my uncle's benefit. A kind of mirror he could look into and know who he was. How much he was worth.

There were so many *things*, it was like my uncle had found a way to ensure there'd be no space for people.

## LITTLE BIRD

Aaron's boss Sergio (Sean "Diddy" Combs), the brash music executive who communicates mainly through barks at his staff, tells us early in the film that everything he does, he does for his family. All the money he makes, all the time he has outside the office—that's for his wife and their six kids. We'll see Sergio talk with Aaron by phone. Between advising Aaron on how to motivate Aldous to comply, Sergio and his wife yell back and forth about where a specific snack is in the fridge. Of the film's three main men, only Sergio puts family first. It's likely no surprise, then, that he is also the most confident, composed, and effective character in the film. He knows who he is and what he wants. Aldous and Aaron, despite the gap in their celebrity, lack this same conviction.

## BACKSTORY

My uncle owned a series of niches in a memorial wall at a Danish retirement community not far from where he lived in Ontario. My great-grandparents, my grandparents, my father, and he would all have their own final resting places, plaqued with a ceramic memorial with their names, the years they lived, the Danish flag.

One small problem: three of them had been inurned in Southfield, Michigan, for decades. We needed to claim their remains, transport them, and inurn them again.

My uncle never asked about my dad's wishes. Still married, living in Arizona where two of his children and all of his grandchildren lived, my dad wouldn't elect to have his remains housed in a remote patch of woods in another nation. But because my uncle was alone, he perceived everyone to be alone. The niches were his last-ditch effort to build a family again. One that would never leave him.

## SEARCHING FOR A FATHER

The reunion between Aldous and his father Jonathan is bittersweet. As they talk, they untangle the mess of years between them—the good years, the difficult years, the silent years, the wistful years. Aldous's stepmother does her best to keep peace and foster good vibes between them. The détente doesn't last long, and Aldous and Jonathan fall into their old patterns, raising their voices and arguing about which of them is responsible for Aldous's success. When his dad breaks a guitar over

Aldous's back in the midst of this explosive argument, the two men finally see each other, really see each other.

The act sets off a raucous fight that ranges all over a suite where they've thrown a party. Before long, broken bottles, panic, and even a little fire have broken out. This reflects our cultural expectation of straight white men when they have no other option but to express their emotions. It's devastating for them, and worse for everyone else. White masculinity's primary toxin is just this: men's inability to relate emotionally to the world around them, but especially to other men. Their only means of expression cosplays in violence. Years of neglect forged Aldous's resentment into an explosive weapon.

## THURSDAY, NOVEMBER 15, 2007

My uncle parked at the cemetery and took a deep breath. "These guys are going to try to fuck us." He snatched a cap he kept in the center console and pulled it over his hair. It featured a pair of crossed anchors with the words "U. S. Coast Guard" embroidered over them in an arch. "Let's see how they deal with an injured veteran." He pulled a metal crutch out from under his backseat, then steadied himself with it as he walked toward the administrative offices. He exaggerated a limp to a comical degree, his face swirled into a grimace. When he committed, he committed.

My uncle served in the Coast Guard in his twenties, so at least that part was true. But he sustained no injuries in the line of duty that I knew of, and he definitely had no visible disabilities. Why he had a crutch in his car, set exactly to his height, mystified me. Then I realized he'd engaged in this particular ruse before, maybe even many times.

I wanted to dissolve into a pool on the asphalt and rush away from all of this. It was a sunny fall day, the kind of day that looks warm through a window but chills you when you walk outside. The trees around the cemetery entrance and those lining the road waved in the breeze, their leaves rustling in a soft woosh. Yet my uncle lumbered through like an uncoordinated Bigfoot, dragging dad and me behind him.

A receptionist sat at a small desk just inside the offices. She greeted us when we walked in.

"We need to claim the ashes of our parents and grandparents." My uncle leaned heavily on the crutch as though it were the only thing between him and a spectacular fall to the carpet.

The receptionist let us in to speak with the director, a middle-aged Black man. He wore a clean white shirt with shiny cufflinks and an austere tie. My uncle lumbered into the room, trying to appear unsteady and uncoordinated. "How do we retrieve ashes?" he asked the man.

"We can just go pull them," he told us.

"Oh," my uncle said.

"But you can't take them out of here without the certificate of cremation."

"Where do we get that?" My uncle swayed on his crutch.

The director nodded to a series of filing cabinets lining one wall of his office. "They're in there. What years were the deaths?" My uncle rattled off the dates in the 80s and 90s. The director sighed. He called to his assistant. "Get the boxes."

My uncle got suspicious. "What boxes?" He tapped the crutch on the ground.

"Records that old are in deep storage," the director explained. "Not a lot of demand for them. But by law we have to keep them. So we keep them in boxes."

The assistant walked in, carrying two or three small rectangular storage boxes each time. In all, there were about fifteen.

"Also, they're...not well organized," the director said. "This is going to take a while."

Each of us took a box to a chair, flipping through every single piece of paper inside. Certificates of cremation looked like little handbills, featuring the deceased's name, years of life, cause of death, and the location of cremation, along with a permit number. All of the records we reviewed were completed by hand or by typewriter, and the deaths ranged in years from the 1940s to the 1980s. We were looking for three needles in these haystacks: Oscar, Thea, Svend. There were so many names that weren't theirs. I picked up a bill, checked the name, and then turned it face down in a pile on the chair next to me, moving through a box from front to back until I was sure the certificates we needed weren't in there.

It took time—hours—but we found them, one at a time. We met each discovery with cheers as though we'd found one of the Golden Tickets from *Willy Wonka and the Chocolate Factory*. Each certificate meant we were that much closer to getting the ashes and getting out of there.

The columbarium that held my family's remains crouched in a shaded part of the cemetery, near a winding water feature and some rolling hills. It looked tranquil, exactly the kind of place you'd want your loved ones to spend eternity—if you believed in that sort of thing. Inside, marble faces held the names and years of life for the occupant of each niche in gold letters. My great-grandparents shared one, while my grandfather's looked only half-occupied, with space for us to install my grandmother's name and her dates beside his.

The cemetery director unlocked the niches and handed us the small cardboard boxes that held their remains. Now four generations of my family were together again. Half dead, half living. My uncle tried to bribe the cemetery director with some cash, but he kindly refused the offer. My uncle didn't know how to receive this. He seemed both relieved and offended. In the end, he took his money, his crutch, and his unconvincing limp back to the SUV with the boxes of remains. He wedged them into a banker's box in the back.

My uncle fired up the engine, turning around to glance at me in the back and then my dad in the passenger seat. "Who's hungry?"

## JACKIE Q

Aldous and Aaron split up in LA. At the start of the film the two men seemed like opposites of each other, but now their circumstances feel eerily similar. Aaron needs to triage his relationship with Daphne. He's been unwittingly butt dialing her every time he's in a compromising position on his journey, making repair of their relationship seem unlikely if not impossible. There's no reason Daphne should even entertain the idea of getting back together. She could take the Seattle job and move forward with her life, unencumbered by Aaron's selfishness and his lack of support for her. Yet, Aaron feels just enough unearned confidence to give it a shot.

Aldous seeks reconciliation with his estranged wife Jackie Q (Rose Byrne). The two of them were a pop powerhouse of a couple, but fallout from the "African Child" single drove them apart. Jackie tells a TV reporter during a live interview—with Aldous sitting beside her—that she's bored in her marriage, and that Aldous can't satisfy her sexually. Aldous breaks his sobriety as a result of the revelation, and the two lovers start living separate lives. When he tracks her down to reconnect, he finds her snuggled in bed with Lars Ulrich, real-life drummer of the band Metallica. When Aldous opens his heart to Jackie and tells her how much he misses her and her son, Jackie reveals a long-held secret: their son Naples was the result of an affair Jackie had with a photographer while doing a shoot in Italy. The news rocks Aldous. The one unshakable relationship he thought he had—that with his son—vanishes.

Aldous shares a quiet moment with Naples. "Call me Aldous," he tells the boy. Naples says, "But you're my dad." Naples has known no other father; Aldous is the only one he wants and needs. Despite the child's insistence, Aldous can't let go of the betrayal. He goes to Aaron's apartment, where Aaron and Daphne are mid-argument. Aldous floats the idea of a three-way. Daphne leaps at the opportunity, resulting in perhaps the most awkward, unsexy, unfulfilling three-way in contemporary cinema. In the end, Daphne calls it off. They can't heal these wounds with their bodies. But Aaron still can't take responsibility for his own actions. Aaron blames Aldous for everything that's gone wrong in his life. Their tenuous bond shatters.

Aldous doesn't know how to resolve conflict—with others or within himself. Yet it thrives all around him. In his marriage. Between his parents. With those who work for him. The only relationship in his life that lacks friction—that with his mother—feels fake. Her parenting style is that of a wax dummy. With no role models in his life teaching him how to safely and lovingly express emotions, Aldous' descent into drug abuse, alcoholism, and sex addiction seem almost predestined. The "loss" of his son—perhaps the only human being Aldous knows he truly loves—devastates him, and in turn, he detonates the only other positive influence in his life: Aaron, who saw the good in him, who ignored the bad, and who, we might say, just wanted to love him.

## THURSDAY, NOVEMBER 15, 2007, CONT

My uncle took us to an Olive Garden en route to dropping us at our hotel. It was the first break we'd had, the first moment we weren't actively wrapping up the loose ends of my grandmother's life or trying to liberate two generations of my family from a marble wall in a Southfield cemetery. Once we were seated and had placed our order, my uncle turned his attention to me, asking me all about my life, my job. I filled him in with the short version of all the stories, not sure how much detail was actually desired, reluctant to offer more than necessary.

He took a sip of water. "Do you have a…" He paused, thinking of the phrase. "Special friend?"

I wasn't there for euphemistic bullshit. We were going to call things by their real names. "You mean a boyfriend? Yes."

My dad put an arm around me. "Charlie's had a tough year in the dating department," he said. "But things are looking up."

My uncle wanted to know what happened. I didn't want to tell the story—not now, not to him, not as I sought to forget what happened. I didn't want to tell again how in love I'd been with a man I saw myself marrying, how much I dreaded reaching my thirtieth birthday. How my birthday collided with an out-of-the-blue breakup that sent me to karaoke, where I dedicated a slurred rendition of "Tainted Love" to the guy who touched me and tainted me. And after, how I begged a man at the next bar to go home with me, just so I could prove to myself how over it all I was. Though he'd turned me down on the hook up, we went out on dates, many dates. I realized you don't get to choose when good guys show up, but you do get to choose if you let some jerk wreck you so much you won't take a chance. The short version, the one I shared, was simple. "I got dumped out of the blue and it was hard."

"Now, I can't believe that." My uncle's face wore an incredulous expression. "A handsome guy like you. He must be an idiot."

He was an idiot, but only I got to say that. "It's complicated."

"I don't know why," my uncle shot back. He gave me an evaluating look, taking in my appearance. "If I was gay, I would go for you."

I choked on the bite of food I'd just put into my mouth. I glanced at my dad. The comment hadn't registered. I sat alone on my island of cringing discomfort in a suburban Olive Garden. I wasn't sure if this was a compliment or a conspiracy to commit a crime, so in true Midwestern fashion, I addressed it all by changing the subject.

"When do we pick up grandma?" I asked my dad.

"Tomorrow morning."

I focused on my meal, the first thing I remembered eating since the Chinese restaurant. I tried not to think about anything else.

## I AM JESUS

Desperate for any kind of human connection, Aldous phones his mother back in London and tells her he won't be doing the show at The Greek. "Can you say something reassuring to me, something reassuring mothers say to their sons?" he asks her, coaching her on the right emotional response to his mood.

"You stay chipper." She struggles to find a platitude, any platitude, that might fit. "And don't get down, and when you get back I'll make you some shortbread."

"Well, I think everything's going to be all right," Aldous says, doing the work for her.

With the concert just a couple hours off, Aldous retreats to The Standard Hotel in downtown Los Angeles. He eschews the huge VIP party in his honor. Instead, he paces the edge of the building, looking over at the pool and party on one side and the empty street on the other. He knows now that he is alone—utterly alone—in this universe. Every family member either resents him or embodies some kind of caricature of the role they play in his life, as authentic as a Muppet movie in which he's the only human in the cast. He has no real connections, no bonds—just fame with its tenuous relationship to reality and shrieking fans who paint all their dreams and desires on the blank canvas of his life.

At home, Aaron watches the live broadcast. An announcer says Aldous Snow, the "most self-destructive man in rock and roll, is not yet in the building." Sergio texts Aaron asking him where the fuck Aldous is. "Fuck him," Aaron mutters. Just then, Aldous calls Aaron and leaves him a voicemail. "I really need to apologize and tell you that I'm gonna jump off the roof of The Standard Hotel now." Then, to be especially English about it, he adds, "If you're not busy…" and hangs up.

Aaron races to the hotel, unsure if he'll make it in time to stop Aldous from killing himself.

## THURSDAY, NOVEMBER 15—FRIDAY, NOVEMBER 16, 2007

My uncle drove the retrieved ashes into Canada after dinner, when he knew Canadian Border Patrol would be at its most lax. Dad and I got up early the next morning to drive with my uncle to the crematorium, its forgotten industrial facility vibe in stark contrast to the bucolic surroundings. The mortician there handed us a cardboard box too light to contain an entire human life. I took it in my hands.

My uncle eyed the guy with suspicion. "You sure that's her?"

The mortician was horrified. "Sir, it absolutely is."

My uncle looked around the facility, as though a cursory glance would confirm there were no other possible bodies handed to us, and that we truly did have my grandmother's ashes in a box.

Since this was the first time I'd spent time with my dad and uncle as an adult, it was also the first time I saw my dad shift into Big Brother Mode. How practiced his words were when speaking to my uncle. His steady tone. The way he knew when my uncle was about to lose his temper and create a scene. Their quick anger with each other, and the speed with which it snuffed out.

My dad touched my uncle's arm. "Let's go."

I sat in the backseat of the car, the box on my lap. It felt heartless not to hold on to her, cruel somehow. When my dad and uncle sunk deep into conversation with each other, I slipped the top from the box and looked inside. A sealed plastic baggie held my grandmother's ashes. What she'd become was dark gray in color, uneven in grain. Again, I was struck by how little of her remained. The human body is 70% water. The majority of my grandmother became steam in that oven. What I held was mostly bone, and whatever part of it didn't burn had been ground up to fit in this box.

My uncle picked up a blanket from between the front seats and threw it back at me. "Cover up."

The car slowed. We gathered into the slow stream of traffic approaching the border checkpoint.

As we crept forward toward the guard, the birdlike weight of my grandmother's remains pressed into my lap beneath the blanket, the only thing shielding me (and her) from discovery by the border patrol.

Since my uncle was a citizen, crossing into Canada was always easier for him than leaving it. U.S. Border Patrol agents were more confrontational and aggressive in the way they spoke to you. The Canadian agents were the Canadian version of this extreme: cautious, but polite; suspicious, but permissive.

My uncle rolled down his window. "Good morning," the agent said. "What's your reason for visiting Canada today?"

"I'm a citizen," my uncle said, "and I'm bringing my brother and his son to visit my place in Sarnia," he said. He offered the agent his credentials and our passports. While the agent spoke to us, another looked in through all our windows. It was November, cool enough that covering up with a blanket wasn't a red flag, but I still felt the exacting gaze of the agent study me.

There was a pause that stretched out for an unbearable length of time.

Finally the agent encouraged us to enjoy our visit. My uncle's window rose back up with an electric hum, and then we were crossing the St. Clair River into Sarnia.

We drove mostly in silence. I had no idea how deep we went into Canada, but the landscape soon became wild and undeveloped, the highway the only evidence of humanity for many miles. The Danish community sat off several backroads, nestled in a stretch of otherwise untouched wilderness. The property included apartments for retired folks, a traditional Scandinavian house that held a Danish restaurant, and some administrative offices. The memorial park was off in the back, among the trees.

The niche wall was simple: rounded stones in an arc held fast with concrete. Glazed plaques, mostly empty, except for the few that read the names of my grandparents and great-grandparents. We placed my grandmother with Svend's remains. Now they were all back together, each couple sharing one niche.

## GOING UP

Aaron shouts from the crowd of fans gathered around the Standard Hotel's pool. "Hey, Aldous, I'm here!"

Aldous jumps, overestimating the power he needs and almost misses the pool. We see part of his body slam against the pool's concrete lip. But then he emerges from the water. Baptized, reborn. And then he says the true thing, the one thing he's never been able to say out loud, much less admit to another person: "I'm lonely, mate. I'm really lonely. And I'm sad. And I ain't got no one except my mom. And she's an idiot." Aldous cries, but his tears disappear into streaks of pool water running down his face.

Aldous recommits to the show at the Greek. Sergio sends Aldous right into wardrobe, gives Aaron some pills to give Aldous. Aaron sees Sergio—and the industry—for what it is now, a cycle that traps people like Aldous in the isolation of fame and money. Sergio doesn't care about Aldous's health or well-being at all. Sergio's only priority is his family, and providing for them. Sergio is the polar opposite of Aldous.

Aldous's performance starts. He stands in front of the name of his band, Infant Sorrow, in giant letters at the back of the stage. The name, which felt comical and inane at the start of the film, now bears the gravitas of Aldous's journey. The sorrow he feels traces all the way back to his own infancy, to the failure of his parents to love each other and him, and to all the betrayals and abandonments that followed up until this moment. And that same sorrow prevents us from developing beyond the all-consuming id of infancy. Aaron, standing off stage watching, is the first person to see Aldous in all his woeful complexity and to love him anyway, even after everything they've been through. It has renewed Aldous, and so we believe him when the first song, "Going Up," prepares to launch into its chorus. "Can you see what's going on?" he asks of those who didn't believe in him. "I'm coming up," the triumphant chorus calls, over and over and over.

And we believe him. After everything he's been through, after everything he's realized about his life, there's nowhere left for him to go but up.

# WESTERN

## STAYCATION, WITH BULLETS

The drive to Tombstone brought us thirty miles south down Interstate 10 from Tucson. Desert pushed civilization away as far as the eye could see, replacing it with low desert cactus, mesquite, and acacia. Then red mountains. Past them, their vague, purple cousins. As we neared the exit for Highway 80, the only road from I-10 into the isolated towns of Cochise County, the vegetation changed to desert scrub, Joshua trees. The cacti vanished. The air thinned and got cooler.

I took my friend Maureen to visit Tombstone during her trip out West from DC. She wanted to escape their wild winter for the warmth of the Southwest. I'd been in Tucson for less than a year and was still learning about what the region had to offer. My boyfriend Brody was finishing his degree at the University of Arizona and I, unable to find a full time job in the wake of the 2008 recession, had cobbled together enough adjunct teaching and contract gigs to keep us eating and paying rent, even if neither of us had health insurance. I found Tucson strange. My friend Jaime once explained to me that in Phoenix, "we pave the desert away, but in Tucson they welcome it up to the front door." The landscape was gorgeous. Being in my mid-thirties, I was struck by Tucson's conspicuous lack of middle age. There were college kids and retirees, but not much in between.

Tombstone, listed on the national registry of historic places, was a largely undeveloped swatch of land atop a mesa in the middle of the desert. Highway 80 curved around its edge before heading further south to Bisbee and, just beyond that, to Mexico. A modern Holiday Inn Express stood next to the Lovely Lookout Inn on the outskirts of town. A few blocks in, a combo lundromat and car wash squatted unused next to a run-down Circle K. It would have been an unremarkable Arizona town hovering dangerously close to "ghost" status were it not for the billboards promising daily gunfights, mine tours, resorts, and miniature golf courses. A few billboards were so large, built so far out of scale, that they dwarfed nearby homes, casting shifting quadrilateral shadows as the sun made its way overhead.

When Maureen and I arrived in town, parked the car, and stepped onto the sidewalks of modern Tombstone, it was eerily quiet despite the clusters of tourists striding by us. Until the gunfights began.

They continued, like clockwork, every thirty minutes.

The cracking of pistols and the throaty booms of shotgun necks made the date fall into place in my memory. It was the one-year anniversary of the violent shooting that left six Tucsonans dead, and another thirteen wounded. Among those victims was Congresswoman Gabrielle Giffords, a relatively unknown third-term Representative. The shooting came on the heels of a year in which Arizona often made the national news for spearheading a series of laws that took aim at what the state legislature considered to be the federal government's inability to curb and curtail illegal immigration. The most spurious of these laws, SB 1130, authorized police officers to conduct citizenship verification in the course of routine investigations if they suspected the subject of their investigation were undocumented.

On January 8, 2011—the day of the shooting—I was temporarily not an Arizonan. I lived in suburban Washington, DC, after relocating to take what I thought would be a dream job but was instead a living nightmare. I took over operations of a financially challenged nonprofit organization, whose board, it turned out, was wary of trusting a new director after their last executive was fired for unscrupulous self-dealing. I was young, and it was my first time being the leader of an organization. I ended up dreading the work day and, after getting lambasted by the board president so viciously he foamed at the mouth and covered my face in spittle, I walked away. For the next year I lived off a meager combination of retirement savings and adjunct pay. Brody and I lived at the edge of our means, scraping by.

When I first arrived in DC, I came face to face with the ignorance and general confusion about Arizona itself. Washington is Hollywood for smart people, but that didn't make the culture there a compassionate one. The city was racially segregated, and defined by the vast income inequality of its residents. People were mean. When I first moved to Arizona, everyone was so nice. Laid back. Welcoming. A lot of the people I met were from somewhere else, open to making new friends. Washington was the opposite. The first time Brody met a member of my organization's board, she said, "Nice to meet you. How many degrees do *you* have?" Brody's answer, at the time, was zero. When people in DC ask you what you did, what they were really asking was who you knew and whether or not you were more successful than they were. It was exhausting and toxic. One colleague of mine joked that I would likely bring in my collection of crystals to the office, perhaps imagining me to be some kind of blissed-out hippie who wrote poems in an RV I parked near a spiritual vortex.

Arizona's bad reputation traces all the way back to 1881, when Wyatt Earp, his brother Virgil, and friend Doc Holliday engaged in what became the most famous gunfight of the Old West—the shootout at the O.K. Corral in the aptly-named city of Tombstone. Only three people, all "outlaws," died in that event, and two of the "heroes," Virgil Earp and Holliday, took wounds but survived. Only the hallowed Wyatt Earp emerged unscathed from the thirty-second hail of bullets. He and his friends went on to thrive in Tucson; the other three joined the rest of the dead in Boot Hill Cemetery on the outskirts of Tombstone.

## THESE VIOLENT DELIGHTS

*Westworld* begins, aptly, with a sales pitch. Guests of the Delos vacation packages, just returning from their time away, converse with a host whose vibe settles squarely between reporter and game show personality. Delos offers the vacation of the future—an immersive virtual reality in which guests visit the exact replicas of the Roman Empire, medieval England, and the American frontier. Unlike those eras, though, Delos guests mix and mingle with robots programmed to serve their every whim, whether it's a quick assignation in the madam's house or a spontaneous gunfight at the bar.

Most of the guests we see are men. Committing acts of sex and violence without repercussion are almost exclusively cis-male fantasies. In fact, the three guests we follow into Western World, Delos's pioneer-themed resort, are men. They don period outfits to blend in, leaving their street clothes, accessories, and shoes in a locker. They look the part. They're ready to act the part, complete with the pistols that fire exclamations into the bodies of robots who run afoul of them. John Blaine (James Brolin), a previous Western World guest, has invited his friend Peter Martin (Richard Benjamin) to join him for a week of shoot outs and hook ups at the resort. Peter's marriage ended six months earlier, and we get a sense early on that divorcing his wife and living away from his kids wasn't Peter's choice. This trip is an opportunity for Peter to forget about his heartbreak and lose himself in the swirling tempest of his malnourished id.

Their first stop is the bar. When the Gunslinger (Yul Brynner), a figure dressed in all black, bumps Peter and spills his drink, John tells Peter to shoot him. Peter does, puncturing the Gunslinger with three perfunctory shots that leave him covered in the too-vibrant red of robot "blood." To celebrate a job well done, John and Peter take two sex workers from the madam's place for a quick encounter in the brothel. The robots' only "desire" is to satisfy their human partners. The men eat it up. No responsibility. No repercussions. No soul.

# HISTORY IS WRITTEN BY THE VICTORS

Fremont Street, where much of the O.K. Corral shootout transpired, became Highway 80. Because of this, it became impossible for the town to accurately reenact the gunfight there. Tombstone's side streets all appeared untouched, recapturing that pioneer spirit of taverns, bordellos, and more taverns. All the historical action took place on Allen Street one block south of Fremont. Guests arriving to Tombstone parked their cars in any of the public lots—at the high school or church—or gambled on finding parallel parking on a side street. Allen Street allowed only pedestrians and carriages, just as in the old days.

I left my trusty Scion on the shoulder of an unpaved side street, lucky to find such a clutch spot in the downtown. My car would need a good wash due to the gusty wind that showered grit and dirt like earthy confetti. We zipped our jackets and headed toward the commotion.

Allen Street's three-block historic stretch had the unreal feel of a Hollywood film set and all the crass puffery of a snake oil salesman. Plank sidewalks lined either side of the dirt street. Small shops ranging from "genuine O.K. Corral tours" to period clothing stores to bars and restaurants offered visitors respite from the bright sunshine and sometimes forceful winds. Scattered among families in their t-shirts, shorts, and fanny packs were men in spurs and chaps, refined couples wearing finely tailored formal suits and dresses. Actors. Props.

"This is like the Renaissance Faire," Maureen said just above whisper, trying to avoid eye contact with all the people around us dressed in period costumes. And like a Renaissance Faire, it was hard to determine who was on payroll and who was enthusiastic about Tombstone's checkered past. Tombstone strived to be a fully immersive, interactive experience—at least above ground.

Maureen and I opted to take a tour of the Good Enough Silver Mine. Our guide Mike wore jeans, a flannel jacket torn open at the seam, and worn-in construction boots. A thin ponytail emerged from the back of his hard hat. When he smiled, his two front teeth were conspicuously absent. Despite his rough-and-tumble demeanor, Mike had a kindness about him and a clear enthusiasm about mining that bordered on glee when he spoke.

The tour began with a quick demonstration of how Tombstone's miners would have done their work. Mike picked up what looked like a jackhammer drill bit, a four-pound hammer with a yellow handle, and then placed a leaking Powerade bottle filled with water near an indentation in a giant stone. "Aside from the plastic bottle, this is how the Good Enough miners would have worked," he said, placing the bit in the shallow hole. He swung the hammer, striking the bit with a musical clink. "You swing and turn," he said, rotating the bit in his hand between swings. After ten swings, he didn't appear any deeper into the hole. "Once they reached a depth of six feet, they'd load in their dynamite and stand back."

Mike pointed out a few legitimate relics scattered about the yard near the entrance. One rusted mine car slumped against a dented iron bucket to our right, while farther off, another stood frozen inside a mine car elevator. "The only piece of machinery available to the miners was that," Mike said, gesturing to a hunk of metal gears, pipes, and winches. "And that was because not a man alive could drag up a mine car filled with two tons of broken rock."

The vista from above the mine was bordered by scalloped hills in the distance, crisscrossed with roads and trails. A sizable industrial building overlooked Tombstone from a perch on the highest of the hills. Desert scrub and cactus littered the ground. The only other modern presence was a chain link fence that would deter the casual hiker from walking too far into what we learned was a paper-thin layer of land above a latticework of tunnels, dead ends, and drops.

The widened mouth of the mine assisted with exploration and made the tour safer. Here, too, a chain link fence, attached to the sheer-rock face bordering the mine's opening, was a rare modern element. "When Ed Shieffelin told some folks he was planning to mine in these hills, they told him he was crazy, that the only thing he'd find out here was his tombstone," Mike said as we and the other tourists gathered around him. "And with those words, this town was born, courtesy of the second-largest silver strike in American history."

Mike described how the opening we stood in was at one time filled with solid silver ore, all of it removed by the miners in the course of their work and shipped offsite for processing. "Miners worked ten-hour shifts, with an hour set aside for the transition between each shift," Mike told us. The tour group gathered around a pile of black rocks, on which a large half-dollar coin sat, glinting under Mike's flashlight. "That meant the mine was going 24 hours a day, so Tombstone was going 24 hours a day," he went on. "It was the Las Vegas of its time. Anything you wanted, you could get in Tombstone, and you could get it any time of day, because of this." He gestured to the rocks and the coin. "Silver ore. Not much to look at, but once it was mixed with mercury and lead, melted down and smelted into an amalgam, and then separated from the mercury into pure silver set in 180-pound bars, well, that was this town's blood."

Those of us on the tour stared down at the chunks of black rocks stacked neatly under the coin. I imagined the Tombstone nobody really thought about anymore—the one where businesses never closed, where everyone within the city limits tried to think up ways to separate the miners—then some of the highest paid labor in the West—from their money. Was the lawlessness overshadowing Tombstone's mining legacy the natural end result of this greed?

## REVERSAL OF FORTUNE

Delos vacations cost guests $1,000 per day in 1972 dollars, or the equivalent of $7,129 in 2023. John and Peter's weeklong trip set them each back $50,000 in today's money. The way they don't sweat the details of their trip assures us this hefty amount is just expendable income to them, while the same amount represents two and a half times the U.S.'s current median annual income. Delos is the playground of the One Percent, the top echelon of wealth most people could never even dream of entering. It's wild to consider that those who are least likely to be arrested and prosecuted for criminal offenses would seek out an opportunity to engage in lawless and obscene acts, but what Western World offers John and Peter is the rare opportunity to commit offenses in the open. No humans are harmed. Just robotic human facsimiles.

The Gunslinger's body goes back to the lab after his untimely death at the bar. Technicians there repair his wounds and upgrade his optical sensors. The team of scientists have been monitoring a troubling spike in robot malfunctions across the Delos property—minor things at first, but more and more robots show symptoms. For the Gunslinger, after his repair, something is different. The Gunslinger tracks down Peter and John at their boarding house, confronting John in the room. His gun is drawn and he's ready to fire. Peter approaches the room door after his bath, towel wrapped around his waist. A housekeeper in the hall, shocked by his state of undress, asks, "Have you no decency?" Without answering her (or, perhaps as an answer to her) Peter bursts through the door and shoots The Gunslinger again, until at last the bloody robot falls through the window onto the street below. Peter mugs at John. "Was he bothering you?" Unlike the previous night, though, there are repercussions for Peter. He's arrested and held in jail by the (robot) sheriff, but John, with the help of a (robot) young woman, delivers dynamite to Peter, allowing him to blow through the jail wall and escape. The two men ride out of town into the desert to avoid capture.

*Westworld*, written and directed by Michael Crichton, feels like a dress rehearsal for a more familiar story, one in which guests at a theme park discover the attractions are much more dangerous than they imagined. That future novel, *Jurassic Park*, became Crichton's most enduring book and one of the top-grossing films of all time. Biogenetically engineered dinosaurs replace *Westworld*'s robots, but the theme remains the same: humanity's intelligence is an uncontrollable weapon when it lacks humility. In both cases, hubris convinces men to try taming something inherently dangerous by corralling it, either behind very real walls, or within a limited set of code.

The Gunslinger's malfunction—or perhaps evolution to superior function—is an unstoppable escalation of the danger guests face. When an animatronic snake defies its programming and bites John in the next scene, it alarms the technicians behind the scientific curtain of the Delos operations center. They're losing control. The hunters will become the hunted.

## HOW THE WEST WAS GUNS

One hundred thirty years after the gunfight in the O.K. Corral, in Arizona's second-largest city, a white man with a gun opened fire on an elected official and eighteen bystanders over the course of a few unbelievable minutes in a Safeway parking lot. Members of the crowd subdued him without causing him harm. The group had gathered to speak with Representative Giffords, ostensibly one of the least controversial members of the Democratic caucus. Several men in the crowd that day carried guns strapped, legally, to their hips, but not one of them drew his weapon in response to the attack. Instead, a woman snatched up the gunman's replacement clip while several others tackled him and brought him to the ground. Even in the most dire of circumstances, with lives on the line, their guns had nothing to say.

Even from my vantage point two thousand miles away, the response to this event was palpable. Media outlets expressed outrage and sadness over the loss of life, but it was tempered with an implication that Arizona's conservative ridiculousness crafted this tragedy. Access to firearms created it, gun control proponents claimed. Others expressed concern that the level of "hate" in Arizona's body politic—the hurtful anti-immigrant rhetoric and legislation, for example—finally boiled over. The quickness to embrace either theory was disconcerting for almost all Arizonans. Culture in the West still holds at its heart a celebration of the maverick, the free-thinking iconoclast. Most folks didn't care what other people did as long as it didn't affect them personally. It was very live-and-let-live. And that's why an armed assault on a member of the government shocked as deeply as it did.

I walked the plank sidewalks of Tombstone on January 8, 2012, my conversation with Maureen punctuated by the popping of fake guns on the street beside us. I felt sick. Men and women in full 19th century costumes passed us, complete with droopy biker mustaches and corsets. They conversed quietly to themselves, walked into stores with a phantasmic calm. Followed the same paths again and again. When Maureen and I crossed the street, a man leaning against a horse pitch told us, "Next gunfight starts in fifteen minutes." More sales pitch than warning.

We walked into the Tombstone Art Gallery, a quaint house with large picture windows. Paintings and photographs inside were hung up on pegboard, each one labeled with the title, price, and author's name, and every few paces a laser-printed paper advised guests that cell phone photography of the work was forbidden without consent of the creator. The gallery was silent and cold. Maureen and I could consider not only the work we saw, but the context in which we viewed it. The pounding of feet on the street outside. The quick snaps of fake gunfire. Shouts. Leaving the gallery, we came upon Wyatt Earp and his gang pacing in the street, talking to the crowd. "Those boys have committed a crime and run off," the Wyatt Earp actor shouted, turning to look at each member of the crowd as he spoke. In his right hand, he held a long shotgun by the barrel, like a baton. "What would you have us do?"

Across the street, a thirtysomething dad in a white sweatshirt, with a three-year-old at his leg, held an iPhone up in front of his face. "Shoot them!" he yelled.

## THESE VIOLENT ENDS

While John and Peter hide in the desert, the Delos resorts erupt in chaos. Robots of all kinds turn on their human masters. In Medieval World, a horny middle-aged man (Norman Bartold), prepared to bed the queen after murdering the Black Knight (Michael Mikler), finds himself on the business end of the knight's sword after a demanding battle in a banquet hall. Bodies litter the gardens of Roman World. Western World's main street, too, becomes an open-air morgue. Unaware of what's transpired, John and Peter wander back into town, tired and dirty. When the Gunslinger confronts them in the street, John volunteers for the duel. The Gunslinger makes quick work of him. The first bullet shocks John. He bleeds. This isn't supposed to happen—only humans have the power to kill. The second shot flips him to the ground. Peter, knowing he's next, runs between buildings back to his horse to ride off into the desert.

The Gunslinger moves with the unhurried confidence of the best slasher villains. His emotionless face and reflective eyes give nothing away. He seems free of desire, yet his relentless pursuit of the man who shot him reeks of that most human impulse: revenge. Violence begets violence. Peter and John believed Western World placed them above civilization's commitment to justice, that their actions would not have consequences. It cost John his life. Peter, more reluctant to indulge his most base desires, even in Western World, may survive.

The Gunslinger follows Peter, getting close enough in range to shoot his hat off. The pursuit is long by contemporary film standards, cross-cutting between Peter's frantic momentum and the Gunslinger's patient trot. Trekking through the desolate desert, Peter interrupts a Delos tech desperately changing the tire on a golf cart. "Everything's broken down. The machines have gone crazy," the tech says. The tech explains there's no way to escape the Gunslinger, that whoever that robot model pursues, he gets. The only way to slow him down would be to assault his optical sensors with acid. Peter, believing he can still outsmart the machine, gallops off with the unearned confidence of a rich white man. Before Peter's out of range, the tech takes two bullets in the chest from the Gunslinger's rifle, dying in the driver's seat of his just-repaired escape vehicle. Peter races past a sign announcing he's leaving Western World.

Peter ends up in Roman World—or what is left of it—before dropping down into an access tunnel that leads him into the bowels of the Delos operation. Everyone is dead.

## ONE SIZE FITS ALL

Over one shop on Allen Street, a sign read, "O.K. Corral fight moved through here," with an arrow directing tourists inside. At the tourist dad's suggestion, Holliday and the Earp brothers disappeared through the door and, I suppose, tracked down the criminals they were about to send to their final resting place. We didn't follow. As we hadn't paid to "watch" the gunfight, we couldn't. But we knew how it ended even if we didn't see it firsthand.

We explored a few of the shops on that recreated street. Maureen and I passed a store with the words "Guns and Ammo" painted in Old West letters on the glass. An old man, looking tired and lonely, sat behind a counter surrounded by handguns, rifles, and shotguns. Boxes of ammunition lined a wall behind him next to a large display of cigarettes.

We didn't pass two adjacent storefronts in Tombstone without encountering a gift shop. Along with the requisite Tombstone paraphernalia—guns, gun-shaped magnets, gun-shaped cigarette lighters whose flames shot out the barrel, and books about guns and Tombstone history—we found green pepper jelly and prickly pear syrup, raccoon hats, States of the U.S. refrigerator magnets, and high-end art alongside sitting frog statues and local wines. One store featured a particularly disturbing selection of racist advertisements from the early 1900s, all featuring Black children with round white eyes and white smiles, often doing something illegal or inappropriate, for the "entertainment" of the viewer.

I studied the various displays of toys and souvenirs. Many shops prominently featured a "cowgirl" pistol set complete with a pearled handle and a pink holster with a star on it. Even girls, it seemed, were not immune to the siren call of Tombstone's violent past. And even cowgirls love pink.

## UNNATURAL SELECTION

Peter moves through the Delos underground facility, passing by a sealed room where the team of scientists monitoring the parks and robots have all suffocated to death. He ends up in the robot repair room, where we previously saw the Gunslinger get his tech upgraded. Now the gurneys are mostly empty, an immobile robot lying here and there. Peter sees exactly what he needs—a bottle of hydrochloric acid, but the Gunslinger is right behind him, terse snaps of his boots echoing down the hall. When the Gunslinger turns the corner, he can't find Peter until it's too late: Peter, lying on a gurney to disguise himself as a robot, throws the acid in the Gunslinger's face. The robot staggers back, his face melting, until he's swathed in smoke. Peter uses the distraction to dash down another hallway, this one leading to the third Delos resort area.

Arriving in Medieval World, he again confronts the Gunslinger in the same banquet hall where the Black Knight made quick work of his human enemy. Peter discovers the Gunslinger's vision is heat-sensitive, a trope that predicts the T. rex's movement-based vision in *Jurassic Park*. By standing below a torch, he vanishes. Peter capitalizes on the Gunslinger's confused state by clubbing him with the torch, setting him on fire. The Gunslinger writhes in the flames, but he feels no pain. Eventually he succumbs to the burning, falling to the floor.

Peter's chance at redemption comes in the form of a woman, as it so often does for white men in trouble of their own making. Peter hears the soft calling of a voice from the dungeon. He finds there a woman (Julie Marcus) chained in a cage, forgotten by her tormentor, mewling for help. Peter unchains her, seats her, and gets water to help restore her from the daze into which she's sunk. It's a moment of valor from a man whose behavior until now has hinged entirely on his willingness to descend into violence and sexual gratification. This woman, unlike the robots of Western World, can feel. She feels fear. She feels pain. This triggers in him the instinct to rescue and protect.

Peter ladles the water into her mouth. Sparks fly and smoke billows from her neck. She, too, is a robot. Nothing in Western World is real. Nothing except Peter and the very real acts of violence he commits.

Like a paranormal killer, the Gunslinger appears one more time, soot-black from head to toe. His desire for revenge overwhelms his instinct for survival. He attacks Peter, but Peter throws him off the steps to the ground, where at last he "dies." Goes offline. Ends function. Falls apart.

Peter has survived the horror of the Delos massacre. One he may have triggered with his own actions. His own desire to exert power over the powerless.

## BLOOD AND STEEL

The carousel of violence that accounted for almost all of Tombstone's economy overtook me as Maureen and I made our way back to the Scion on the little dirt side street at sundown. Here, actors and shopkeepers separated tourists from their money while propping up the romantic notions Americans hold of good versus evil, of might being right, and the bad guys always wearing black.

We didn't say much on the drive back. The sun dipped behind those mountains, leaving behind a glorious Arizona sunset in its wake, until the black of night wiped the color from the sky and left us chasing the glow of the car's headlights to Tucson.

The identities of Tombstone's heroes and villains were etched into headstones. Recounted in stories as archetypal as myths. Explored in books. Celebrated in big budget Hollywood films. America loves to see good triumph over evil and is only too eager to assign those qualified labels—"good" and "evil"—without much consideration of their values. In my childhood, games of "cowboys and Indians" were common, the good/evil binary so entrenched in our history and our culture that numerous generations of white people never thought twice about how good or how evil either one was. At the center—what exists now, our culture now, our perception now—is the firearm, the idea of justice, and the sense that lawlessness, however archaic a reality, can never really be washed away.

# FISH OUT OF WATER

**EXT. BRENTWOOD–DAY. / INT. BRENTWOOD MANSION–DAY.**

I followed Elton's instructions to a home in Brentwood, the Westside community still best known as the location of the savage murders of Nicole Brown Simpson and Ron Goldman. The wide streets with sweeping curves drew me up into wooded hills, a world away from the sleepy freeway-adjacent neighborhood of Highland Park where I rented a century-old one-bedroom house. In my little gray Scion, sputtering up the hills, I felt like a trespasser. A poor trespasser. Elton told me to dress with the holiday spirit in mind. Not one for ugly sweater parties or general Christmas cheer, the closest thing I could find was a fitted red sweater that looked vaguely *après-ski* and a pair of dark jeans. I didn't know what I'd be doing, just that I'd be part of a young gay pop singer's music video for a Christmas-themed single. I had no designs on fame or a career in the music industry. When Elton floated the idea a couple weeks earlier, I thought it sounded fun.

The house Elton directed me to was actually a mansion. The driveway ran parallel to the façade, the front door embraced by a tall, ornate wrought iron gate peeking through a line of hedges. When no one answered my knock on the door, I slipped inside, worried I'd set off an alarm or— worse—alert a pack of hungry Dobermans.

The house, a cavernous space, gaped at me like a toothless mouth. Not one stick of furniture remained. The light marble floors gleamed with morning light streaming through a wall of windows overlooking Brentwood, Santa Monica, and the ocean beyond. The distinctly 60s architecture was chic, but you could tell by looking at it how close it came to the brass accents and crocheted wall-hangings of the 70s. It was the kind of mansion the women might visit in an episode of *Charlie's*

*Angels*, where a scheming millionaire roosted with his henchmen before carrying out some vicious plot.

The entryway split into a hallway that stretched both left and right, angling out of view. I wandered left toward the murmur of voices I thought emanated from that direction. That's where I found them, standing in a lounge area complete with a built-in bar smeared with glittering tinsel, wrapping paper rolls, and bows. "Charlie!" Elton walked over to greet me with a hug. "Come meet everyone."

Elton introduced me to the star of the video, Young Gay Pop Singer. He had the effortless cool of someone whose well of confidence ran all the way to his core. Dark hair fluffed from his forehead just above his eyes, and a few days' growth of beard matured him out of twinkhood. His speaking voice had a beauty and resonance to it I was sure only grew more powerful when he sang. He had that *thing*. That sparkling energy that made you want to be around him. The thing that separates civilians from celebrities. Our director Sergei was the opposite of Young Gay Pop Singer in so many ways. Sergei stood tall and lean, dressed in all black, radiating a bird-like nervousness. He spoke in a clipped accent I assumed was Russian. I knew from conversation with Elton and he and Sergei had been seeing one another for a couple months, trying to make something happen despite the demands of their work. They were in a situationship, and it was complicated. There were six other co-stars for the shoot, everyone with a unique body type, background, and look.

Several folks were already done up in holiday drag: an elf, a union suit with a fur-lined hat. Elton looked me up and down. "Let's get you into costume," he said. "Nick," he called to a twenty-something white twink sorting Christmas tree decorations. "Come with us."

Elton approached some plastic shopping bags set on the floor in the hallway, filled with clothing items, accents, and accessories. Next to the bags was a set of angel wings, the kind worn over the shoulders with elastic straps. Elton squatted down to rummage through them. "Okay, for Nick," he said, stretching out the name as he rifled around,

"I have this." He pulled out a pair of gold lamé shorts right out of *The Rocky Horror Picture Show.*

Nick held them up on front of him, dumbstruck. They were a whisper of fabric. While he was lean and on the short side, they were still going to barely cover his heritage. "I can't wear this," he said.

Elton gave him a stern parental scolding. "You'll be fine. In ten years you'll wish you'd worn stuff like this all the time." He gave Nick a halo and the angel wings and told him to go change in one of the empty bathrooms. "If it looks terrible, I'll give you something else," he assured Nick. "But you at least have to try."

Nick sighed and wandered off. "And for you, sir." Elton peeked into bag after bag. "Here we go." He handed me a neatly folded stack of items less than one inch high.

"Elton," I said.

"What?"

"I will die if I wear this."

Elton gave me the look, a look I was more than familiar with from him and from others. It was the look of exasperation I got whenever my insecurities about my body bubbled to the surface. "I know CPR," he said.

"What's wrong with my sweater?" So what if it was my only holiday-adjacent look? And I looked cute—maybe a little Carlton from *The Fresh Prince of Bel-Air,* but cute. And fully clothed. Fully covered.

"Just have fun with it, Charlie." I couldn't argue with him, in part because Elton was almost my physical opposite in every way: short where I was tall, round where I was lean. His mixed Bangladeshi and Caribbean heritage gave him a head of dark textured curls and a medium complexion with freckles across his cheeks. Meanwhile, I offered a white, cornfed Midwesterner look. Virtually hairless skin aside from the friendly mutton chops reaching down my cheeks to connect at my mustache. Short brown hair. Legs for days. To complain to him about my insecurities would, in a way, emphasize his own. No one likes a normal-sized person who complains about being fat, even if that's how I felt, focused entirely on the subtle roll of Chipotle, Skittles, and pizza that circled my torso just under my belly button. I knew I wasn't "fat," but I definitely did not feel like I was the kind of person who should parade around half-dressed with any kind of confidence. I loved being clothed. Being covered gave me confidence.

I took the paper-thin stack of fabric into an empty bathroom and removed my many layers to replace them with this partial one: a pair of red Christmas socks. Silver sequined suspenders. A pair of boxer briefs with an all-over candy cane print. A Santa hat.

## LOOK AT HER

*The Neon Demon* is less a feature film than a set of loosely connected music videos and visual tableaux. The first shot of the film presents Jesse (Elle Fanning) supine on a satin sofa, umoving. Ominous industrial house music throbs on the score. She wears a shiny minidress, her braided hair wrapped in a crown on her head, large sequins adorning her face. She's so still, in fact, she might not even be real. A man's face appears in the shadows, evaluating his work. Blood covers Jesse's neck. It runs down her arm into a puddle on the floor. It's a violent image. The camera pulls back as flashbulbs snap around her, revealing the staging of a set in an otherwise vacant space. It's meant to evoke both an edgy fashion shoot and a crime scene. The motif of violence against women will be a constant and unnerving thread in this story, though most of it will be inflicted upon Jesse by other women, rather than the men whose patriarchal power they uphold.

The movie offers Jesse to us as the quintessential naïf. In fact, she's still just a girl—sixteen, not even old enough for the work she's trying to book. She conjures up the tale of Little Red Riding Hood, blithely entering a wood she knows nothing about. The wolves sniff her out quickly: Ruby (Jena Malone), a makeup artist who befriends her after that first shoot, and Ruby's model friends Gigi (Bella Heathcote) and Sarah (Abbey Lee). There's something off about these initial exchanges. The film feels written by someone who never lived in Los Angeles, but perhaps saw it from the air or read about it in a Joan Didion novel. It looks gorgeous in *The Neon Demon*, glimpsed in sweeping panoramas behind windowed walls, past terraces, beyond cliffs. The director, Nicholas Refn Winding, has an eye for shot composition. Only the sumptuous interior shots rival these panoramic vistas.

Ruby's too outgoing, too welcoming, too eager to befriend Jesse. When Ruby invites Jesse to a party in their first conversation, it rings false. Jesse's eagerness to attend also rings false. Jesse stands awkwardly by Ruby, Gigi, and Sarah, spying a creepy man we'll later learn is Jack (Desmond Harrington), a photographer. In the restroom, Gigi reapplies lipstick, a color Ruby tells her is called "Red Rum," launching a conversation about how women are more likely to buy a lipstick if it's named after food or sex—plum passion, black honey, peachy keen. No one mentions the fact that "Red Rum" is murder spelled backward and an unsubtle reference to *The Shining*. Ruby asks Jesse what her lip color would be called. "Are you food or are you sex?" she asks Jesse, laying out the entire conceit of the film. Jesse doesn't answer.

In the world of *The Neon Demon*, these are the two functions women can occupy. Sex and the fashion industry are natural connections. But how Jesse becomes food is the film's laughably bad attempt to turn the metaphor into something literal.

This scene is shot with an ongoing focus on the bathroom mirrors, showing us Ruby, Sarah, and Gigi in reflection when they don't occupy the foreground of the shot. This suggests those characters have hidden motives. Dual natures. But they're also obsessed with reflections—not just how they see what they look like, but how others perceive them. Gigi asks Jesse if things about her body are real—her hair, her nose— and then details some of her recent cosmetic surgeries at the hand of

Dr. Andrew, whom Gigi says has nicknamed her "the bionic woman." Jesse wonders aloud if that's a compliment. Gigi's charm vanishes as easily as taking off a mask. "I hear your parents are dead," she jabs at Jesse. "That must be really hard."

As Gigi and Sarah's fakery drops away, they reveal themselves to be mean girls threatened by Jesse's beauty and her lack of social skills. This, too, is not reflective of Los Angeles. People in the city don't take the time to be mean. They just end conversations and leave. No one wastes energy, and certainly not on a barely-verbal, untested model. The filmmaker wants us to believe Jesse's beauty is so intimidating that it maddens the people around her, driving them to desire her, or desire to destroy her. Meanwhile, Jesse herself remains an empty vessel, a character without motivation or point of view, a cipher. A mannequin.

## INT. BRENTWOOD MANSION–DAY.

I looked at myself in the mirror. The costume exposed virtually everything I felt insecure about. I was 35 years old and could count each of the years on my body as easily as the rings of a felled tree. I should have been more muscular, more defined. Living in Los Angeles can do this to you, and fast. Not everyone is beautiful. But almost everyone goes to the gym. A lot.

*You'd wear less at the beach*, I reminded myself. Another voice piped up in response, more rational but perhaps less forgiving: *But also at the beach, you're not the one people are looking at—and certainly not being filmed*. This voice had spoken to me since adolescence, when my gangly body, in too much of a rush to reach full-size, lengthened and thinned with a monstrous intensity that left me clumsy, awkwardly proportioned, and full of disgust. I weighed two hundred pounds now, having exercised and protein-shaked my way into a filled-out physique that, while not magazine-cover worthy, was light years from where

I started. Despite the wisdom of both voices, I knew I wasn't seeing myself the way I actually was, but the way I feared I was.

I stopped by the bag of costume supplies before I joined the others. I wanted to see what else there was, what other options. There wasn't much to choose from. I found a Santa suit belt in the third bag, a wide piece of black vinyl with a plastic buckle. I cinched it around my waist, giving myself at least one less thing to obsess about while I was in front of the camera. As an added bonus, it hid the suspender clips where they attached to the underwear, and made the outfit look more seamless.

I wandered over to Elton. "Do I look okay?"

I towered over him. We'd met at a gay beach day over the summer. My gay hiking group shared a member with a separate circle of friends Elton was part of. I'd shown up with the guy I'd been sleeping with for a few weeks. During a quiet moment when that guy was off talking to others, Elton asked me how long I'd been dating him. "Oh, we're not together," I said. "I have a boyfriend back in Arizona." Elton looked at me and I could tell he saw exactly what I felt. I loved my boyfriend Brody, and our relationship was settled, comfortable, and important to me. We were best friends and always had fun together. But boyfriend or not, I was catching feelings for the guy I brought to the beach, though I couldn't acknowledge it that day. In hindsight, our affection for one another wasn't even subtle— the care we took checking in with one another. The closeness of our bodies on the sand. Those feelings were electric, and they lit me up like a marquee on opening night. I would come to know Elton's sharp insight was his superpower, gleaned through years of cutting through entertainment industry bullshit.

Elton began his music career in Orlando, part of a boy band that didn't go far. But it got him to Los Angeles and started him on the path to writing and producing music for others. He was an effortless DJ for club nights around town, including the 90s hip hop/R&B dance night at an east side gay bar that became my obsession for the year it ran. But that day on the beach, he was just someone new I met in Los Angeles, someone with a dream, someone with a hustle, someone just trying to clear the next career hurdle while juggling the complex matrix of queer communities in which he hoped to find someone to love.

Elton gave me a once over. "You look great." He turned his attention back to props and set up for the first scene: ornaments, tinsel, a fake tree, empty boxes wrapped with paper and tied up with bows. The video would follow Young Gay Pop Singer on a normal day of sunbathing by the pool—at a mansion, like we all do—when wild Christmas revelers show up to imbue him with the holiday spirit. The lyrics of the song referenced how the love of a man was a gift he'd been waiting for.

I picked up a box of ornaments and started unpacking them, adding hooks and placing them in crates for easier decoration between shots. "How did you guys get this house?" I asked Elton.

Elton nodded at Young Gay Pop Singer. "It's his family's. They just bought it, but they're going to demolish it and rebuild on the lot. Meanwhile, we can do whatever we want to it."

I was kind of stunned. I knew rich people existed but I never knew any—not this kind of rich, not mansion-rich, not house-overlooking-the-ocean rich. Part of me assumed Young Gay Pop Singer was on the hustle like everybody else in LA—he showed up with a dream, and he'd made progress. I wasn't getting paid for my time. Only Elton and Sergei were. Now I knew Young Gay Pop Singer had grown up in the rarified air and tony neighborhoods of this city, living in a house as large as my city block. Surely he had financial support from his family that made it possible to take huge career risks like producing an independent holiday song and accompanying video. At the end of the day, I'd drive an hour back to my rickety old claptrap at the end of a dead-end street. I wondered where he'd be sleeping. I wondered what he'd dream about.

## THE METAPHOR IS COMING FROM INSIDE THE HOUSE

The most effective moments in *The Neon Demon* have no talking. This is both because the dialogue is almost universally bad and poorly delivered, but also because Winding's strongest skill as a filmmaker is in blending the aural and visual experience. The lush soundscapes of the film alternate between tense, pulsing beats and synths, and expansive strings and chimes. The party Jesse attends with Ruby and the other women transitions into a "performance." In a pitch-black room, a woman, bound by straps, floats and turns in the air, dark music thumping around them. The woman is lit only by a strobing light. The same effect lights the faces of Ruby and Jess, Gigi and Sarah as they look on. They are the only people in the room.

Just a few scenes later, Jesse goes on a date with Dean (Karl Glusman), the photographer from the first shoot. They drive up to Mulholland Drive, where tourists go to get that stunning vista of the city's lights spread out around the glittering towers of downtown. Now the music is soft and ethereal, like Jesse's flowy dress tousled in the wind. The heaven/hell dichotomy feels tangible, emphasized, and, like many things in the film, literal.

When Jesse returns to her Pasadena motel room that night, she's startled by a figure in the darkness. She begs the manager Hank (Keanu Reeves) to check it out. When they burst through the door, they find the prowler on the bed: a mountain lion, one of Los Angeles's most elusive creatures. They typically eschew the human world, preferring the wild territory of Griffith Park and the foothills that run the length of the valleys to the north. Yet, here it is, not only skulking around the rundown streets of East Pasadena, but right in our heroine's rundown motel room. The film doesn't explain why. The film knows the mountain lion is a metaphor made flesh.

## EXT. BRENTWOOD MANSION POOL–DAY.

Sergei directed the guy in the union suit to walk out of the house with the bare tree while Young Gay Pop Singer relaxed on a zero-gravity chaise beside the pool. Bright morning sun lit the valley in the back of the shot, obscuring the blue of the ocean with blinding white light. One by one, the rest of the cast brought out wrapped gifts, ornaments, garlands, and decorated the tree. Young Gay Pop Singer bolted up in the chair and feigned trying to get us to stop. Instead, Sergei filmed us dancing around the tree. "More excitement! It's Christmas!" It was August. It was hot. It was the least Christmasy environment I could think of. From my place in the circle of dancers, I tried to forget I was wearing less fabric than the tree and plastered a smile across my face.

Sergei circled us, getting different angles, asking Young Gay Pop Singer to react differently each time. Then the singer relented and joined us in the dancing. I shimmied past the camera, grinning and waving. Then turned and shook my butt right up next to the lens. Too late, I realized the most embarrassing thing I did all day would end up in the final cut of the video. My quivering ass cheeks would be immortalized on the Internet.

We danced for over an hour. I was tired, starting to break a sweat, and running out of ideas on how to move my body. Even faking a smile was getting difficult. The filming process sucked all the joy and fun out of Christmas.

## [TITLE CARD: FLASHBACK: 2012]

Early in 2012, a friend of mine in LA sent a mass email to let a bunch of folks in her network know she'd be transitioning to her dream job, leaving open her prior position at an arts advocacy organization in Los Angeles.

Brody and I had been in Tucson for about seven months. In 2010, I had walked away from a difficult job on the East Coast and spent the time since subsisting on adjunct teaching and nonprofit consulting. Brody enrolled at the University of Arizona to complete his degree. Our apartment was far outside the city at the edge of a canyon, surrounded by snow birds whose units were mostly vacant during the hot summer months. At the peak of my underemployment, I taught nine sections in one semester at various institutions while squeezing in ten hours a week of communications work at an arts nonprofit. I couldn't find a full-time job anywhere in Tucson. The arts community was still in the throes of recovery from the housing market crash and the ensuing loss of donors and earned income. But I read my friend's email and felt my heart rate rise. "Hey," I shouted to the other room, "do you mind if I apply for a job in LA?"

"Go for it," Brody shouted back. So I did. I got the job. I spent the next weeks packing up whatever could fit in my tiny car and finishing out my teaching contracts. On the last day of classes, I woke up before sunrise, drove to campus for my 7:10 am class, collected final papers, drove home just after lunch, packed my car, and headed to LA around four o'clock. The scenery on the seven-hour drive resembled the rotating background of a Road Runner cartoon. I pulled up to the house where I was renting a bedroom at midnight. I was exhausted. I unpacked my things, blew up my air mattress, and fell asleep.

My boss met me bright and early the next morning at the entrance of the high rise where our offices were hosted by a larger, more affluent nonprofit. She walked me around, introduced me to about one hundred people, and started training me on my new job while giving me pointers about LA. "If someone mugs you on the sidewalk, don't get in a car and go with them to a second location," she said. "It's better to die on the street than never be found." Around one-thirty, I just couldn't even keep my eyes open anymore. "You're wiped out," she said, her disappointment palpable. She sent me home.

My first months in Los Angeles were a blur. Moving to the city allowed me to reboot my career. Once I settled in, I found I loved the job. Working in advocacy was exciting and energizing, and I met so many people in the nonprofit arts community. I learned the complex geography of Los Angeles County's eighty-eight cities and eighty-one school districts in just weeks. I reconnected with one of my best friends from high school, Jen, who'd been living in the city for a few years and helped me get oriented. The best part, though, was the full-time employment money along with the reduction in my living expenses. For the first time in years, I had disposable income. I could get a drink. I could grab a pizza. I started making friends and going out, drinking too much, dancing too recklessly, indulging in whatever desire I had when I had it. I couldn't remember the last time I wasn't accountable to another person, responsible for their safety or happiness. I was living my life just for me. I felt free.

## A DOLL IS A FETISH OBJECT WHOSE POWER COMES FROM THOSE WHO HOLD IT

Jesse is untethered. No family, no real friends. This isolation becomes literal when Ruby invites Jesse for test shots with Jack. In the bright light of the all-white studio, he's gaunt, skeletal. He moves her against a blank cyclorama wall—no corners, no horizon line, just an unbroken sheet of blank space. He leaves here there, then dismisses everyone else from the studio for a closed set. He tells her to take off all her clothes and turn around. He cuts all the lights but for one spotlight that now traps Jesse in blackness. He approaches her, smearing her body with thick gold paint. He takes picture after picture, a gilded girl carved in onyx.

We don't know how Jesse got to Los Angeles, or why she chose a Pasadena motel as her home base. Navigating the city would be time consuming from that starting point. But the film doesn't want to get bogged down in details. It may fundamentally misunderstand the nuanced geography of one of the nation's most sprawling urban centers, a county with the square mileage of Connecticut whose population would constitute the US's tenth largest state. *The Neon Demon* cares only about how it looks, nestling it square inside the most common perception of Los Angeles culture and the fashion industry writ large.

Not only does Jesse not have a backstory, she is allegedly so beautiful that the professional models around her want to destroy her before her career even takes off. At lunch, Ruby tells Sarah and Gigi Jack thinks Jesse's going to be a star, that she has that "thing." In the next scene, iconic designer Roberto Sarno (Alessandro Nivola) chooses Jesse over Sarah for a high-stakes runway campaign. She single-handedly wrecks Sarah's fragile ego. Enraged, Sarah shatters a mirror in a bathroom and shreds her portfolio—a completely normal reaction a professional model would have to losing a booking. Jesse hears the crash and enters the bathroom, comforting Sarah as if a novice model has anything meaningful to offer a seasoned colleague. "I thought you did great. Honest," Jesse says. When Jesse cuts her hand on a shard of mirror, Sarah shoves the wound into her own mouth.

This is the first instance of the film's forthcoming body horror pivot. Having established Sarah is not exactly well, seeing her try to digest her colleague isn't exactly the shock it might be if we watched Bella Hadid do it. Adding to the confusion in the film's narrative is how Jesse travels from the go-see back to her Pasadena flophouse with a massive flesh wound on her hand and no dressing to stop the bleeding. Dean arrives to offer her flowers, but she faints from blood loss and he wrenches each shard from her palm with tweezers. *The Neon Demon* wants to be both embodied and ethereal. But only when it's convenient.

Back at the Sarno's runway show, he selects Jesse to wear the finale look, becoming along the way his new muse. He dresses her with the care of a priceless porcelain doll. At the end of the show, she kisses her own reflection in a set of mirrors.

Jesse takes Dean to Musso and Frank to meet Sarno after the show. Gigi's in the booth with him. Sarno says beauty can't be manufactured and compares Jesse to Gigi. "Look at Jesse. Nothing fake, nothing false. A diamond in a sea of glass." He waxes poetic. "True beauty is the highest currency we have." Everyone in the film constantly trips over themselves to talk about how beautiful Jesse is until she herself tells others how easy it is to be so beautiful. It takes mere weeks for this rise in career and self-esteem to climax. Jesse is just sixteen years old.

## INT. BRENTWOOD MANSION ENTRYWAY–DAY.

Sergei set us up in front of the house, standing in a long line of gift givers waiting to come in. We'd each get the chance for a featured shot, posing with a gift, before we entered, while Young Gay Pop Singer stood to the side checking off a list. Elton handed me an enormous stuffed bear. It was almost as big as I was.

Sergei wanted to keep this moving so we didn't fall behind schedule. We each took our turn in the doorway. I held the bear like a I spouse I was about to carry over the threshold, dancing and dipping to the beat of the song. Finally, we stood together behind the narrow glass panel next to the door, waving and inviting Young Gay Pop Singer to join us inside.

Then we set up in front of the fireplace, where Elton had rigged a smoke machine to create a little atmosphere. Young Gay Pop Singer sat by the fire. "Tell him what you want for Christmas," Sergei told us. We were to sit there, one at a time, for a private audience with Young Gay Pop Singer, enjoying mugs of cocoa filled with marshmallows. Stockings hung on the flagstone fireplace behind us—two, of course, one for Young Gay Pop Singer and the other for whomever turned out to be his "gift." A sparkly garland drooped between them. I was nervous about being filmed sitting down, knowing everything I disliked about my midsection was going to bunch up into rolls. While the sexy elf filmed her part, I ran back to the costume area to find a cover-up. I rifled through those bags for anything that might make me feel more comfortable. The closest thing was a scarf. "Charlie, you're up," Sergei called from the other room.

I rushed in and sat down. The scarf looped once around my neck and dangled in front of me, obscuring most of my bare midriff. Sergei paused. "What are you wearing?"

"It's cold."

Sergei put a hand to his forehead. The day was stressing him out. He and Young Gay Pop Singer were the only ones who couldn't leave early. The rest of us would be out of here as soon as our group and individual shoots were finished. He weighed whether or not to argue with me. The fact that I had even stayed mostly naked for this one was probably a lifelong personal record for me. The fact that I was doing it with a camera present was truly a measure of personal growth. Sergei sighed. He looked at Elton, standing just off behind him, and I sensed he wanted to complain about me. But maybe because he knew Elton was my friend—because he didn't feel like opening a can of situationship worms that might haunt him once the shoot was over— he changed his mind. "Fine." He picked up the camera. "Action."

I realized at that moment I had no idea what to say. I knew there'd be no sound recorded, so I just babbled. I emoted and gestured to make it seem like I was enervated by the conversation. "I don't know what to talk about," I said. "There's nothing I really want! Except maybe a raise. Or a limitless bank account someone else would fill for me." I went on and on, whatever floated into my mind.

"Get closer to him." Sergei nodded to Young Gay Pop Singer. He scooched down the hearth until he was right up next to me, his leg touching my leg from hip to knee. He draped his scarf over my shoulder. His arm followed, pulling me close. Then he was pushing a marshmallow into my mouth. I moaned, eating it up—figuratively and literally. I imagined it was the best marshmallow I'd ever tasted.

## HUNGER IS A FORM OF DESIRE

Late after the Sarno show, Jesse returns to her motel. She has a nightmare of being attacked by Hank, then wakes up to discover someone trying to break into her room. When she locks the door, the assailant goes next door, forcing Jesse to listen to the woman next door pleading for her life. Jesse calls Ruby, who tells her to come over right away. "You're gonna be safe," Ruby tells her.

Jesse walks into Ruby's mansion. It's not likely to be Ruby's house, since she's a make-up artist who moonlights as a mortician's assistant. Ruby clarifies that she's housesitting. Ruby tries to seduce Jesse, going so far as to pin her to the bed until Jesse throws her off. This reveals Ruby to be just another rendering of the psychotic lesbian trope, a lineage stretching back all the way to *Rebecca*'s obsessed Mrs. Danvers. The next shot of Ruby shows her drawing x's on a mirror with lipstick, obscuring her own eyes as though disguising from herself what she's about to do.

Ruby goes to work and masturbates on top of the corpse of a woman vaguely resembling Jesse at the mortuary. And despite Ruby's attempted assignation, Jesse remains at the mansion. For some unknowable reason, she spreads glittery makeup around her right eye, then puts on a dress laid out on the bed for her. Hours pass. Night falls, and Jesse walks out to the empty pool in the blue-bluish dark, where she stands on the diving board mostly for visual effect.

Ruby walks to the deep end of the pool, staring up at Jesse, who both towers over her and seems to float, weightless. Jesse monologues— the most words she's said at one time in the entire film by far—about her mother, about her own beauty. "Women would kill to look like this. They carve and stuff and inject themselves. They starve to death, hoping, praying one day they'll look like a second-rate version of me." Her entire characterization swerves 180 degrees away from the mousy small-town girl we first met. Sarah attacks her inside the house, and when Jesse shakes her off, Gigi chases her. They both grab knives from the kitchen, but Jesse doesn't want to fight; she wants to fly away. She ends up back at the empty pool, cornered by Ruby, Gigi, and Sarah. Without much fanfare, Ruby pushes Jesse over the edge of the pool. A pool of blood seeps from beneath her as she suffers, barely alive. The three women look at each other knowingly.

They eat Jesse. There's no delicate way to say this, and it doesn't exactly make sense. But Gigi, Ruby, and Sarah consume her flesh. We don't know why. Maybe something about consuming the flesh of your enemy, or about the vitality of youth to keep the other three women young and beautiful. Explanations like this are distractions from Winding's vision.

In the next shot, we see Ruby in a bathtub, her entire body slathered with blood. Gigi and Ruby shower together nearby. The camera, taking Ruby's point of view, obsesses over each inch of their naked skin, eroticizing the moment as a pulsing beat and shiny synths radiate around her. The film tells us beauty's only purpose is to be consumed, whether it be through the lens of a camera, a sex act, or a meal.

## INT. BRENTWOOD MANSION LOUNGE–DAY.

Between set ups, we drank juice boxes and munched on snacks Elton brought to keep us energized. I tried to consume as little as possible. I wanted to hold on to the magical "morning skinny" as long as I could. The minute I swallowed food, I knew my gut would paunch out. I didn't want to put anything into my body that might end up visible to the viewer.

Sergei started to transition the shoot to the final set up. I took that opportunity to wander the house, just taking it all in. How many more times would I find myself in a mansion? Albeit an empty and kind of creepy one. I followed the main hallway away from the shoot. One doorway led to an office with built-in bookcases and a window overlooking greenery past the end of the driveway. Another to a bonus room that could have been used for a billiards room, a fitness room, a craft room—a place someone could burn hours of leisure time.

At the end of the hallway, two heavy wood doors swung into the master suite. My steps echoed as I walked in. One set of windows took in that glorious view, the one we'd had from the pool area. Los Angeles tumbled down a hill all the way to the ocean, the horizon invisible under a tide of fog. The en suite bathroom alone dwarfed my house. It contained a bathtub large enough for a family, as well as a walk-in shower, dual sinks, and a dressing area. Without furnishings, the whole room felt like a waste. A warehouse. And soon it would just be dust and rubble on this lot. I wondered who built this house—surely someone in the Industry bought the plot of land and envisioned this two-winged home here, each hallway like an arm reaching forward to embrace the swimming pool. I wondered if they were happy here. I wondered if they were sad to leave it. I wondered if they knew, or cared, that the place they once loved was about to meet its natural end at the hands of ambitious new buyers who had their own vision of happiness, one that didn't include this architecture.

I felt poor, though I was far from it. To encounter great wealth like this is to realize how wide and broad that economic gulf really is. I earned less than the median income of the region, but I could afford my rent. I could afford my bills. I could afford a little fun. But I would never be mansion-rich. I would never be rich enough to forget I wasn't this rich.

I walked back to the shoot. We had two more major set ups before we wrapped for the day. We'd be writing items onto a giant Christmas list Young Gay Pop Singer unrolled. We'd dance and hide behind a short wall of presents while Young Gay Pop Singer flirted with us. The list writing was straightforward and went quickly. For my part, I popped a hip at the camera, flirted with my eyes, and scribbled on the paper. It took a single take. For the last part, Young Gay Pop Singer slapped me on the butt. I giggled and dashed away. For the other actors' featured shots, I crouched behind a short wall of wrapped gifts. At some points I was completely hidden from the camera.

## YOU ARE WHAT YOU EAT

Gigi has a photo shoot in Malibu, in another mansion, this one by the sea. Sarah goes with her. Jack, the photographer who snapped Jesse nude, has Sarah join the shoot. The women wear severe pleather minidresses with S&M accoutrements, hair in cornrows, big sunglasses covering half their faces. The whole scene feels off as a viewer—for almost all of the film, we are in Jesse's point of view. Seeing what she sees. Living what she lives. With a few extremely notable exceptions, such as Ruby's sexual violation of a corpse, Jesse is the center of our world. Now, she's dead, and we're tagging along as her killers (and consumers) punch back in for a day of work.

Things are fine until they aren't. Gigi rushes off set clutching her gut. Sarah goes after her, finds her gripping a small couch with both hands, choking back vomit. When Gigi finally throws up, Jesse's eyeball drops onto the carpet, maybe a coy suggestion Jesse is still with us after all. "I need to get her out of me," Gigi sobs. She grabs a nearby pair of scissors and slices her own gut open. After she dies, Sarah falls to her knees—in grief? No, in hunger. She eats the eyeball and struts away. This is how the film ends.

What does it mean? The surface of the film offers many critiques. There's the obvious exploration of the way the fashion industry turns people into objects to be looked at, evaluated, and dehumanized. Jesse begins the film as a shy naïf but in just a few weeks (?) becomes so full of herself, so bloated with her sense of her own beauty, that she drives her obviously-fake friends to murder her—and this after Jesse has headlined one fashion show by one designer. But past that there's the way capitalism makes ravenous consumers of us all, so much so that an industry devoted to beauty won't hesitate to consume that beauty to perpetuate itself. Under capitalism, all things have value, and all things with value can be exchanged. Jesse is interchangeable with other young women. There isn't much that seems to make Jesse unique from them aside from her stunning beauty.

In the end, though, Jesse doesn't accomplish anything. Not really. She doesn't reach Gigi or Sarah's level of fame. Her legacy won't last longer than Sarah's digestive cycle. Perhaps the film astutely points out how the labor of the poor serves only to further enrich the wealthy. Neither Sarah nor Gigi need help being more beautiful. But they believe that by ingesting Jesse, they take on her power. They take on the benefits of her labor. They become somehow more beautiful, more unignorable with Jesse inside them. They become richer.

## INT. BRENTWOOD MANSION–DAY.

The last shot of our day was an easy one. Elton laid cookies on a tray. When Sergei yelled "Action!" each of us snatched a cookie from the tray at the same time, revealing in their absence the tray's cheery message—"Merry Christmas." We did a few takes, and then most of us were wrapped.

I stepped back into my normal clothes. We'd burned most of the day away and now the sun was setting for my drive east. I went to find Elton to say goodbye before I left. I found him huddled with Sergei in a quiet corner of the house. Now, literally working together, being in the same city, things didn't seem to be improving between them the way Elton had hoped. I recognized everything Elton's demeanor was saying. The stifled frustrations. The wishing things were easier. The conflicting desire to open up and be vulnerable at odds with the need for self-protection. I slunk away unnoticed, joining the rest of the remaining actors until Elton was free.

When Sergei poked his head around the wall, he called for Young Gay Pop Singer to join him in the bathroom for the next set up. Elton walked past Sergei into the room with us. "I'm going to head back," I said, touching his arm. "Thanks for inviting me."

Elton reached his arms around me. "You're a good sport." The hug was warm and sincere.

I paused as we broke apart. "Are you okay?"

Elton nodded. "Oh yeah," he said in that too-cheerful tone that means *Not at all, but don't press me on it.*

"If you need me—"

"I'm fine." I knew he would be—maybe not today, but Elton knew how to survive. Disappointment was part of the hustle. But if there was anything I learned from Elton in the time I had known him, it was to maintain a cautious optimism undeterred by inevitable disappointments. It was how he approached work and, I intuited, his entanglement with Sergei. If things never worked out between them, Elton would be sad, of course. But he'd also pick himself up and carry on. Something better was waiting down the road. Why? Because it had to be.

I took one more glimpse around the mansion. How long until it would be gone—days? A couple weeks? All the people who'd lived here, their memories razed. Maybe it was only ever one family. Maybe mansion-replacement is the natural evolution of this neighborhood. One falls, another rises. It was a world I knew nothing about. The home that sprouted here would cradle the dreams of Young Gay Pop Singer's family. They'd host their Christmases in it, maybe preserving that view from the pool in the new architecture, the ocean unfurling like a big blue carpet past the tree and the presents. Surely there would be so many presents. Though it's the thought that counts, I felt fairly sure whatever would be inside them also counted a great deal.

# PSYCHOLOGICAL THRILLER

## SUMMER 2012

I'm already drunk when he takes me by the arm and says hello. We're at a bar. It's crowded. Men in twos and threes fuck each other on several televisions mounted high on the walls. There's music—something forgettable. We introduce ourselves. He offers me a shot of something, and I drink it. We talk, but I won't remember this conversation. Nothing sticks in my memory until I realize I'm kissing him in the parking lot after last call. His friends have shoved themselves into a yellow Ford Fiesta idling a few feet from us. The horn bleats with insistence.

He invites me to join them, but I know when my hourglass has run out. We exchange information. I'll hear from him again. What happens next will unlace everything about my life: where I live. Who I am. Who my boyfriend is. How much I want to live.

## BLACKOUT

*Black Swan* is the story of a woman who is just trying to keep it together during a period of intense turmoil, scrutiny, and uncertainty. Set against the backdrop of the prestigious New York City Ballet at Lincoln Center, the film leverages the excruciating physical demands of ballet—exacting technique, the punishment of repetitive movement, the crushing expectations of bodily perfection—against the pliable psyches of the dancers, the artistic director, and the people they orbit.

Artistic Director Thomas Leroy (Vincent Cassell) re-envisions *Swan Lake*: "We strip it down, make it visceral and real," he tells the company during a warm-up at the start of the film. He looks around the room at the women. "But which of you can embody both swans?" This will be the guiding tension in the film, and the introduction of its theme of dualities. Binaries. Reflections. The light and the dark, never meant to coexist, somehow finding balance in the body of a single woman.

## SUMMER 2015

I study a much-photocopied sheet of instructions, the type gray and faded, before the first meeting of my Adult Beginning Ballet class. It instructs me to buy shoes, to wear comfortable clothing to class. I should be prepared to move. I find the nearest dance supply store and after trying on what feels like every shoe in their backroom, I find the pair that hug my feet without strangling them. "When you get home, attach the elastics so that the slipper fits snugly but not uncomfortably," the salesperson tells me, showing me with her finger where I should sew it with thread. I go home, pull out the sewing kit I have never used before, and do my best.

The studio is a large square space with high ceilings and a wall of windows looking onto The Broad, Los Angeles's new contemporary art museum. It stares back at us with its architectural oculus, a window bulging through the concrete of the museum's façade. The room gets a lot of natural light and feels spacious.

As a clumsy, self-injuring oaf even on flat surfaces, dance always felt like it was out of reach for me. I am in this room at age thirty-eight with no prior dance experience because my life has fallen apart. I don't know who I am anymore. But now I have nothing left to lose.

The teacher, Amy, is in her forties with dirty blonde hair and a petite frame covered from head to toe with a light jacket, long pants, and leg warmers. She has a direct demeanor and speaks with an occasional accent that I can't pin down. We all help pull out the barres and place them in straight lines around the room. She asks us our names and memorizes them almost immediately, then launches into a series of steps at the barre. Her nylon pants rustle like dry leaves while her feet become blurs near the floor, flicking, pointing, tapping. Her arms swoop up over her head and trail back down in graceful arcs that are so perfect they seem robotic.

I try as best I can to repeat these movements with my own limbs, with varying results. At 6' 4", I tower over my petite classmates. They wear leotards and sheer wrap skirts and look much better prepared than I do in my striped tank top and gym shorts.

Though I am barely moving, I break a sweat. Then a hard sweat.

I see myself in the mirror, a praying mantis among swans.


## BLACK MAGIC

There's a lot of mirror imagery in *Black Swan*. This makes sense—mirrors line the walls of every ballet studio. The dancer must observe herself to assess her movements, make corrections, understand her placement on the stage, how she travels through space. But the obsession with reflection threads deeper. In one of the first shots of Nina (Natalie Portman), she rides a subway train, staring into the glass, where her own face is a ghostly reflection in the darkness outside the car. Then she sees a different image: a woman in the adjoining car, dressed similarly, hair in the same kind of bun. Nina strains to watch this figure exit the car and push through a crowd. We learn later this is the company's new dancer, Lily (Mila Kunis).

It's easy to say Lily is Nina's enemy in *Black Swan*. The vivacious, carefree dancer is in almost every way her opposite. Nina would certainly agree. But Nina's enemies are more numerous than the woman Nina thinks may snatch the role of the white and black swans out from under her. Thomas, who sexually assaults her as he tries to teach her the art of seduction, is an enemy. Her mother (Barbara Hershey), who both lives through her and tries to stop her from succeeding so she can never leave her, is an enemy. Beth (Winona Ryder), the prima donna she replaces, is an enemy who suggests Nina's ascent is due only to fucking Thomas, not her talent or passion.

*Black Swan's* mirrors reflect more than the physical world. They reveal Nina's fracturing psyche. She makes a half-hearted attempt to seduce Thomas into giving her the role, and in response, he kisses her aggressively until she bites him, shocking him. He's seen enough to believe the black swan may exist beneath her rigid, virginal exterior. She passes a mirror in the bathroom as she enters a stall to call her mother and share the good news. When she hangs up and exits the stall, the word "WHORE" streaks across the mirror in red lipstick. She frantically wipes it away. Later in the film, alone in the rehearsal room, Nina goes over and over her routine so much the pianist finally gets up and walks out. She stays back, practicing the black swan's solo. As she sees herself in the mirror, her reflection stops matching her movements. She backs toward another mirror, where out of the corner of her eye she sees her reflection turn toward her, a menacing grin on her face, before the lights go out. The black swan *is* within her, and the more Nina tries to perfect the role, the more that dark energy consumes her.

In another scene, walking alone through a construction corridor, Nina passes a figure who for a moment has her own face, a Cheshire smile blooming there, unnerving the real Nina. Her ultimate enemy is herself, her own distrust in her abilities, her own fears. She learned this: to doubt everything, except her own ambition.


## AUTUMN 2012–AUTUMN 2014

The man I met at the bar becomes a regular hookup. I keep his identity, and the identities of all my hookups, secret from the rest of the people in my life. Except for Brody, my partner of six years, whose blessing I have to participate in this ethical nonmonogamy.

For a while, it was good. And then, all of a sudden, it wasn't. Hookup guy tells me one night at a bar he's not in it for the long haul with me if Brody is around. When he leaves my house that night, he leaves with a duffle bag of clothes and toiletries and ephemera, wrecking me.

Brody tries to be there for me from 500 miles away. Despite how much Brody and I both want it to help me, it doesn't. I drown in the murky soup of my sadness. That's when I notice it—a crack in our foundation. Maybe it was always there. Maybe the three times Brody and I loved each other across a long distance caused it. Or maybe it was our joint agreement to sleep with other people. Maybe all of it. Maybe none of it. But once I see the crack, I can't unsee it. It widens. It becomes as unstable as the faults zigzagging through the earth under my feet in Los Angeles.

I love Brody. He is my best friend. Over our years together, we grew to complement each other's shapes. A comfortable alchemy. But one morning, I realize I don't get enough of what I need  that, in fact, the only time I ever needed to lean on Brody was when my mother died, when we shared our grief. Now, this grief I'm feeling is my own. Brody can't come with me. And I realize how alone I am as I shower before work, sobbing into the stream of hot water reddening my whole body. I know I have to let go of the only thing that ever felt sacred to me. The thing I know will not return.

Over the course of a few weeks, all the love I felt disappears from my life. I no longer know who I am.

A few months later, the guy from the bar reaches out to me again. I let him back in. Just us.


## THE BLACK SWAN

Lily doesn't understand why Nina is so serious. Why she can't let loose, have fun, live a little. Lily is free, liberated. She chases experiences more than achievements. It's what Thomas loves about her, the way she loses herself in life and in dancing. "Watch the way she moves," Thomas says to Nina as Lily dances. "Imprecise, but effortless." Nina is a perfectionist. Her self-awareness overpowers all her other desires. She knows when she is being watched, and she knows she is always being watched.

Nina wants to be like Lily. The closer Nina gets, the more she realizes she can't have it both ways. She can't be the technically proficient and demure white swan if it also means being the dark, seductive, calculating black swan.

The white swan, like Nina, is aware men are watching her and so she performs for them. The black swan, like Lily, performs so that men will watch her. It's a subtle difference, but ultimately the one that defines them: who wields the power.

## [TECHNIQUE]

What strikes me about ballet in the beginning isn't necessarily how hard it is. I once took a break in the work day to watch New York City Ballet alum Wendy Whelan teach the advanced students of my school's Dance Academy, my first real peek behind the curtain of what goes into a ballet performance. Wendy's body, made only of muscle and bone, swam through space, calculated to be perfect yet graceful— precise but effortless. I watched the students follow her instruction, her adjustments, having no clear idea what was happening within their bodies to make these steps come to life.

And that, for me, is the struggle in ballet. The carriage of the body, even its placement at rest, requires muscles I've never thought about before. To stand in first position—heels together, feet turned just above nine and three o'clock—engages the thigh and hip. Fifth position, the most challenging to feel comfortable in, looks almost comically difficult, feet stacked and pointed in opposite directions. To stand in this position is a feat; to stand with grace, to seem natural, is athleticism.

## BLACK AND WHITE

Those around Nina convince her she's not good enough to be both white and black swans. Nina knows they're wrong. After all, she's smart enough to get to the top of the company. The face she presents to the world—uncertain, flappable—invites them to underestimate her, but we, the audience, know with greater certainty what lurks within.

However, their words resonate in her. Her psyche splits. She feels pulled taut between mastery and misery. Rather than battling her critics and her rivals, she fights herself. This becomes literal during the opening night performance. Nina goes to her dressing room to change from white to black swan, but she sees Lily at her mirror, making herself up to dance the black swan. When she turns to face Nina, Lily's face morphs into Nina's face. They attack each other. White Swan Nina shoves Black Swan Nina into a full-length mirror, shattering it. Black Swan Nina chokes her, stretching her neck with such grotesque force it lengthens like a swan's. White Swan Nina grabs a shard of mirror and stabs Black Swan Nina in the gut, killing her. Nina's disintegration—or, perhaps, integration of dark and light—happening via a shattered mirror is significant. It all becomes very bloated with metaphor.

*Black Swan* suggests that psychological dismantling is necessary for artists to reach their full potential. Nina dances Odette, the white swan, and Odile, the black swan, expertly. She embodies Odile's allure and violence, and Odette's fragility and pleading. *Swan Lake* is almost happening within her. At the climax of the performance, when she, as Odette, leaps off the peak to kill herself, we see her plummet through an overlay of mirror shards, recalling the shattered glass from the dressing room encounter with her own dark self. Her identity, we should assume, has been irreparably broken. Her face is pure ecstasy. She's done it. She defied all the expectations, her own included, and earned stardom. Yet, when she lands on the mat backstage, we realize she, White Swan Nina, has been stabbed, implying in that moment the fight between Black Swan Nina and White Swan Nina was some kind of vivid fantasy with mortal results. The wound is extensive, perhaps even fatal. And cruelly, the film withholds her fate from us.

Earlier in the film, Thomas, pacing around the rehearsal room, waxes poetic about Odette's tragic fate. "In death," he says, "she finds freedom." The film campaigns for us to believe the art transcends its maker. Art trumps life. Nina fulfilled her purpose. Nothing else about her matters.

Thomas fails to add that Odile was already free.

## 2014-2015

It starts off with little things.

Getting ready to go out to a bar with him for a second, third, or fourth time that week, I pull off my shirt and reach for a new one. My boyfriend steps into his jeans. My chest, a glass-smooth sea mostly unbroken by hair, catches his eye. He says, "You know I'm really only attracted to hairy guys, right?"

Playing a board game with another couple, when he senses I'm going to win the game, he targets me and me alone. He places roads and settlements to stunt the growth of my empire, leaving me to languish and lose, even as his focus on me has allowed one of our friends to take and hold the lead until the end of the game. His pursuit of me is punishing, and personal. I am not allowed to beat him, even if destroying me means destroying himself.

Another night, a bar night like most of our nights, he leaves me waiting for the karaoke DJ to call me up. Maybe he's smoking outside.

Maybe he's chatting with friends in the back. But then he's standing in front of me. I see his eyes bobbing on whisky's choppy waves. The dread rushes into me. He puts his arm around a short man next to him who can't be more than twenty-six years old. "This is Sam," my boyfriend says. Sam's face has a dog's eagerness all over it. As I shake Sam's hand, my boyfriend leans toward my ear. "Let's take him home with us."

We've never spoken about this kind of thing—what it means to us, what it might do to us. I've learned to stay sober no matter how late the night gets to stop mistakes like this from happening. "No."

He doesn't say a word. Just turns and storms out of the bar. Sam stands there, reading me with his optimism. He holds up his phone. "Can I give you my number?"

Another night, a neighbor pounds our door at four in the morning. It yanks me out of a deep sleep. My first thought: police. A crisis. An accident. Still mostly asleep, I answer the door, hiding my body behind the wood. The neighbor points to a rideshare service idling in the street. The back door yawns open and the interior light reveals my boyfriend, cradled in the back seat, passed out. The driver shakes him. He's unresponsive.

I drag him to the couch and go back to bed.

Over time, it becomes a kind of dance. I work hard not to be noticed, to anticipate what will set him off or open myself up for criticism, and correct it before he can comment.

And the undermining. Well. Eventually, I hit bottom.

The exhaustion I feel pulls me toward the earth with its own gravity. I pass out before ten almost every weeknight night, usually in front of the TV while he struggles, through ADHD, to complete his graduate school coursework.

I go into therapy for depression. Between the complexities of my work environment and the needling at home, I have no peace.

We explode. Shouting from one end of the apartment to the other.

Me screaming (again) that it's over. My body filling up with despair like a cistern in a hurricane. Then I'm crying. I'm telling him how much he's hurting me. I ask him to help me feel better. He tells me he just can't with me, that I need to much, ask too much, that I'm draining him dry, that I'm holding him back, that he can't anymore.

I remember saying the words, "Maybe I shouldn't even be alive anymore."

He locks himself in the other bedroom.

I have been shrinking and shrinking for months but now I can feel how close I am to blinking out.

The voice who could say those words. I don't recognize myself.


## BLACK AND BLUE

Nina's body weathers aggression throughout *Black Swan*, both as a dancer and as victim of self-harm. In an early scene, her mother notices a rashy patch of skin on her back. Nina doesn't know what it is and shrugs it off. It's the last injury she'll ignore in the film. Later, that area on her back bleeds, reveals a deep scratch. Her toenail snaps in half while she practices *pirouettes en pointe*, and she yanks a hangnail from her finger during a celebratory gala. All of these wounds manifest the stress Nina is under. As viewers, we worry both that they are real and that they are imagined. Because a ballet dancer's body is the tool of their art, it is sacred. Nina cares for hers like a priceless violin. When it begins to break down, she's stressed and concerned.

Yet the physical harm can't compare to the self-harm she endures at the film's climax. Or is the self-harm the inevitable evolution of the harm she endures from others? Beth's slut-shaming. Thomas's psychological abuse. Her mother's overprotective and volatile attention. Lily's constant glittering on the periphery of her vision. The ire of her company members. The being-a-woman in a world where everything about her—her body, her sexuality, her interiority—are owned by everyone else around her.

By the end of the film, Nina resolves to defy others' expectations and embody herself and her opposite. She thinks she is doing this for herself, but it is the outcome those around her have been pushing her to realize. And it (probably) kills her. And perhaps, in death, she'll find freedom.

## SUMMER 2015

The moment I walk in, I know something is wrong. Off. Hollow. The way the sound of the door opening echoes when it should absorb. The click of my steps on bare tile.

The realization swoops into me with a breath I feel all the way in my gut.

I look in the bedroom. The closet gapes, the bare hangers there dangling like teeth in a broken grin. I rip open a dresser drawer: disemboweled. The master bath, his bath, empty, even the shower curtain gone.

I call him. It rings and rings.

I call him. It rings and rings.

I call him. It rings and rings.

I feel like a conduit. Electric. Things are rushing into me (air, panic, images) and rushing out of me (breath, anger, sweat).

I text him. *You moved out?*

I see the bubble with three dots pull up on the screen. I don't wait. I call him again. He declines the call.

Then the message appears: *I do not want to talk right now.*

I text back that he can go fuck himself.

The phone shaking in my hand.

The emptiness of the rooms, how hollow and dead they feel. A discarded cocoon.

The fear and panic and anger and devastation washing over me in waves, taking turns.

Was this freedom?

## AUTUMN 2015–SPRING 2016

There are weeks when being a failure in the ballet studio is the very best thing I can do for myself. The fall ballet teacher, Lucy, is Amy's opposite in almost every way. She has red hair, is maybe ten years older than Amy, and has a Southern accent that fades in and out depending on how informal she's being. She's loose, casual, funny, loves chatting throughout class, and laughs loudly and often.

I attempt one of the *valse* combinations Lucy demonstrates. It's a delicate waltz-based step with a PUM-pum-pum rhythm and combinations of steps forward and pauses. I just can't do it; I get so deep in my head about what each foot is supposed to do and how my arms are supposed to wave and swan around me.

Lucy stops me and gestures to stop the music. "Why don't we do this." She presses my arms to my chest. "Let's not worry about these. Just step to the music." She claps out the waltz rhythm with her hands and demonstrates for me a significantly dumbed-down version of the footwork. I've been assigned ballet for babies. I don't protest. I follow her instructions.

I'm grateful for the opportunity to actually do something, and do it right.

Then there is the day Lucy asks us to spin across the room with our arms up, bent at the elbows, fingers touching our shoulders. This, she says, is to force us to spot, which in turn prevents us from becoming dizzy, which in turn allows us to spin and spin and spin. To spot, you choose something on the wall ahead of you and hold your gaze there as your body turns, your head stationary, until the very last second when you whip your head around and snap back to that same spot, over and over. Unless you are me, in which case you reel around until the floor rises up to catch you.

I am awful at ballet, and yet I find myself leaving each class in high spirits—smiling even, ready to try again the next week. There are weeks the drive home from ballet is the only time I feel any joy at all.

## BLACK SHEEP

*Black Swan* does a great job of keeping Lily elusive from the audience. We are so forced inside Nina's perspective—even experiencing Nina's delusions and fantasies with her, unable to discern what is real and what isn't—and Lily is always just outside our view. Her role in this film, and in Nina's psyche, is to always be just out of reach. This is the dance of the black swan: to be available, but unattainable.

We don't know why Lily is so free and confident. She's just a company dancer, and she doesn't even seem to take it that seriously. Thomas chooses Lily to be the alternate for Nina's starring role, despite her rejection of everything Nina holds sacred about dance. Lily routinely shows up late to work. During one rehearsal, she *pirouettes* so carelessly she bumps right into another dancer. At the fundraiser, she commiserates with Nina in the bathroom. She unapologetically removes her panties and shoves them in her purse. Lily even smokes in the ballet studio after rehearsal, a double whammy of rule-breaking. Lily, with her dark hair and black ballet clothes, is already a black swan. Nina, who is practiced and technically perfect, lives in constant fear and doubt. Yet of all the characters in this film, it is she who should be confident.

But successful, accomplished women in our culture don't get to be the objects of desire. They spend years honing their skills, making progress, achieving. Some women feel socialized to minimize their own talents and triumphs when interacting with men so as not to draw their ire, their jealousy, or even their violence. The old saw "men are afraid women will laugh at them, while women are afraid men will kill them" feels connected to these impulses somehow. That women who surpass the men around them deserve scorn instead of desire.

Beth is as accomplished and flawless as Nina. But she's ancient in ballet years. Not only is she "too old" to do her job, she's too old to be desired. This, too, is a distinctly female problem. The sketch show *Inside Amy Schumer* satirized this by giving women self-awareness of their expiration date, their "last fuckable day," by toasting Julia Louis-Dreyfus as she makes the transition from desirable to disgusting. But why is this film, in which we occupy a woman's psyche, blind to this double standard? Beth is aware of what's happening, and Nina is too. Nina is younger, stronger. She's also meeker, more pliable to Thomas's whims. At the same time, Nina cannot ignore Lily, who is years behind her in technique and training and, with her work ethic, will never reach Nina's level of success. Nina has assessed all the wrong threats, and she won't look far enough down the road to accept her own obsolesence. When Beth's fate will become Nina's fate.

As the audience, we see Lily is no threat to Nina on the stage—only in life, where she has learned to live, while Nina has learned to succeed.

## WINTER 2016

I'm out at a bar with friends. My now-ex-boyfriend leaps out of nowhere, lands in front of me, and says, "Hi." Before I even know what my body is doing, I turn on my heels and scurry away, heart pounding. I'm not ready to see him. He has been engaged to a man for several months. The insult and injury are inseparable from one another. Rather than deal, I don't.

I walk into the room with the dance floor. The Boulet Brothers, dressed in their trademark twin drag looks, have just announced they need three volunteers. They clutch their mics with taloned fingers painted blood red. I don't know what they're looking for, but I raise my hand anyway. They choose two young men and then, straining through the crowd, they say, "You, the daddy with the mustache, come on up."

I climb onto the stage, joining the others. Below me, the crowd is packed shoulder-to-shoulder with men: men in tank tops. Men with glitter beards. Men holding beers. Men as far as the eye can see.

"Now what we're doing here is a dance contest," the taller Brother says.

"You have one minute to strip down to your underwear. Make it sexy. Make the crowd love you," the shorter Brother says.

"We'll judge the winner by audience vote."

"Gentlemen, are you ready?"

My hands start to sweat. The other guys are in their twenties. I see triceps popping on one of them, groomed eyebrows and a flat tummy under the tight shirt of the other. They nod at each other with respect, but I'm off to the side, maybe not even registering them.

"DJ, music!"

The beat drops, hard and loud and demanding. I don't waste time. I whip my shirt right off. The crowd cheers for us, hollers. I hear an encouraging "Yes, daddy!" bubble up through the music. I unbuckle my belt, but I have never, in my whole life, felt less sexy. I unbutton my pants. I lower the zipper, grateful I had the foresight to wear cute underwear. I slide the denim down my thighs, rippling with the muscles ballet class has earned for me. I show them my ballet butt, bouncing my hips to the music. Eventually I forget the other men on stage. I forget about the men in the crowd. All I hear is the music, the breath flowing in and out of my body.

When the audience votes, cheering loudest for me, I win a crisp $100 bill. It feels like dignity.

## SUMMER 2016

Amy returns to lead the class for summer. Her style feels radically different after my year with Lucy. Amy's teaching asks us to focus our bodies on activating the right muscles. She wants precision in movements and positions. I stand in *sous-sous* on the balls of my feet, one heel crossed over the top of the other foot, trying to maintain balance as I raise my arms over my head in fifth position. She wants us to keep our legs "sewn shut" using the inside thigh muscles we mostly don't use for any other reason. "Charlie! Keep your legs closed!" she calls across the room. "I can see light through them."

But Amy's insistent methods come at precisely the right time. Now that I'm more or less familiar with the positions, the names of our movements, and a bit of the technique, I can address skill. And Amy's astute eye catches all. At one point, seeing my struggle to balance on my *demipointe*, she hunkers down to the floor, putting her hand on my right foot. My body weight rests on the four small toes. She tilts my foot so that I plant from only the big toe and second toe. The shift is fortifying. I stop struggling to stand straight. She gets up, looks me in the eye. "That's easier, right?"

In the next class, she corrects my *chaines* turns. "You're keeping your arms too low," she says. "When your arms are low, you lean forward. When you lean forward, you don't make complete turns, and then you don't cross the room in a straight line." She demonstrates my movements through exaggeration, zipping around drunkenly like a toy top. She stops, returns, and pushes her shoulders back. "Keep your arms here." She makes a perfect oval with her arms and raises it just shy of perpendicular to her body. "Then when you turn through," she goes on, sweeping her right leg and her right arm open and slamming closed again by pulling her left leg and arm toward the right, "everything stays connected." I try the turns again, keeping my arms elevated. Now instead of nearly toppling over, I'm turning—maybe a little too fast. "Good!" Amy says as I move. When I walk back toward her, she looks me in the eye again. "That's easier, right?"

## BLACK BOX | MID-SUMMER 2012

Natalie Portman took a year of intensive ballet prior to filming *Black Swan*. During production, she fell in love with her ballet teacher, Benjamin Millepied, who would go on to serve as the artistic advisor to the pre-professional Dance Academy where I worked.

There's a moment where all these lives and stories converge. A happier time. A few weeks after meeting him in the bar, I snag free tickets for my future ex-boyfriend and I to see Millepied dance in the galleries at MOCA. We stand in the crowd, watching Millepied leap and turn in an empty room, surrounded by squiggly art and two floodlights pushed into the corners.

I am falling in love, though I don't know it. Before the year is out, my life will be unrecognizable to me in this moment.

I look to my left as Millepied dances. There, next to me, stands Natalie Portman. Her eyes fix on her husband, drinking in his performance with an eagerness that is equal parts love, pride, and learning.

I hold the hand of a man who will never look at me like that.

## WINTER 2017

When the new semester begins, ending our holiday hiatus, Lucy joins us again in the studio. She wears her all-black leotard, red hair pulled back into a low pony. "I know some of you have been away from the barre for a few weeks, so we'll ease back into it," she says. We start with *tendus,* our backs to the barre, to warm up the feet and ankles, then move into *pliés* from each position, and then into *fondus*. It feels good to be back again.

Near the end of the barre exercises, Lucy waxes poetic for a moment. "Ballet is a process," she says. "We come into the studio each day. Our goal is to be better than we were the last time." She nods to Kathy, our accompanist at the back of the room. "Just like with piano. There's a layering of experience. We just want to get better. We just want to *be* better."

We move to center floor and *chaînés* turns. You can see shoulders slump on everyone when Lucy announces it. No one likes these. But we do them. I do them. In fact, I do them well. My feet feel stable. I even spot successfully. We move into a combination that ends with a *jeté*, a full leap into the air with legs extended in either direction. Lucy instructs us to throw our arms directly over our head as we launch into the air to direct all the energy in our bodies straight up. The move takes power, confidence, and complete coordination of mind and body.

I complete the first steps across the floor correctly and then, my feet land on the floor in perfect time, on the correct beat. I leap like taking a giant step. My legs extend. My arms rise over me with the authority of an exclamation. I feel so light. My body hovers over the ground. And then the floor and my feet meet again, softly, gently, and I'm done.

Lucy gives me loud praise, "Great work, Charlie." She claps enthusiastically. I blush. "This is going to be your year," she tells me. I believe her.

# ACT III

# SPECULATIVE FICTION

## HYPOTHESIS

The examination room at the sprawling Kaiser Permanente LA Medical Center campus felt like a broom closet. The windowless box accommodated an exam table, a countertop just big enough for a sink, a plastic chair pressed up against the wall, a wheeled stool, and a rolling cart on which a computer teetered acrobatically. I waited for my new doctor to arrive. The only thing I knew to expect was that he was handsome. Kaiser allowed you to choose your doctor on its website, providing medical school information, a brief physician's statement, and a headshot. I scrolled through doctor after doctor, looking for a man close to my age or younger, someone who had recent medical school training. Of these, Dr. Bartholomew was the best looking, exactly the kind of doctor you'd expect to be working in a Hollywood-adjacent clinic, and therefore more trustworthy to me.

A spring in the hinges shrieked and doinged when the door opened. Dr. B swooped into the room in his white lab coat, trailed by a young woman with blonde hair. He barked his name at me and waved an arm at the woman. "This is my resident Dr. Jeffries. If it's all right with you, she'll sit in on our consultation today." She smiled at me as she eased into the plastic chair. She looked bright, interested, and like Dr. B, attractive. It felt as though I were visiting the set of *Grey's Anatomy*.

Dr. B squatted on the rolling stool and pulled himself toward the computer. "You're interested in Propecia," he said.

"Yes."

"Dad bald?"

"Yes."

"Siblings? They bald?"

"Bald or balding." He tapped notes into my chart.

"Maternal grandfather? He bald too?"

"Dead. But was bald."

Finally, Dr. B turned toward me. He was excruciatingly handsome. His gold wedding band winked at me, reflecting fluorescent lights. Dr. Jeffries looked on, an eager kind of expression on her face, like she wanted to please us both by saying and doing nothing. Dr. B looked at me from beneath his own perfect coif of sandy brown hair. "It's genetic, you know. Balding."

Of course I knew. I'd known my whole life this day would come. The men in my family were cursed with luscious heads of hair in childhood, but all of us made our own march toward reflective scalps. My brother Gary began to lose it in college, and Dennis in his thirties. I hoped and prayed that whatever genetic milkshake made me gay would also exempt me from this fate. And for a while, it seemed it might. I spent most of my thirties in a relationship with Brody, a hair dresser who cut my hair and kept me apprised of how my family curse progressed. Eventually, he started frosting my tips to hide the thinning—lighter hair doesn't appear quite as thin when you're white—and for a few years I got to stave off the inevitable: shaving my head.

I was thirty-eight. Not ready to be bald. Not ready to let go.

Dr. B finished typing some notes in my chart. "Try minoxidil for six months," he said. "It's available over the counter. If that doesn't work, come back and see me again."

He popped up off the stool and swooped out of the room. Dr. Jeffries glanced around the door as she left. "It was nice to meet you."

"You too," I said to the empty room.

## DESIGNER BABIES

In the utopian future of *Gattaca*, your genes shape your destiny. Babies fresh from the womb get a blood stick test, and a machine analyzes their probability of developing various maladies, from poor eyesight to heart disease to mental illness. After newborn Vincent's genetic test, they read his report aloud to his mother (Jayne Brook), still lying prone on the delivery cot, and his father (Elias Koteas), who stands by like he's hearing the death sentence for a child he hasn't even held yet.

The next scene shows the couple at a boutique fertility clinic, where they evaluate four potential embryos and identify their preferred genetic traits. They customize everything, right down to eye color. This embryo divides and divides into the son Vincent's father deems worthy to carry his name, and Vincent's brother Anton arrives not long after his older brother.

Anton (Loren Dean) and Vincent (Ethan Hawke) echo Hercules and Hephaestus. The younger brother, the Hercules, becomes a physically perfect specimen: handsome, smart, strong, confident. Hephaestus, like Vincent, was considered imperfect—in fact, deformed—at birth. Anton's height quickly outpaces Vincent's. Vincent wears glasses to correct his poor eyesight, while Anton needs no assistance. Vincent harbors big dreams—he wants to explore the outer reaches of the galaxy. Anton shrugs and tells Vincent, "I bet I could be [an astronaut], if I wanted." With any number of career options at his fingertips, Anton seems void of any actual ambition. Their parents dote on Anton, but take a stern hand with Vincent, wanting him to accept his genetic limitations. His father tries to temper Vincent's ambition of entering Gattaca, the nation's space academy: "The only way you'll see the inside of a spaceship is if you're cleaning it," he says.

This comes to pass. Vincent leaves home in the night. He ends up exactly where his dad predicts, on the janitorial staff with a bunch of other so-called In-Valids, or people whose genetic makeup precludes them from success. Anton, as a Valid, will have all his doors opened for him.

The name "Anton" describes something of inestimable value—a

fitting moniker for the family's golden child. Curiously, "Vincent" means "conqueror."

## SIDE EFFECTS

I took a photo of my head before I started the treatment, in an effort to help me document any progress. For weeks after, I pumped minoxidil mousse into my palms, twice a day, and massaged it into my scalp. It gave me a vaguely burning sensation, like the sun hitting the crown of my head during a long day at the beach.

After two months, I saw no change, and my scalp felt a little tender all the time.

I packed up my half-empty apartment in Pasadena, my ex-boyfriend having moved out without a word weeks earlier. He still came by every few days to pick up mail, and, I suspected, to give me a chance to apologize to him. But I wasn't going to do that. Instead, I reached out to Chip and Julie, the folks who'd rented me their little house in Highland Park, to see if they had anything available, even a short-term rental. They offered me the in-law apartment in their house in Mount Washington. My friend Kaitlin lived there for about a year, and after she moved out they'd converted it to an Airbnb. They gave me six months. While the rent was much higher than I'd paid anywhere else, I welcomed a new sanctuary where I could focus on me, my healing, my future.

I went back to the Kaiser Permanente website to find a new doctor, one who worked at the closer Pasadena clinic. Dr. Ramos, like Dr. Bartholomew, was handsome (but not *too* handsome) and he had a physician's statement about how much he loved helping patients find their own healthy lifestyles. When I finally met him a few weeks later, he revealed himself to be the Dr. Jekyll to Dr. B.'s Mr. Hyde: kind, happy, engaging, interested in helping me. After our brief consultation, he sent a prescription for finasteride, the generic form of Propecia, to a nearby CVS.

In its 5 mg form, finasteride reduces swelling in the prostate. It followed through on this promise in clinical trials, but researchers noticed it had the curious effect of stopping hair loss in some patients and even causing some lost hair to regrow. Like many drugs, a surprise side effect made it more marketable. Doctors now prescribe it in a 1 mg dose for the express purpose of stopping and sometimes reversing hair loss in men.

The male body converts testosterone into dihydrotestosterone, which then binds itself to various organs in the body. In men who are predisposed to hair loss, DHT latches onto the hair follicles and, well, the hair stops growing. Finasteride reduces the production of DHT and effectively stops hair loss before it starts. In some cases, finasteride brings hair back from the brink, turning the tables on male pattern baldness.

My first week taking finasteride, I plummeted into depression.

I lost interest in just about everything except sitting around my temporary apartment feeling terrible. I tried to write, but nothing came. I started tinkering with a series of poems I'd written in the form of a reading comprehension exam, a project I'd finalize as the chapbook *Story Problems* and which would ultimately serve as the spine for my third poetry collection *Instructions between Takeoff and Landing.* The poems, written before, during, and after the recent breakup, focused on the complex alchemy of midlife—looking backward at what cannot be changed, battling the anxiety for what was to come, and contending with what I perceived to be the fragility of my mortality. I ended up so devastated by my own words that I sat at my desk and cried. I barely got myself together—showered, dressed—to get to work. I came home at night and it took all my strength to put ingredients together for a meal. I sat in front of the television doing nothing.

A fraught relationship exists between medication and emotions. It was familiar to me. Following an extended hospitalization for asthma when I was seventeen, I took a course of steroids meant to keep passageways in my lungs open and dilated. They also acted on the rest of my body. I broke out in acne on my face, chest, and back, hyper-fueling the explosion that raged across my skin since I was thirteen. The mood swings were even more noticeable. A bonfire of anger was just a hair trigger away from lighting up, sending my voice booming through a room and my heart racing. While on the medication, my moods felt normal. They felt earned. The world around me became hostile, and I became hostile in return. I don't know how my parents dealt with me during those two terrifying weeks. I suppose it's hard to distinguish a normal hormonal teenager from one whose hormones have been hijacked by mood altering meds. When I finished the steroids, my asthma symptoms and the rage vanished.

I took Zyban to help me quit smoking while I completed my MFA degree in creative writing. None of the usual remedies worked and I felt desperate. Psychologists prescribe Zyban under the name Wellbutrin to treat patients suffering from major depression and seasonal affective disorder. Just like with finasteride, initial users demonstrated an unexpected side effect: they lost interest in smoking. Dismantling addiction, especially one as entrenched as nicotine, requires intensive work on the part of the user, so learning there was a drug, a miracle cure, for addiction to cigarettes felt like a gift from God. While taking Zyban, I stopped requiring sleep, and I felt a surge of inspiration and creativity, often working on poems into the early morning hours and waking up refreshed after three to four hours of sleep. I also lost interest in smoking, slowly but surely. This would have been a scientific breakthrough if, at the same time, I wasn't riding a wild, rickety roller coaster of emotions. I'd laugh uncontrollably at something moderately funny someone said to me, and within five minutes I'd be sobbing into my palms. It felt terrible. It felt worse than smoking. I gave up on Zyban but not cigarettes.

A few years later, Big Pharma marketed a new prescription treatment for nicotine addiction: Chantix. This drug blocked nicotine from entering the pleasure center of the brain, making the user feel less and less addicted to smoking until they finally quit altogether. What the commercials didn't mention is that Chantix blocks everything from reaching the pleasure center of your brain. Within a few days, all the color drained out of the world. I lived in a plotless black and white movie. I lost interest in everything: food, hobbies, sex—anything that offered pleasure offered me nothing. I stopped smoking, having lost interest in that too.

Chantix has complex psychological effects on users. For a close friend of mine, this included a sudden but, he said, completely rational suicide attempt. After a mild disagreement with his partner, he walked into their bathroom and swallowed a handful of pills. He survived, but he quit Chantix. I experienced something different. I joined my friend James and Brody, whom I was just weeks into dating, at the country-western gay bar. I couldn't shake the feeling that the two of them were ganging up on me, making fun of me, laughing about me. The conspiracy started in the tiniest seed and sprouted in time-lapse until anger roiled out of me. I insisted we leave. As soon as we were in the car, I gave them each a vicious lambasting so severe not one of us has forgotten it in the decade since. Words tumbled out of my mouth with gymnastic precision. That either one of them forgave me was yet another miracle. I also quit smoking for good.

I existed in the finasteride-induced dulled state for days on end. As the drug wove its way into my bloodstream, it tinkered with how my body produced and used testosterone. I felt like crawling under a shroud and waiting to die.

## THE FLAW IN THE DIAMOND

Vincent always thinks about hair.

His hair holds the key to his genetic identity, along with all the other shed cells of his body. Vincent's dad was right—there's no way Vincent would make it into Gattaca. If he's going to succeed, Vincent needs to become someone else. He'll become what society calls a "borrowed ladder" or "de-gene-erate." The terms turn the In-Valids' disadvantaged status into a sense of being physically lower than everyone else, a common trope society has used to marginalize people for everything from the color of their skin to their romantic and sexual desires.

He enlists the help of a black market dealer named German (Tony Shalhoub). German knows just the person. The candidate's "impeccable credentials" include better than perfect vision, a heart strengthened with decades of exercise, and "an expiration date you wouldn't believe," German assures Vincent. "He could run through a wall."

As they step into his home, a man in a wheelchair appears from behind a column. "If only he could still run," German adds. As Vincent notes in voice over, "there is no gene for fate." This man is Jerome Morrow (Jude Law), an Olympic swimmer whose career was cut short by a car accident that broke his back. "You could go anywhere with this guy's helix tucked under your arm," German whispers, sure he'll make the sale. Since Jerome's accident happened outside the country, there's no official record that Jerome is anything but the Valid he always was.

To slip into Jerome's identity, Vincent needs an *Extreme Makeover* upgrade. Contact lenses to correct his myopic and match color. A haircut matching Jerome's portrait. Learning to write with his right hand. Vincent thinks that's all he needs, but Jerome's profile says he's 6'1"—two inches taller than Vincent. In order to seal the deal, Vincent needs his tibiae lengthened, a painful procedure involving a bone saw and weeks of immobilization. The cost of this upgrade? German takes 25% of everything Vincent earns. Forever.

Once he cons his way into Gattaca, Vincent must strip himself of all loose cells each morning. This choreographed routine ensures no strand of hair, not even an eyelash, travels into Gattaca with him. He exfoliates under a blue light inside what we first think is some kind of shower. Despite his biological disadvantages, adult Vincent has a good physique, and, like Anton, looks handsome enough to pass as a Valid—with some help. When Vincent finishes his ritual, we discover the shower is actually an incinerator, burning stray traces of himself so that he can move into the world with the identity of Jerome Morrow, the man from whom Vincent rents his virtual identity and Valid status.

Though society has evolved to ensure genetic supremacy, Valids seem very paranoid about the unlikely event a de-gene-erate might infiltrate their ranks. Gattaca has a finger-prick entry gate that requires a drop of blood to ensure only Valids can gain entry. Vincent undergoes routine urinalysis, which again, seems primarily focused on confirming the presence of his DNA double helix rather than, say, illicit drug use.

At work, Vincent sucks up all the loose cells that may have fallen into his keyboard, then replaces them with Jerome's cells. We see a close up of Vincent's fingers tangling one of Jerome's hairs around the hairbrush Vincent keeps in a desk drawer.

Irene (Uma Thurman), Vincent's amorous coworker, plucks this hair from his drawer and has him "sequenced." Sequencing is how Valids confirm their love interest is who they say they are—the equivalent, perhaps, of diving deep into someone's Instagram grid or trolling their public Facebook posts. In *Gattaca*'s world, having someone sequenced is just as casual, even if the depths they plumb are invisible to the eye, buried in the secrets of each cell's nuclei. Irene joins other Valids at a teller window where she provides the sample of the hair she retrieved and, moments later, receives a print out of Jerome's genetic makeup. She does not know Vincent planted Jerome's hair in his work station for exactly this reason. The sequencing confirms Jerome's identity and, we intuit, that he is somehow out of Irene's league. Her face crumbles. Though Irene herself is a Valid, she was born with an unexpected heart condition mild enough to get her into Gattaca, but she'll never leave Earth with even this potential for fallibility. Perhaps she hoped Jerome, too, kept such a secret within his body.

Vincent sculpts his hair with thick pomade in the style of the society but also in a way that prevents it from moving, much less falling out.

When the dead body of a Gattaca director is found in the offices, Vincent hovers in the background of a group of bystanders, troubled. An eyelash drops from his face and lands on a piece of molding, where it waits to be vacuumed up by police.

## ENVIRONMENTAL FACTORS

The shroud of depression covering me that first week lifted like fog burning off in the afternoon. As time went on, I returned to a mostly normal state of emotional affairs. I worked in a toxic office environment where infighting, back biting, and ego-bolstering were de rigeur. After a month or so on the drug, I felt dead inside. This was a welcome change from the emotional turmoil I'd been experiencing at work and in the wake of the break up that upended my life.

"Dead inside" was the softening of highs and lows.

"Dead inside" was an even emotional keel I'd never in my life experienced.

I embraced "dead inside." I felt grateful for it. I loved the evenness of my feelings. I remained calm. A kind of detachment from events that, paradoxically, gave me the strength to counter them.

The men in my family have a notorious scorched-earth temper. I dedicated time and energy to taming it in my twenties through therapy and mindfulness. But with finasteride, any anger I felt was akin to a blown-out birthday candle—a puff, and it was gone. I didn't morph into Pollyanna overnight. I still experienced part of anger, the logical part, when you know something isn't fair or right. These thoughts just didn't trigger an emotional response or even changes in breathing, sweating, etc.—the physiological markers of anger. Anger retreated into intellect.

## DEATH BEFORE DISABILITY

*Gattaca* reminds us that public displays of emotion have always belonged to the realms of oppressed classes—the In-Valids of society. The Valids have no reason to feel anything but happiness, joy, love, and for that reason they can't understand why anyone else wouldn't. Everything about society benefits them, and that privilege both shields them to the plight of others and convinces the Valids they've earned their comfort. Even Jerome barely ever raises his voice, despite the fact that all the luxuries and opportunities afforded to him by his Valid status don't rescue him from debilitating malaise. Jerome's loss of joy makes him feel In-Valid, but the privilege he enjoyed until his accident inspires him to fuck with the system that no longer serves him. The same privilege convinces Jerome he has the power and freedom from consequences to enter the arrangement with Vincent in the first place.

Jerome burns himself to death at the end of the film. Thoughtfully, he leaves behind a lifetime supply of his cells, his blood, his urine, for Vincent to use upon his return to Earth. But he doesn't do this for Vincent. He does it because he'd rather die than live out his life as an In-Valid. And this is perhaps the most damning indictment of privilege in the entire film—most Valids will never have cause to consider the circumstances of their birth, while In-Valids will spend their lives thinking of nothing else. Jerome is the rare trespasser who moves in the direction opposite Vincent. Valids simply cannot fathom living the In-Valid life. Death is preferred to abdicating privilege.

The prohibition on extremes in the Valid emotional spectrum makes it impossible for the police to suspect any Valids of the murder of the Gattaca director, the man who threatened to cancel Vincent's mission to Titan. Once Vincent's eyelash identifies him, and confirms him both an In-Valid and in the vicinity of the crime scene, Detective Hugo (Alan Arkin) pursues Vincent with the fervor of a starved dog, certain only an In-Valid could be capable of such anger and violence. The other detective doesn't think Vincent did it. He wants to find who had the strongest motive to commit the crime. But Hugo, relentless, screens every Valid at Gattaca, sure the guilty In-Valid (Vincent) is in their midst.

We can't tell if Hugo is a Valid or an In-Valid. His relationship to the other detective is mostly deferential, as though the obviously-Valid younger detective supervises Hugo. Hugo himself looks shabby enough to pass convincingly for In-Valid. His rumpled clothes fit him poorly, and tufts of hair poke out from beneath his hat. His gruff demeanor, unlike the restrained even keel of the Valids around him, further implies Hugo's status. It makes sense that police would recruit In-Valids as part of their work. Empowering oppressed people to become agents of the very state that keeps them oppressed seems like a form of enlightenment, but instead turns those In-Valids into traitors to their class.

We learn about halfway through the search that Hugo's boss is Anton, Vincent's brother, and we believe that's why he won't pursue Vincent as a viable suspect. He knows deep down Vincent isn't capable of violence of this kind, that Vincent wouldn't have done all the work to con his way into Gattaca only to blow it by murdering his boss's boss. Even still, he wants to find Vincent. He needs to see Vincent for himself, to believe any of this could be true.

## RESULTS MAY VARY

I didn't see hair regrowth results from finasteride for quite some time.

Initially, it appeared my hair was falling out even faster than before, and I experienced other unexpected physical changes. The increase in my level of circulating testosterone meant I saw subtle improvement to my ability to build muscle mass throughout my body. With less money to entertain myself and no one at home to distract me, I had so much more free time to fill on my own. Along with writing, I did the only other thing that felt meaningful: I worked out six days a week, a combination of morning weightlifting, evening yoga, and a Sunday ballet class that kicked my ass. Visiting the gym like this suited the post-break up heartbroken person I'd become. The routine added several new days and types of workout to what I had been doing. In return, my body changed faster than I'd ever seen it respond to exercise in my life. By the fall of 2015, I had a six-pack of abs. The limited amount of hair I had on my body faded away as well, leaving my arms and legs smoother than ever.

Since finasteride meddles with one of the male body's sex hormones, it can have some undesired effects. In worst cases, it causes erectile dysfunction and a loss of interest in sex entirely. Many websites peddling the drugs assure potential users how rare these occurrences are, close to just 2% of cases. And while the effects can be permanent, many men who experience these effects find they go away when they stop taking the drug. After a few months on the drug, I noticed a sloughing away of my sex drive. It had always been high for me. So high in fact that I sometimes pursued hook ups through apps too desperately. I felt trapped between feeding my physical needs and the emotional needs I felt in the wake of the breakup.

A reduction in sex drive didn't seem like a bad thing. It felt like a refocusing of my energy and attention. Sex fell several rungs down the ladder of my life priorities, and I became more interested in other things. I read and wrote. I still went on dates, sure, but how those dates ended became less of a concern for me. I also came less when I did have sex, and it changed from appearing bright white to mostly clear.

When I revealed to a few of those dates that I was taking finasteride, they asked me, "Does your dick still work?" I went out with a man who told me he was also taking finasteride. He wore his hair in a style that masked the recession of his hair line, sweeping long bangs over his forehead and to the other side of his scalp; the effect was only a little convincing.

Like many men who lose their hair, he was hairy all over his body. In fact, he was the hairiest person I have ever seen, the hair on his chest so thick it was almost a kind of sweater. I mentioned I'd been taking the pills but wasn't seeing results. "It takes about a year," he told me. He explained hair grows on a cycle and that it would likely take that long for most or all of the hair to finish the current cycle, that I'd start to see effects as each follicle started over. He also mentioned the drug ebbed away at his sex drive. "I used to jerk off six to eight times a day," he said, as casual as can be. I think my jaw hit the floor. "Now I'm down to more like three to six."

I loved sex. I'd spent nearly my entire adulthood, though, in monogamous relationships, so I hadn't experienced much of hook-up and app culture until I lived in Los Angeles. I thought hooking up would be a good antidote to the loneliness and hurt I felt from the breakup, and sometimes it was. And sometimes it brought more emotional entanglement than I could handle. I ended up hurting some good men in the process. It's hard to date someone who's dead inside. It was hard to date me.

## NATURE V. NURTURE

Driving home after a date, Vincent and Irene encounter a mandatory traffic stop related to the search for the Gattaca killer. Vincent leans over the side of her convertible and, in a smooth motion, plucks two contacts from his eyes—the ones that help him pass as Jerome in real life. They make it through the checkpoint due to the society's overreliance on genetic data in lieu of firsthand observation. Later, Irene parks on the side of a busy road, running across it between cars, wanting to show Vincent a place that is special to her. We see the road through Vincent's eyes: blurred headlights whiz by at frantic speeds. He has to follow her or risk being found out. He may also die trying.

But he makes it, and they watch the sun rise. He has beaten the odds—repeatedly. When Irene confesses to Vincent she had him sequenced to see his genetic makeup, she's ready for his rejection. She offers him a strand of her hair so he can return the favor, but he lets it float away on the wind. "I can save you the trouble," she says, disclosing her own heart issue.

Vincent understands this vulnerability. "They've got you working so hard to find any flaw that, after a while, that's all you see."

## PROGRESS, NOT PERFECTION

Some weeks later, my ex-boyfriend's new ex-boyfriend, Nick, reached out to me via Facebook message. I didn't know who he was at first, having never heard his name mentioned. Just that my ex, four months after our breakup, had gotten engaged. The news cut through me like a spike. At the same time, I felt suddenly freed. Every lingering connection I felt to my ex and that relationship released and vanished like the tubes plugged into Neo's real-body skin in *The Matrix*. Despite everything I had been through, I somehow felt like I was the failure, the unlovable one, the damaged goods. The engagement seemed to confirm it.

Nick's message said something like, "Hey, you don't owe me anything, but did you think your ex was abusive?" I wanted to tell him to fuck off, and I almost typed it out. But I didn't. I took a breath. The anger snuffed out.

Nick and I talked it through. Somehow we offered each other the support we each needed to make sense of what had happened to us. We agreed to meet for coffee, where we traded stories and compared wounds. Nick's break-up with my ex was as terrible as—maybe worse than—mine. The end for them came when our ex got drunk at a wedding and started antagonizing Nick. When Nick retreated to the hotel room to escape his laser-sharp attention, our ex pounded on the door and shouted obscenities for so long he had to be dragged away by security.

Disentangling their shared life was an ongoing process for Nick. Nick moved out of their apartment. But once he was settled, Nick noticed our ex left himself logged into Facebook on one of Nick's devices. Nick found an interaction between our ex and finasteride guy—as if we didn't all live in a city of more than four million people. The two of them worked in the same industry. Our ex was trying to find work to cure his chronic unemployment; finasteride guy was offering to help. But first, they talked about me.

Encountering the private conversations two people have about me is not high on my list of life priorities. I'm happier not knowing. But Nick offered to share them with me, and out of a morbid sense of curiosity, I agreed to look. Finasteride guy made fun of a pair of very short shorts I wore to a retro roller skating night I'd gone to with some friends—they'd made him jealous, I guess?—and my ex was like, "Yeah lol." Finasteride guy continued with his takedown and I won't forget the summary he offered: "So we agree: he's a fat, bald, middle-aged man who wears short shorts." This is not how I'd prefer to self identify, but if someone sought to catalog my flaws, these are the most obvious.

It was the balding part that hurt me most. I can't change my age and I'll never apologize for wearing short shorts. My ex complained about my hair when we were together. He kept telling me to give up and shave my head because I was embarrassing him. He'd say it to me privately at home and in front of our friends when we were out. I suppose that was really how the insecurity took root. I suppose that was why, after our break up, I sought out finasteride.

And that was why, eventually, my hair grew back.

The most significant results I saw were in the front, where my hair filled in all the thinning areas so much so that it grew as thick as the hair on the sides and back of my head. Lizzy, the stylist who'd been cutting my hair, even commented on it. I'd been seeing her for a little over a year, since I moved to Mount Washington and then after I'd settled into a permanent roost in East Hollywood. Because the crown wasn't filling in quite as fast, I kept the style short, envying the luscious undercuts and long swooping bangs of the men in Silverlake, Echo Park, and Los Feliz. But I was making progress. I was finally getting somewhere.

## UNDERDOG

Vincent knows he'll never measure up genetically to the people at Gattaca, to Jerome, to Irene, even to his brother Anton.

The director's murderer is revealed to be a Valid, Director Josef (Gore Vidal). The hunt for the real Vincent ends. Anton confronts Vincent about his masquerade. It's clear even Anton doesn't believe Vincent is capable of what he's trying to do, despite everything Vincent has already achieved. They fall into a childhood pattern, daring each other to swim out into the ocean as far as they can; the first one to turn back is a chicken.

They strip down and dive in. They call to each other as they crawl through the water. "How did you do it?" Anton wants to know.

Vincent is honest. "I never saved anything for the swim back."

Anton founders and slips under the waves, but Vincent pulls him back up, swims him to shore. The weaker rescuing the strong. Vincent has fulfilled the promise of his name: he's defeated his genetically perfect brother. He's beaten the system that would hold him back for even the likelihood of a physical defect. And he's about to go into space for a yearlong mission, his life's dream.

But he doesn't get to do any of these things as himself. He'll remain Jerome Morrow, at least virtually, until the day he dies.

## ASK YOUR DOCTOR IF FINASTERIDE IS RIGHT FOR YOU

I still take finasteride. If I stop, my hair will fall out at will, and eventually I'll look like all the other men in my family. I would love to understand better why I want my hair to stay where it is. It's not vanity, necessarily. I find bald men and men with shaved heads attractive. I also look enviously at men with full, thick heads of hair they can style however they want.

But I do feel better. I feel like *me*. In these past few years, that, above all else, has been the most important thing to give myself.

In the story of Samson, a man is imbued with strength by God, as long as he never cuts his hair or shaves his beard. He tears apart a lion with his bare hands and defeats an army of 1,000 men using only the jawbone of a donkey for a weapon. I understand that. Having hair does make me feel more powerful than I felt when mine was noticeably thinning. Samson makes poor choices in love, though. He falls for a double agent, a woman sent to seduce him and rob him of his great strength. You know her name. Delilah discovers the source of his strength and removes it, betraying her lover by cutting his hair and turning him over to his enemies in this weakened state.

I would love to be the kind of man who can embrace this change openly—the kind of man who can shave his head. But I'm not there yet. And thanks to science, I don't have to be.

It seems such a trivial thing, hair.

But I know that I feel like the best version of myself when I have it. Even if it forces me to become a person my DNA never meant me to be.

# ACTION/ADVENTURE

## MAY THE ODDS BE EVER IN YOUR FAVOR

Just past the Double Tree's grand ballroom, flanked by a horseshoe of vendor tables, a folding table in the hallway presented a comically small sign with the *Jeopardy!* logo on it. Below the Art Nouveau-inspired font, I read instructions in small type telling auditioners to fill in some forms and wait.

I leaned against a wall for a while, watching the other hopefuls wander in. The hotel's brass and beige glamour reeked of the 1980s. Fluffy couches provided seating, but I was too wired with nervous energy to sit. Other people—my competition—arrived, glanced at the sign, took a form, and spread out around the hallway alcove. We kept wide space between us. We regarded each other like feral cats whose territory was under threat.

It was 8 am on a Friday in October, still summertime in Los Angeles. The forecast promised a hot and hazy day reaching 90 degrees. Even this early, the sun blazed through the plate glass windows at the far end of the hallway, flooding an open reception space with light and heat. Air conditioning whispered from vents over my head, doing little to stem the rising temperature around us.

At precisely nine o'clock, four people burst from a meeting room into the hallway. The energy level went from 0 to 60 in fewer than three seconds. A tall blond man clapped his hands and rubbed them together. He welcomed us and asked us to line up by the wall in a series of quick barks. We'd be going into the room shortly. But first they would take a photo with a Fuji Instax camera. I ended up near the front of the line, smiled at the camera—wondering as I did if I *should* be smiling—and then walked into the room.

Rows of tables jutted out from the walls, draped with cloths to look a little fancier than they were. The *Jeopardy!* logo lit up a projection screen hanging from the ceiling. It looked like the meeting room for any kind of motivational seminar. I took a seat somewhere in the center of the room, not wanting to be too close or too far away from whatever was going to happen.

There were about twenty auditioners in all, ranging in age from eighteen to around fifty. Everyone was white. Most folks seemed to be on the precipice of middle age, making me one of the older people in the room. The staff introduced themselves: Bryan, the tall blond; Melinda, with big round glasses that made her look a little like Annie Potts in *Ghostbusters*; Corrine, a little wisp with a lot of enthusiasm; and Tammy, with a loud, raspy laugh.

We went around the room, introducing ourselves with "big energy," the kind of thing that would translate on television. Almost every potential contestant in that room was the kind of person who did *not* like to bring big energy to anything, especially an introduction. Imagine grown-up versions of your high school's chess club and you'll have a sense of the majority of my fellow hopefuls. There was a freshman student from Chapman University, a theater executive director from San Diego, the associate dean of a university honors college, a homemaker from Texas. Most folks lived in the Southland, although a few had driven out from Phoenix to be there.

We got a brief overview of how *Jeopardy!* works. Then we launched into a 50-question written test. A game clue, just like on the TV show, flashed on the screen. We wrote down our response (not yet in the form of a question) on an answer sheet. For the most part, I felt confident. There was one clue I had to guess. Another I blanked on until seconds before I had to turn the paper in, scribbling in the name of a writer-actor who'd had remarkable success in the last decade.

We took a short break. I tried to strike up a conversation with the folks around me—the Chapman student, the theater guy—but talk quickly petered out. I grabbed another water and listened to a group of folks talk to each other in the back of the room until the break ended.

That's when the practice rounds began. First, we did a group raise-your-hand game of answering easy clues, practicing answering in the form of a question. No one raised a hand for the last one, which sought the name of the original street in Los Angeles where the city was founded. I raised my hand. "Olvera Street," I said. I had the hometown advantage.

Groups of three went to the front of the room and took *Jeopardy!* buzzers from Corrine and Melinda. Melinda was running this part of the day. "I'm going to interview you like Alex," she explained, and then flipped through our audition paperwork, asking us about things we'd written down on our questionnaires. We had to say everything "loud" and "with energy." Anytime I spoke, Tammy, at the back of the room, shouted, "Louder, Charlie!" By the end, I, too, was shouting.

Playing the game was fun. Of course, we were only standing in a little conference room in a Double Tree on an industrial street in Culver City, and not playing for actual cash on an iconic set on the Sony lot.

I looked around the room. Only 400 potential contestants from the auditions held across the country would be invited to play. I wondered who among us would be chosen.

## I BELIEVE THAT CHILDREN ARE OUR FUTURE

All the children of District 12 walk to the square, where their names wait on scraps of paper in two bowls, separated by gender. This is the Reaping, the annual selection of tributes for the nation of Panem in *The Hunger Games*. The chances of any one person being drawn are slim, but, for two unlucky children, that chance will be 100%. Effie Trinket (Elizabeth Banks), the District 12 Hunger Games coach, appears. Her clothing and makeup look like a gauche mash up of Restoration France and Imperial Japan.

To viewers, the look and feel of District 12 will conjure up images of Appalachia. This district's industry is coal mining, providing essential fuel for other districts' industries and to the Capital, which produces nothing but consumes the fruits of each district. It feels as though an economic and emotional depression have taken root in District 12. The colors in the clothing, mostly blues, are all washed out.

Unlike Effie, Katniss (Jennifer Lawrence) and her younger sister Primrose (Willow Shields), wear modest and traditional braids. Their plainness feels like a kind of religion, though their poverty is inflicted upon them by the political forces of the nation. Like coal miners themselves, exploited by an industry notorious for endangering the lives of its labor without compensating them for the risks they face, the residents of District 12 occupy an isolation that has settled into their bones. They are the last district. They are the most remote district. They are the poorest district. All they have is themselves.

Effie draws one name each from two huge fishbowls. Each child under eighteen has at least one card with their name on it. Those whose families have bartered with the Capitol for more essential resources, like grains, have an additional card for each shipment received. In Panem, the cost of life is life. The first name Effie draws is Peeta Mellark (Josh Hutcherson), the child of the District's bakers. He joins her on her platform in front of his community. Effie reaches into the girls' bowl and pulls out a familiar name: Primrose Everdeen. Prim, barely twelve years old, panics. Katniss panics. Prim would never survive the blood bath of the Hunger Games, and sending her to them would ensure her death. Before she knows what she's doing, Katniss volunteers to take her sister's place.

The name of this event, The Reaping, implies both "reaping what you sow"—harvesting ripened plants, for instance—and resonates with the specter of "reaper," as in "grim": the harvester of souls. In this case, the children themselves are the bounty, their souls a currency.

## I VOLUNTEER AS TRIBUTE

At every step in the audition process, *Jeopardy!*'s staff say, "We'll call you any time in the next eighteen months" to participate in the next step of the process. This is what the online test tells you after you complete it, and this is what they said at the in-person audition in Culver City.

I got the call three weeks later. Alan, a contestant coordinator, ran down all the information I needed to know about competing on the show. Each tape day consisted of five games of *Jeopardy!*, played back-to-back with a lunch break in between. Contestants were advised to bring multiple changes of clothing to sustain the illusion each game was played on a different day, the way it would be televised. Alan emailed me a big packet of information I needed to complete before coming in. I'd have about two weeks to prepare. Because I was an LA local, I was one of two "alternates" they called in for my tape day. One alternate was sure to play in the final game of the day, while the other was the insurance policy they could run all five games, even if a player or two didn't make it to the studio because of travel issues or illness. At the end of the day, they'd flip a coin for the last game to determine which of the alternates would play. The other would be sent home.

I had no idea how to prepare. For a few nights each week, I binged the episodes available on Hulu and Netflix, trying to connect with the pacing of the game, the structure of the clues. Most *Jeopardy!* clues contain at least three significant suggestions of their answer: the category name, which limits the correct options; the straightforward request for information, which further delineates the number of possible responses; and, finally, the clue's use of adjectives and descriptors. The correct question becomes a kind of triangulation of these elements. If you know what both the clue and descriptors point to, you know the question. If you know one of the two, you can probably make a guess in the right direction based on category. And so playing *Jeopardy!*, in part, becomes a kind of gamble.

## TEACH THEM WELL AND LET THEM LEAD THE WAY

After days of training, Capitol Gamemaker Seneca Crane (Wes Bently) and his staff—all men—assess each tribute and assign them a numerical score indicating how lethal each tribute will be to the others. Katniss is last to go. She picks up the bow and arrow provided but—uncharacteristic of her—misses her shot at the mannequin. The men laugh, chalk it up to District 12's lack of skills. They see her as a poor country bumpkin, not a killer. She tries again, this time piercing the bull's eye on the mannequin. But no one's watching her. They're lost in their own conversations, marveling at a plattered pig. It pisses Katniss off. She takes aim at the group of men and when she lets her arrow go, it strikes the apple crammed in the pig's mouth in a fleshy burst, startling the men. "Thank you for your consideration," she says, her voice saturated with smarm, as she bows to them.

The gamble works. Katniss is given one of the highest scores. But it also makes her a target. The kids in their late teens, volunteers from Districts 1 and 2, will try to eliminate her first. The film refers to this group as the "career tributes." They've been training to compete in the games since early childhood. It's a way of gaming the system. Any Hunger Games not won by a career tribute is considered a historic upset. Peeta, too, seems embarrassed at being bested by Katniss. She chalks this up to Fragile Male Ego Syndrome and just wants to ignore him. But Peeta realizes just how mortal he is compared to Katniss. He has no real skills beyond camouflaging himself with makeup application, a talent gendered culturally to women.

This reinforces the existing gender dynamics between Katniss and Peeta and—well, Katniss and everyone else. Peeta is the One to Be Rescued—a damsel in distress—while Katniss is the hunter (provider), the guardian (warrior), and the desired (hero). She is mother and father to her own sister. Both Gale (Liam Hemsworth), her District 12 sort-of boyfriend-slash-best friend, and Peeta wait to be chosen by her, to let them love her.

She echoes the myth of Adonis, the storied hunter pursued blindly by Venus. Though Venus was the ravishing goddess of love, Adonis couldn't be distracted from his true passion—the hunt. This is what ultimately kills him. The Hunger Games is the hunt that promises to eliminate Katniss even as she tries to vanish into her elements: the wilderness, the use of a bow and arrow, her protection of Peeta and District 11 tribute Rue (Amandla Stenberg).

## HOPE IS THE ONLY THING STRONGER THAN FEAR

By the time I got to the studio on tape day, all the other contestants had arrived and were completing their intake paperwork. The energy in the room was electric. The other folks were nervous, excited, uncertain. They ranged in age from maybe their late-20s to mid-60s, with most folks landing on the younger end. There were slightly more women than men. Melinda had us go around the table to confirm our biographical details, which would be read by iconic announcer Johnny Gilbert when our episodes began.

I got my turn in the make-up chair last, since I wouldn't be playing until the end of the day, if at all. The artist asked me my name, then wrote it in eyeliner pencil on a blending sponge in case I'd need touch ups later in the day. "I'm going to make you look handsome," she said, regarding me with brush in hand, then second guessed herself and added, "I mean, you already are." I wasn't going to turn down the help.

The contestants moved out onto the set. It's smaller than it looks on TV, but everything is lacquered and shiny and glowing with lights. It felt big. The studio audience held maybe 100 people, including the contestants waiting to play. Tammy filed us into the audience to sit down while Melinda and Corrine corralled three players and three on-deck players to do some practice rounds with Jimmy McGuire, a member of the *Jeopardy!* "Clue Crew" you often used to see in video clues, serving in the host's role. The practice rounds had easier clues and categories, but the experience was helpful. Timing is a key element of playing the game. As soon as Jimmy finished reading a clue, columns of lights on either side of the game board—visible to folks in the studio but not those watching at home—flashed to indicate we could buzz in. If we buzzed in too early, we'd be locked out for a quarter of a second. Not only do you need to know the correct question, you have to beat out the other players with the buzzer, but not buzz in so fast that you beat the lights. It takes some practice.

Everything about *Jeopardy!* is randomized and selected by blind draw. The game boards played within each game and the order they appear. The challengers. The podium they each occupy during the game. There are strict laws about these elements, many of which stemmed from the game show scandals of the 1960s. *Jeopardy!* was transparent with us about these randomizing tactics, explaining at each step what was happening.

When we'd had our chance to practice, the staff rushed us back toward the green room. We saw our friends and family lined up, waiting to be seated, for a brief second. In the room, the first two challengers were drawn to face returning champion Jonathan. A frenzy of activity—last make up touch ups, restroom breaks—and then we filed back into the studio. The games were about to begin.

## SHOW THEM ALL THE BEAUTY THEY POSSESS INSIDE

Katniss rides a platform into a field encircled by woods. She and the other tributes surround a "cornucopia," where the game's weapons and supplies have been stockpiled, daring the tributes to rush there. Haymitch (Woody Harrelson), Katniss's mentor, calls this the lure of certain death, but Katniss sees a bow, a quiver, and knows it is her best chance to survive.

A clock counts down, each tick a resounding thud, until the beats give way to the shrill whine of a stringed instrument on the soundtrack. The tributes scatter. The film's sound effects vanish, replaced only by the urgency of its deconstructed music, tense and dissonant. As Haymitch promised, a blood bath ensues. It's horrific to watch these children eviscerate each other in near-silence, divorcing us from their pain. Katniss grabs a backpack of supplies, then runs into the woods to find camouflage and shelter.

She collides with another tribute, a girl she'll think of only as Foxface (Jacquelyn Emerson), and they tumble to the ground. We'll see Foxface over the course of the film. Like Katniss, she's a clever survivalist. She outsmarts the career tributes' hoarding of supplies and weapons, which they circle with buried landmines. Katniss, evaluating how best to eliminate these resources, watches Foxface traipse through the mines to steal some food, then leap and twist out with the grace of a professional dancer. In the moments after the Games begin, though, neither wants to fight. They seem to see this in each other and run off in opposite directions.

Katniss finds refuge in a tree. She evaluates the supplies in the backpack (a canteen, bungee cord, wire, a thermal sheet), then seeks fresh water using her tracking skills, hunts and cooks a squirrel, and retreats back into the tree, tying her body in place with the bungee.

## MAKE SURE THEY REMEMBER YOU

Rounds of *Jeopardy!* went fast. Even sitting in the audience waiting to play, it felt electric. Clues flew by as fast as we could think about them. Players buzzed in. Game board dollar amounts vanished into blank blue screens.

Between rounds, production took breaks for the "commercial." Tammy dashed up to the players with bottles of water, each cap numbered with their player position (1, 2, or 3). Alex popped off his stool behind the podium and sauntered toward the audience, encouraging them to ask him questions about the game, himself— whatever they wanted to know. If the question was even a skosh off the topic of the game, he responded either with a groanable dad joke or some kind of witty barb, which he seemed to possess in equal measure.

Jonathan lost in the first game to Canadian Zorn, who lost in the next round to Jessica from Texas. In the audience, conversation was quiet, a little uneasy. There was a sense we were just waiting for our own chance to be killed on live television by some more powerful intellect. I sat next to Evan, a comedy writer from Georgia, who whispered the answer to each clue. He was trying to get into the rhythm of play, and maybe boost his own confidence. After Jessica's first win, Melinda called the next two contestants to face her: Siobhan, an attorney from Little Rock, and Evan. He took a breath and went to the dressing room to prepare. As contestants played and lost, they were invited to remain in the audience, sitting with their loved ones, in the opposite aisle from the remaining potential champions. Our side of the aisle thinned as the games ended.

David, a retired mixed martial arts athlete who'd previously appeared on *Who Wants to Be a Millionaire*, moved into the seat next to me. He was average height but had a thick build under his suit, tattoos peeking out at his wrists and on his hands. I imagined he was used to competition, the anxiety of performing before an audience and even on television. But *Jeopardy!* flowed like a raging river compared to the sweet meander of *Millionaire*. This would be more like fighting in the octagon than sitting across from Meredith Viera.

Jessica won her the third game of the day, and everyone— contestants, staff, Alex, and the audience—dispersed for lunch. Bryan walked us across the Sony lot to the commissary. We were cordially invited to eat whatever we wanted—for some, this would be their last meal. The restaurant had the frenzied buzz of a dorm cafeteria. Studio staff swarmed the place, waiting in lines for burgers, salads, sandwiches, and hot entrees-of-the-day. The remaining potential contestants— Anneke, Dave, Sarah, Jocelyn, champion Jessica, and me—sat together in two cautious groups. I congratulated Jessica on her run and asked her what it was like to play. "It goes fast," she said. We talked about some specific clues she answered. Jocelyn's anxiety about playing was visible. She knew she'd be up in the next few games. Of those remaining, only Sarah and I weren't sure which of us would play that day. It was up to the luck of the draw.

Back in the studio, with a new audience watching the taping, Anneke and Dave were drawn for the fourth game. Despite his calm demeanor, Dave didn't do well. He ended up digging himself into a hole he couldn't get out of. By the end of Double Jeopardy, he was in the negative and couldn't participate in the final round. After a slow start in the first round, Anneke dominated Double Jeopardy She beat out Jessica in Final Jeopardy by one dollar, becoming the new champ.

Jocelyn practically gnawed off her own hand in the audience. She knew she was up, and she'd had all day to marinate in her nerves. Melinda drew one of two index cards. It had Sarah's name on it. I wouldn't be playing that day. I was relieved and disappointed, and unsure what it meant for my future on the show. The three women were strong competitors. The game was a nailbiter. First Jocelyn was up, then Sarah pulled back in, and finally Anneke surged ahead. It was thrilling and exciting to watch. The Final Jeopardy clue stumped all three of them, though, and Anneke, with a cautious wager, remained the champ.

I watched alone from my side of the aisle, the last potential challenger remaining.

When the game ended, I met Corrine at the base of the stage. "We love you," she said, pulling me into a hug. "You'll definitely be back. We'll call you."

This was the final tape day for the week, and the week after was Thanksgiving. They wouldn't tape again until the Tuesday after that. I asked Corrine if that's when I should plan to come back in. "Oh, no," she said. "It could be anytime in the next eighteen months."

I'd have time to study. To look at maps of continents whose nations and borders had evolved since I'd last been in a classroom. To brush up on some trivia. To watch more rounds of the game on TV and practice.

## GIVE THEM A SENSE OF PRIDE TO MAKE IT EASIER

*The Hunger Games* makes some bold but realistic assumptions about the unifying nature of class identity. Marvel (Jack Quaid) and Glimmer (Leven Rambin) from District 1, have names honoring the kinds of luxury goods produced there for the Capital. Cato (Alexander Ludwig), named for a Roman soldier, and Clove (Isabelle Fuhrman), referring to a cleaving weapon, are from District 2, where masonry and military strength are centered. As Districts geographically close to the Capital, they align most with its consumerist ideologies, representing both capitalist excess and the military-industrial complex. Districts 11 and 12, which Rue and Katniss call home, are the most impoverished, and their labor centers—agriculture and mining—represent more dangerous and less economically developed industries than the other districts do. They don't receive dedicated training for the Hunger Games like career tributes do. The children from the poorer districts already have "careers." They labor alongside their parents to keep their families alive.

The tributes from Districts 1 and 2 are the predators, and everyone else in the game is their prey. Katniss hears them approach. They make no effort to be quiet because they're not afraid. But Katniss isn't ready for what she sees next: Peeta traveling with them. They chase her into a tree. Cato tries to climb up after her, but he's heavier, clumsier. He didn't grow up in a forest and doesn't know how to use a tree's natural shapes to support his path up. Glimmer shoots a half-hearted arrow toward her, but Katniss dodges it. Even Cato's attempt with the bow flies right by her. Peeta suggests they sit and wait, that eventually Katniss will need to come out of the tree or starve to death as a result.

Peeta's not a rich kid from an inner district. He's worked in his parents' bakery since he was a child. He hasn't known the lure of luxury and excess the way the others have, nor was he trained from childhood to win the Hunger Games for his district. His only benefit to them is locating Katniss and potentially drawing her into a trap. Then his utility to the rich kids will expire. They'll kill him too. Katniss thinks Peeta's only prolonging the inevitable and losing his best chance of survival: staying hidden.

## THEY HAVE TO HAVE THEIR VICTOR

Tammy called the following Monday. "Charlie, can you come in tomorrow? One of our contestants can't travel due to a blizzard."

My heart buzzed. "Uh," I said, clicking around to look at my calendar, which I knew was empty. I'd held the date in case I played on the last tape day and ended up being a returning champion. "Uh... yes," I said, knowing my family wouldn't be able to come on such short notice, that I'd probably not have anyone in the audience watching.

So I went back. This time I arrived just as the busload of contestants from the hotel pulled in, all the new chickens clucking nervously as they pulled their garment bags of hope and their suitcases from the back of the van.

I saw Anneke, the champion from the previous tape day, among them. I walked over to say hi and we gave each other a quick hug. "It's good to see a familiar face this time," I said. Because we'd been through the whole shebang before, Anneke and I took a seat together on the couch in the green room while the other players went through their paces. We talked about our Thanksgiving holidays, about the games we'd seen and that she'd played last time we were here, the contestants we enjoyed meeting, other general pleasantries. I found myself liking her—my enemy.

Tammy, Bryan, Corrine, and Melinda made me feel welcome. I believed they believed I had a chance to win—but of course, the individual outcomes likely didn't mean as much to them as the stories that came out of winners like Ken Jennings and James Holzhauer. Still, I admired the way they kept each of the contestants calm and optimistic through the warmth, humor, and encouragement they offered us. Melinda and I reviewed which stories Alex might ask me about during the brief interview segment. It came down to two options: how I started writing poetry or a celebrity encounter that meant a lot to me. She asked which I preferred. "Seeing Kristen Bell at a stoplight," I told her.

She swiped over that note with a highlighter. "Ok, just remember Alex is going to ask you about whatever he wants, but probably this." She moved on to the next contestant.

After the training talks and rehearsal with Jimmy, we all dashed back to the green room in a frenzy. I'd been told on stage to change out of my shirt, which had a very subtle pattern on it that wouldn't look good on camera. I ducked right into the "Jeopardy Champion Dressing Room" to swap it out for another in my bag. I thought, with some concern, that it left me only one other shirt in case I won my game.

"The first two players are…" Melinda called to the room, pausing for dramatic effect as she opened up the index cards. "Suzy! And…" Another pause. "Charlie!"

As if on cue, I popped my head out the door of the dressing room. "I'm ready!"

We had one last check with make-up and then we were on the stage. The game was about to begin.

## LET THE CHILDREN'S LAUGHTER REMIND US
## HOW WE USED TO BE

Rue and Thresh (Dayo Okeniyi) are the only Black tributes in the 74th Hunger Games. Though they live in relative freedom in their district, the Capital forces them, like District 12, to remain in an abject poverty. They work themselves to death merely to keep surviving.

Katniss knocks a deadly tracker jacker nest from the tree to escape the tributes waiting for her at its base, getting herself stung in the process. Rue nurses Katniss back to health, then applies leaves to her skin to camouflage her from other tributes while Rue hides nearby. When she's recovered, Katniss hunts food for them. They talk. These are some of the calmest scenes in the film. We know these two children will not attempt to kill one another. They plot to blow up the careers' stockpile of food and weapons, which they've surrounded with landmines. This single act is a metaphor for Katniss's entire character arc over the course of the film series. She knows cutting off resources from the Capitol will put its isolation and superiority to an end. And once power is no longer isolated, it becomes dynamic, scattered, messy, and seizable.

Marvel—tasked with guarding the now-destroyed resources—runs into the woods to find out what happened. He runs Rue through with a spear. Katniss, in pure reflex, pierces him with an arrow. This is the only murder she commits that isn't done out of mercy. It's revenge. In order for Katniss to remain sympathetic to the audience, she cannot commit to winning the games. She can only commit to her own survival, and the protection of those she deems innocent enough to save. Rue was one of these people. The other is Peeta.

The film never addresses the gulf of privilege between Katniss and Rue. While their emotional connection appears genuine, the death of the only girl of color in the entire film is a troubling plot device. It's a narrative practice known as "fridging," a term tracing its roots back to comic book storytelling. A villain kills a female character and stuffs her body in a refrigerator for the hero to find, torturing him through his failure to save her. In *The Hunger Games*, Rue's death operates as virtue signal that identifies Katniss as "good." Katniss honors Rue by surrounding her body with flowers. The act becomes character development for Katniss, underscoring her deep well of feeling and heroism. In response, the residents of District 11 salute Katniss rather than honoring Rue. Her death does more to make Katniss sympathetic than it does to make the audience mourn Katniss's most important partner in the games.

We see Thresh only a few times in the arena: once at the cornucopia during the bloodbath when he escapes carrying a scimitar, and then near the end when Katniss comes face to face with Clove again. Thresh saves Katniss. He tells her it's because of her relationship with Rue. He runs off. We only see him once more, when he's attacked and killed by muttations, giant dog-like creatures designed to kill all but the final player, bringing the games to a quick and decisive conclusion. His death, as unceremonious as Rue's, occurs after he saves the white girl.

## EVERYONE LIKES AN UNDERDOG

I wrote my name on the center podium screen. The lacquered stage looked wet under the stage lights, the game board rising like an ancient tablet across the room from us. To the left of it, just above the cameras, hung three digital screens, our way of seeing what our dollar amounts were—and what our opponents had—during the game.

The *Jeopardy!* theme played in the studio. Shortly after the familiar strings fired up, we heard Johnny's booming voice speak the iconic phrase, "*This...is...Jeopardy!*" He ran through our brief introductions. Then Alex read off the categories as each one flashed on the screen: "Exotic Wildlife." "Olympians." "Connectiquette."

"T…Y." "Windmills." "Found in Translation." These were not my dream categories. But I was hoping the clues themselves would tip me off.

Play moved quickly. Buzzing in was hard; I had to find the right rhythm. Lights come on, press the button. I knew a lot of the right questions, but I didn't buzz in unless I was sure I was right. At the same time, there were a bunch of things I didn't know. I played it safe. Wrong answers would deduct hard-earned money from my score. I knew I couldn't risk any slippage against Anneke. I found the Daily Double in the "Connectiquette" category, wagered $1,000, and wildly guessed it right.

At the first commercial break, I was in the lead with $2,800. Tammy approached us with our water bottles, using soft comforting tones. Alex popped off his stool to take audience questions during the break. When filming resumed, Alex appeared next to Suzy's podium to interview her about her career as a social worker. He moved on to me. He mentioned that I started writing poetry as a teenager, then asked, "What's become of that?"

My brain rattled, unprepared for this change of subject and even of discussion. I was ready to talk about the morning I pulled up to a stoplight in downtown Los Angeles and saw Kristen Bell in a puffy vest standing next to my car window while filming *House of Lies*. "Well, I have a career as a poet," I said. I don't remember everything that tumbled out of my mouth, but it felt haphazard and I know it included me acknowledging that being a poet "pays zero dollars."

Alex slid down to Anneke. "She is working on writing, not poetry, but something *more* people can relate to," Alex said. He meant a cookbook, but he also meant she wasn't wasting her time earning zero dollars. Touché.

We resumed game play. The women were formidable opponents, and I strived to buzz in on categories that were not my strong suit. I correctly identified the animal involved in "dressage" because I'd once read a queer YA book about a teen cowboy who learns the refined way of riding. I ended up at the bottom by the end of the Jeopardy round, but all three of us were pretty evenly matched. I felt great. No nerves. It was almost like the practice rounds we'd played that morning. I knew all of the "T…Y" answers, but only managed to sneak in on "toxicity." Oddly, I answered the most clues in the "Connectiquette" category, I state I visited only one time and, to be honest, slept through while riding a bus.

The categories of Double Jeopardy appeared like six horsemen of my personal apocalypse: "Euro Coins." "Terms of Endurement." "The Story of My Life." "In the Cloud." "Dressed Alike." "They Got the Memo." I ended up knowing more clues than I anticipated, but I struggled to buzz in before my opponents or, worse, made the fatal error of buzzing in before the lights appeared. The timing was hard. The lights only flashed on when Alex finished his reading of a clue and were controlled by operators seated a table at the base of the stage. One of the "In the Cloud" clues flashed a photograph of a miniature schnauzer, a dog that had lived in my very home for the past 14 years, asking us to name the breed. I wasn't able to buzz in on time. I felt like I'd betrayed my own child. My proudest moment, though, was identifying which celebrity Aubrey Plaza dressed exactly like at a film premiere. I knew it was an event for the film *Ingrid Goes West*, so the answer was Elizabeth Olsen (queen). Elizabeth later posted a video of clue to her Instagram account but cruelly trimmed off the part where I named her.

I was significantly behind moving into Final Jeopardy. I knew I had to go big or go home, so I wagered everything but $100 of my total, hoping the other two might answer incorrectly. The category was "Familiar Phrases," something I assumed a writer like me wouldn't struggle to identify. I also knew from watching my share of Final Jeopardies that I either had the correct question immediately, or I didn't know it at all. There was no ability to reason with the clue, and the extended time Final Jeopardy offered to panic, second guess, and fumble made it harder than answering clues during the game. The clue asked for a folk term for a chronic rash that gained fame as the title of a play and movie. I jotted down *"Seven Year Itch,"* holding in my mind the image of Marilyn Monroe standing over a subway grate as her skirt blows up around her, an iconic image from American film history if ever there was one. All three of us answered correctly, and Anneke prevailed again, maintaining her championship streak by besting Suzy's score by only $401.

## EVERYBODY'S SEARCHING FOR A HERO

Peeta eventually hides, using his makeup camouflage skills to disappear into the underbrush. Katniss almost trips over him. Peeta reveals the career tributes turned on him early and wounded him. Katniss hides him in a cave while she tries to find a way to heal his wound—a dilemma solved by the generosity of medicine sent via one of her spectator sponsors. As if to foster their tender moments, a voice announces a policy change: the games may have two victors if they come from the same district. That means if Katniss and Peeta survive, they can be the first co-victors in the history of the Hunger Games.

President Snow (Donald Sutherland) meets with Seneca Crane in his rose garden. He explains The Hunger Games have been specifically designed, that the Capital could have rounded up 24 children from each district to execute them each year, to punish those districts for their insurgence. "Do you know why we have a winner? Hope. It's the only thing stronger than fear. A little is effective, a lot of hope is dangerous." Katniss never hears this conversation, but she realizes as she plays the game that the Capital, more than anything, needs its victor.

Peet and Katniss escape the muttations by climing onto the Cornucopia. But they're not safe—Cato is also there. He attacks them, pinning Katniss dangerously close to the edge until Peeta, using the strength he demonstrated in training, tosses Cato off her. In response,

Cato scrambles up and grabs Peeta as a human shield. "Go on! Shoot," Cato yells. "Then we both go down and you win. Go on. I'm dead anyway. I always was, right?" Cato realizes that despite the wealth and luxury he enjoyed in life, he was always just fodder for the cannon. Expendable. Collateral damage that kept everyone else in his district living in privilege. Katniss shoots the arm Cato has around Peeta's throat, making him flinch, lose his grip. Peeta pushes him off into the waiting jaws of the muttations.

Katniss and Peeta remain the only tributes standing. Before they can celebrate, a new announcement: the co-victor rule has been canceled. Only one tribute can remain. Katniss wants them both to survive, but in this moment she realizes it won't be possible. Katniss must kill Peeta, or Peeta must kill Katniss. These are the only outcomes.

This is the death of hope. We watch it die in Katniss's expression when she realizes there is only one feasible outcome. If Katniss were to kill Peeta, she would become as treacherous as the Capital. She would reinforce the system that oppresses her, Peeta, their families, their district, the entire nation. But she also knows the entire nation—including President Snow and the rest of the Capital—is watching her. The Capital thinks her sense of self-preservation will win out over her love for Peeta, over her sense of what is right. And for many other tributes, this may have been the case. But Katniss also has a keen sense that she's been forced the play the game by the Capital's rules, and the only way to break the machine is to break those rules.

She offers Peeta a handful of poisonous berries. They will both die. There will be no victor. For the districts, this means there will be no hope. Before she and Peeta can eat the berries, a harried announcement comes. "Stop!" the voice cries, shaking with nerves. The Capital anoints two victors. Peeta and Katniss have won.

Peeta and Katniss return to District 12, but a revolution begins. Her willingness to disobey sets off resistance in the outlying districts. District 11, distraught over the deaths of Rue and Thresh, rebel. It is the people of color in Panem who throw the first stones, willing to risk their lives for justice and freedom. Just as it has happened in America. People of color fought back against Jim Crow laws and voter suppression to ignite the Civil Rights movement. Trans people of color initiated the acts of resistance at Stonewall. Feminism owes its progress to women of color. There has never been a movement for freedom that didn't hinge on the initiation and participation of communities of color.

## GUESS THE ODDS AREN'T EXACTLY IN MY FAVOR

I couldn't disclose the outcome of the game for weeks after I played, though I was encouraged to tell people I was going to be on the show and invite them to watch. I hosted a party with friends when it aired two months later. So many people who knew me offered support and excitement about my appearance: I felt loved. Even the Internet was fairly kind to me, limiting its mockery of me to *Saturday Night Live* Turd Ferguson (Norm MacDonald as Burt Reynolds) references. I didn't mind the comparisons to Burt one bit.

I got to relive the excitement again when the episode aired a second time in the summer of 2020, during the stay-at-home orders implemented to mitigate the pandemic. In conjunction with the Tournament of Champions, of which Anneke was a part as a five-day winner, they replayed memorable episodes featuring those contestants.

Anneke and I kept in touch after we filmed, mainly through our connected social media accounts. Our conversation the morning of the game made me a fan of hers. I told her this shortly after we played, and in response she said, "You were so nice, I almost felt bad beating you." I loved the sentiment, and I loved the careful inclusion of the word *almost*.

That's what it means to be a victor—to have a heart. But not too much heart.

# CLOSING CREDITS

# ACKNOWLEDGMENTS

I am grateful to the editors of the following publications, in which these essays previously appeared, sometimes in a slightly different form:

*45th Parallel.* "Coming of Age" as "A Crack in the Closet // *Were the World Mine.*"

*American Literary Review.* "Buddy Comedy" as "Get Them to the Niche // *Get Him to the Greek.*"

*Exposition Review.* "Psychological Thriller."

*The Florida Review.* "Sexual Thriller" as "Hot for Teacher // *Fatal Attraction.*"

*Lunch.* "Western" as "Trigger Effect."

*Passages North.* "Suvival Horror."

"A Crack in the Closet // *Were the World Mine*" and "Monsters in the Closet // *Scream*" comprised the chapbook *Cross Cutting*, winner of the 2020 Outwrite Nonfiction Chapbook Award, published in 2020 by Neon Hemlock Press.

Writing a book as weird as this one required a lot of guidance, help, and support. I first and foremost want to thank Andrew Gifford from Santa Fe Writers Project for his enthusiasm for this book. I had the tremendous fortune of being paired with editor Adam al-Sirgany. I cannot express enough how important his comments and suggestions were in making this book what it is today, and his confidence in these essays helped me believe in this weird little book I never thought would see the light of day. Thank you both for giving this work a loving and supportive home.

I also want to thank Tyrese Coleman for choosing *Cross Cutting* for the Outwrite Nonfiction Chapbook Award. Before that recognition, I had no idea if these essays would ever amount to anything, and Tyrese's recognition emboldened me to press on with this project. Big thank you to dave ring, Publisher and Managing Editor of Neon Hemlock Press, for his careful stewardship of the essays and the great design work on that cute little chapbook.

Thank you so much to Annlee Ellingson and Mellinda Hensley, Editors-in-Chief of the *Exposition Review*, who nominated "Psychological Thriller" for the 2022 Best of the Net anthology. Their support for the essay, the most difficult to write and share, will never be forgotten.

During the writing process, I relied on the cheerleading of and feedback from R. J. Gibson, Matthew Hittinger, Fulton Jackson, and my brother Gary Jensen, and my amazing writers group of Tihi Hayslett, Dan López, Dudley Saunders, and Tony Valenzuela, who have steadily helped me become a stronger prose writer and specifically helped me reconfigure the first chapter in this book. I'm grateful especially to Beau Hamilton for giving me his blessing to tell a difficult story he lived with me.

I got helpful input from Gordon Grice, Alison Singh Gee, Shawna Kenney, and workshop classmates at the UCLA Extension Writers' Program, and I'm grateful for the incredible team of folks I have worked with there on the daily, who keep my life rooted in writing and community: Ashley, Bree, Carrie, Chae, Jeff, Jennie, Merrill, Mijoe, Nutschell, and Pascale.

Thank you to Corina Nusu for giving me clearance to write about my appearance on *Jeopardy!*, and to her and the rest of the team there for ensuring all contestants had a wonderful experience on set.

Several incredible professors taught me to read films during my undergraduate years, and their lessons were crucial to crafting this work. Thank you to Laura Czarnecki, Michelle Lekas, John Mowitt, and Rob Silberman in particular for giving me the keys to do this work.

I am so thankful to have Bill Greening as my partner in this life, and for all the ways he supports my writing practice, champions my work, consoles me through disappointments, and shows up every day of our life to remind me that this work is always worth doing.

# FILMOGRAPHY

*Beverly Hills, 90210*. Created by Darren Starr, performances by Jason Priestly, Shannon Doherty, Luke Perry, Tori Spelling, Jennie Garth, Spelling Entertainment, 1990.

*The Birds*. Directed by Alfred Hitchcock, performances by Tippi Hedren, Suzanne Pleshette, Jessica Tandy, Rod Taylor, Universal International Pictures, 1963.

*Black Swan*. Directed by Darren Aronofsky, performances by Natalie Portman, Mila Kunis, Barbara Hershey, Vincent Cassel, Searchlight Pictures, 2010.

*The Bride of Frankenstein*. Directed by James Whale, performances by Boris Korloff, Elsa Lanchester, Colin Clive, Universal Pictures,1935.

*Can't Hardly Wait*. Directed by Deborah Kaplan and Harry Elfont, performances by Ethan Embry, Lauren Ambrose, Seth Green, Jennifer Love Hewitt, Columbia Pictures and Tall Trees Productions, 1998.

*Charlie's Angels*. Created by Ivan Goff and Ben Roberts, performances by Kate Jackson, Farrah Fawcett, Jaclyn Smith, Tanya Roberts, Spelling-Goldberg Productions, 1976.

*Clueless*. Directed by Amy Heckerling, performances by Alicia Silverstone, Stacey Dash, Brittany Murphy, Paul Rudd, Paramount Pictures, 1995.

*Compulsion*. Directed by Richard Fleischer, performances by Orson Welles, Dean Stockwell, E.G. Marshall, Diane Varsi, 20th Century Fox, 1959.

*The Craft*. Directed by Andrew Flemming, performances by Robin Tunney, Fairuza Balk, Neve Campbell, Rachel True, Columbia Pictures, 1996.

*The Descent*. Directed by Neil Marshall, performances by Shauna Macdonald, Natalie Mendoza, Alex Reid, Saskia Mulder, Celador Films and Northmen Productions, 2005.

*Dressed to Kill*. Directed by Brian De Palma, performances by Michael Caine, Angie Dickinson, Nancy Allen, Cinema 77 and Film Group, 1980.

*Educating Rita*. Directed by Lewis Gilbert, performances by Michael Caine, Julie Walters, Acorn Pictures, 1983.

*Extreme Makeover*. Created by Howard Schultz, appearances by William Dorfman, Sam Saboura, Anthony C. Griffin, Lighthearted Entertainment and New Screen Entertainment, 2002.

*Eyes without a Face*. Directed by Georges Franju, perfrmances by Pierre Brasseur, Édith Scob, Alida Valli, Juliette Mayniel, Champs-Élysées Productions and Lux Film, 1960.

*Fargo*. Directed by Joel Coen, performances by Frances McDormand, William H. Macy, Steve Buscemi, Peter Stormare, PolyGram Filmed Entertainment and Working Title Films, 1996.

*Fatal Attraction*. Directed by Adrian Lyne, performances by Michael Douglas, Glenn Close, Anne Archer, Jaffe/Lansing Productions, 1987.

*Freaky Friday*. Directed by Gary Nelson, performances by Jodie Foster, Barbara Harris, John Astin, Dick Van Patten, Walt Disney Productions, 1976.

*The Fresh Prince of Bel-Air*. Created by Andy Borowitz and Susan Borowitz, performances by Will Smith, James Avery, Alfonso Ribiero, Tatyana Ali, NBC Productions and Quincy Jones Entertainment, 1990.

*Gattaca*. Directed by Andrew Niccol, performances by Ethan Hawke, Uma Thurman, Alan Arkin, Jude Law, Columbia Pictures and Jersey Films, 1997.

*Get Him to the Greek.* Directed by Nicholas Stoller, performances by Jonah Hill, Russell Brand, Elisabeth Moss, Rose Byrne, Apatow Productions, Relativity Media, and Spyglass Entertainment, 2010.

*Ghostbusters.* Directed by Ivan Reitman, performances by Dan Ackroyd, Sigourney Weaver, Harold Ramis, Ernie Hudson, Columbia Pictures and Delphi Films, 1984.

*Grey's Anatomy.* Created by Shonda Rhimes, performances by Ellen Pompeo, Chandra Wilson, James Pickens Jr, Justin Chambers, Shondland, Mark Gordon Company, ABC Studios, 2005.

*Heavenly Creatures.* Directed by Peter Jackson, performances by Kate Winslet, Melanie Lynskey, WingNut Films, Fontana Productions, New Zealand Film Commission, 1994.

*A History of Violence.* Directed by David Cronenberg, performances by Viggo Mortensen, Maria Bellow, William Hurt, Ed Harris, BenderSpink, Media I! Filmproduktion, München & Company, 2005.

*House of Lies.* Created by Matthew Carnahan, performances by Don Cheadle, Kristen Bell, Ben Schwartz, Josh Lawson, Cinema Vehicles, Crescendo Productions, Matthew Carnahan Circus Products, 2012.

*The House of Yes.* Directed by Mark Waters, performances by Parker Posey, Josh Hamilton, Tori Spelling, Freddie Prinze Jr, Miramax Films, 1997.

*The Hunger Games.* Directed by Gary Ross, performances by Jennifer Lawrence, Josh Hutcherson, Liam, Elizabeth Banks, Woody Harrelson, Color Force and Lionsgate, 2012.

*Ingrid Goes West.* Directed by Matt Spicer, performances by Aubrey Plaza, Elizabeth Olsen, O'Shea Russel, Wyatt Russell, Star Thrower Entertainment, Mighty Engine, 141 Entertainment, 2017.

*Inside Amy Schumer.* Created by Daniel Powell and Amy Schumer, performances by Amy Schumer, Kevin Kane, Kyle Dunnigan, Kim Caramele, Irony Point, It's So Easy Productions, Jax Media, 2013.

*Jeopardy!* Created by Merv Griffin, performances by Alex Trebek, Johnny Gilbert, Jimmy McGuire, Jeopardy Productions, Merv Griffin Entertainment, Columbia TriStar Television, 1984.

*Jurassic Park.* Directed by Stephen Spielberg, performances by Sam Neill, Laura Dern, Geoff Goldblum, Richard Attenborough, Universal Pictures, Amblin Entertainment, 1993.

*A Kiss Before Dying.* Directed by Gerd Oswald, performances by Robert Wagner, Jeffrey Hunter, Virginia Leith, Joanne Woodward, Crown Productions, 1956.

*M.* Directed by Fritz Lang, performances by Peter Lorre, Otto Wernicke, Gustaf Gründgens, Nero-Film A.G., 1931.

*The Matrix.* Directed by Lana Wachowski and Lilly Wachowski, performances by Keanu Reeves, Laurence Fishburne, Carrie-Anne Moss, Warner Bros, Village Roadshow Pictures, Groucho Film Partnership, 1999.

*Mean Girls.* Directed by Mark Waters, performances by Lindsay Lohan, Rachel McAdams, Lacey Chabert, Amanda Seyfried, Broadway Video, 2004.

*My Fair Lady.* Directed by George Cukor, performances by Audrey Hepburn, Rex Harrison, Stanley Holloway, Wilfrid Hyde-White, Warner Bros, 1964.

*My So-Called Life.* Created by Winnie Holzman, performances by Clare Danes, Bess Armstrong, Wilson Cruz, Jared Leto, a.k.a. Productions, The Bedford Falls Company, ABC Productions, 1994.

*The Neon Demon.* Directed by Nicholas Refn Winding, performances by Elle Fanning, Jena Malone, Bella Heathcote, Abbey Lee, Wild Bunch, Gaumont, Space Rocket Nation, Vendian Entertainment, Bold Films, Danish Film Institute, 2016.

*A Nightmare on Elm Street.* Directed by Wes Craven, performances by Heather Lagenkamp, John Saxon, Johnny Depp, Robert Englund, New Line Cinema, Media Home Entertainment, Smart Egg Pictures, 1984.

*A Nightmare on Elm Street 2: Freddy's Revenge.* Directed by Jack Sholder, performances by Mark Patton, Kim Myers, Robert Englund, New Line Cinema, Heron Communications, Smart Egg Pictures, 1985.

*Notorious.* Directed by Alfred Hitchcock, performances by Ingrid Bergman, Cary Grant, Claude Reins, Lous Calhern, RKO Radio Pictures, Vanguard Films, 1946.

*Paris Is Burning.* Directed by Jennie Livingston, performances by Dorian Corey, Pepper LaBeija, Venus Xtravaganza, Willi Ninja, Academy Entertainment and Off White Productions, 1990.

*Popular.* Created by Ryan Murphy, performances by Leslie Bibb, Carly Pope, Christopher Gorham, Sara Rue, Murphy/Matthews Productions, Shephard / Robin Productions, Touchstone Television, 1999.

*Pretty Woman.* Directed by Garry Marshall, performances by Julia Roberts, Richard Gere, Laura San Giacomo, Héctor Elizondo, Touchstone Pictures, Silver Screen Partners IV, Regency International Pictures, 1990.

*Psycho.* Directed by Alfred Hitchcock, performances by Janet Leigh, Vera Miles, Anthony Perkins, John Galvin, Shamely Productions, 1960.

*Pygmalion.* Directed by Anthony Asquith and Leslie Howard, performances by Leslie Howard, Wendy Hiller, Wilfrid Lawson, Leueen MacGrath, Metro-Goldwyn-Mayer, 1938.

*Queer As Folk.* Developed by Ron Cowen and Daniel Lipman, performances by Gale Harold, Hal Sparks, Peter Paige, Sharon Gless, Cowlip Productions, Tony Jonas Productions, Channel 4, Showtime Networks, Warner Bros. Television, 2000.

*The Real World*, season three. Created by Mary-Ellis Bunim and Jonathan Murray, performances by Pedro Zamora, David "Puck" Rainey, Pam Ling, Judd Winick, Bunim/Murray Productions, 1994.

*Rebecca.* Directed by Alfred Hitchcock, performances by Joan Fontaine, Laurence Olivier, Judith Anderson, George Sanders, Selznick International Pictures, 1940.

*Rebel without a Cause.* Directed by Nicholas Ray, performances by James Dean, Natalie Wood, Sal Mineo, Jim Backus, Warner Bros., 1955.

*The Rocky Horror Picture Show.* Directed by Jim Sharman, performances by Tim Curry, Susan Sarandon, Barry Bostwick, Meat Loaf, Twentieth Century Fox, Michael White Productions, 1975.

*Rope.* Directed by Alfred Hitchcock, performances by James Stewart, Farley Granger, Joan Chandler, John Dall, Transatlantic Pictures, 1948.

*Saturday Night Live.* Created by Lorne Michaels, performances by Kenan Thompson, Seth Meyers, Fred Armisen, Kate McKinnon, NBC Studios, NBC Universal Television, Broadway Video, 1975.

*Saved by the Bell.* Created by Sam Bobrick, performances by Mark-Paul Gosselaar, Mario Lopez, Elizabeth Berkeley, Tiffani-Amber Thiessen, Peter Engel Productions and NBC Productions, 1989.

*Scream.* Directed by Wes Craven, performances by Neve Campbell, Courteney Cox, David Arquette, Drew Barrymore, Woods Entertainment, 1996.

*The Seven Year Itch.* Directed by Billy Wilder, performances by Marilyn Monroe, Tom Ewell, Evelyn Keyes, Sonny Tufts, Charles K. Feldman Group, Twentieth Century Fox, 1955.

*Shadow of a Doubt.* Directed by Alfred Hitchcock, performances by Teresa Wright, Joseph Cotton, Macdonald Carey, Patricia Collinge, Skirball Productions, 1943.

*She's All That.* Directed by Robert Iscove, performances by Rachael Leigh Cook, Freddie Prinze Jr., Matthew Lillard, Paul Walker, Tapestry Films and FilmColony, 1999.

*The Shining.* Directed by Stanley Kubrick, performances by Jack Nicholson, Shelley Duvall, Danny Lloyd, Scatman Crothers, Warner Bros, Hawk Films, Peregrine,1980.

*The Silence of the Lambs.* Directed by Jonathan Demme, performanes by Jodie Foster, Anthony Hopkins, Scott Glenn, Strong Heart Productions, 1991.

*Suddenly, Last Summer.* Directed by Joseph L. Mankiewicz, performances by Elizabeth Taylor, Montgomery Clift, Katharine Hepburn, Horizon Pictures, Academy Pictures Corporation, Camp Films, 1959.

*Swoon.* Directed by Tom Kalin, performances by Daniel Schlachet, Craig Chester, Fine Line Features, 1992.

*Today.* Created by Sylvester L. Weaver Jr, performances by Savannah Guthrie, Hoda Kotb, Al Roker, NBC News,1952.

*V for Vendetta.* Directed by James McTeigue, performances by Natalie Portman, Hugo Weaving, Stephen Rea, Stephen Fry, Silver Pictures, Virtual Studios, Studio Babelsberg, DC Vertigo Comics, Anarchos Productions, Inc., 2006.

*The Way We Were.* Directed by Sydney Pollack, performances by Barbara Streisand, Robert Redford, Bradford Dillman, Viveca Lindfors, Rastar, 1973.

*Were the World Mine.* Directed by Tom Gustafson, performances by Tanner Cohen, Nathaniel David Becker, Wendy Robie, Judie McLane, The Group Entertainment, 2008.

*Westworld.* Directed by Michael Crichton, performances by Yul Brenner, Richard Benjamin, Jmes Brolin, Metro-Goldwyn-Mayer, 1973.

*Who Wants to be a Millionaire?* Performances by Meredith Vieira, Chris Harrison, Cedric the Entertainer, Buena Vista Television, Celador Productions, Disney-ABC Domestic Television, 2002.

*Willy Wonka and the Chocolate Factory.* Directed by Mel Stuart, performances by Gene Wilder, Jack Albertson, Peter Ostrum, Warner Bros, 1971.

# ABOUT THE AUTHOR

Charles Jensen directs the Writers' Program at UCLA Extension and was designated a Cultural Trailblazer by the City of Los Angeles Department of Cultural Affairs. He's the author of three poetry collections and seven chapbooks that cross the boundaries of genre and form. A cinephile and bookworm since childhood, he studied film and creative writing at the University of Minnesota and Arizona State University. Originally from a small town in Wisconsin, he lives in Long Beach, California, with his partner Bill, and is a proud *Jeopardy!* second runner-up. He's the recipient of the 2018 Zócalo Poetry Prize, a Dorothy Sargent Rosenberg Prize, and an Artist's Project Grant from the Arizona Commission on the Arts. His poetry has appeared in *American Poetry Review, Crab Orchard Review, The Journal, New England Review,* and *Prairie Schooner.* He hosts *The Write Process,* a podcast in which one writer tells the story of writing one project from concept to completion. Find him at: charles-jensen.com.

# Also from Santa Fe Writers Project

## Negative Space
### by Lilly Dancyger

Despite her parents' struggles with addiction, Lilly Dancyger always thought of her childhood as a happy one. But what happens when a journalist interrogates her own rosy memories to reveal the instability around the edges?

*"Candid, thrilling, wickedly smart,* Negative Space *is one of the greatest memoirs of this, or any, time."*

— T Kira Madden, award-winning, author of Long Live the Tribe of Fatherless Girls

## We All Scream
### by Andrew Gifford

Suicide, bankruptcy, and a missing fortune...What happened to the iconic Gifford's Ice Cream franchise and the family behind it? Few know the truth...

*"This amazing, harrowing tale of the D.C. ice cream family makes it deeply clear that what looks sweet on the surface begs for further investigation— a brave, dark story of dysfunction."*

— A.M. Homes, author of May We Be Forgiven and The End of Alice

## Smoking Cigarettes, Eating Glass
### by Annita Perez Sawyer

Annita Sawyer's memoir is a harrowing, heroic, and redeeming story of her battle with mental illness, and her triumph in overcoming it. Hers is a unique voice for this generation, shedding light on an often misunderstood illness.

*"This utterly gripping, sharply written memoir pulls no punches. With cauterizing honesty and a blessed sense of perspective, Sawyer takes you into and through her dark experience to the shores of wisdom."*

— Phillip Lopate, author of Being With Children

## About Santa Fe Writers Project

SFWP is an independent press founded in 1998 that embraces a mission of artistic preservation, recognizing exciting new authors, and bringing out of print work back to the shelves.

 @santafewritersproject | X @SFWP | sfwp.com  sfWP)